Global Theo of the
Arts and Aesthetics

Edited by Susan L. Feagin

Blackwell
Synergy

Copyright © 2007 Published for The American Society for Aesthetics by Blackwell Publishing Inc.

Blackwell Publishing, Inc.
350 Main Street
Malden, MA 02148 USA

Blackwell Publishing, Ltd.
960 Garsington Road
Oxford OX4 2DQ
United Kingdom

Library of Congress Cataloging-in-Publication Data has been applied for.

ISBN 978-1-4051-7355-1
ISSN 0021-8529

Contents

GLOBAL THEORIES OF THE ARTS AND AESTHETICS
Susan L. Feagin, Editor

SUSAN L. FEAGIN

Introduction

I. GLOBAL THEORIES

The word 'global' in the title of this collection of papers characterizes its focus on theories and practices in relation to the arts around the globe, in particular, those that have been ignored or marginalized by analytic or Anglo-American aesthetics and philosophy of art. Debates over the very possibility of cross-cultural understanding and whether concepts of the arts and the aesthetic have universal application across cultures are important, but they are sidelined here in order to focus on the substantive contents of thoughts and practices that in fact stretch the Western imagination, potentially enriching and extending theories of art and the aesthetic.[1] Each paper is, of course, an expression of the views of its author or authors from his or her own perspective at this point in time in relation to a project whose core purposes are defined in decidedly Western terms.

One way that differences in ideas about art are revealed is through the conflicts that arise between traditional forms of thought and practice, on the one hand, and the pressure, often unwanted, to become artistically—or economically, religiously, politically, or in other ways—viable in the contemporary world. Philip Alperson, Nguyễn Chí Bến, and To Ngoc Thanh tell of how protracted wars and economic demands necessitated by globalization threaten musical traditions in the Vietnamese central highlands, traditions that flourished as part of a network of social and economic practices for hundreds of years. Jale Nejdet Erzen describes some difficulties in adapting an Islamic worldview, which traditionally extended across all aspects of human life and experience, to a more secularized contemporary world. In contrast, Mary Bittner Wiseman describes how Chinese visual artists have recruited contemporary forms of Western art along with practices that are deeply rooted in Chinese history and culture to serve their own contemporary political purposes.[2]

Not every culture has an intellectual tradition or philosophical methodology that is comparable to the analytic tradition of aesthetics or philosophy of art in the West. Careful, literal, discursive explanations of the concepts being explicated may well structure the discussion of those concepts in ways that are alien, to some degree, to the cultures and traditions in which they emerge. An analytic philosopher might wonder what the claim that "the spirit of bamboo is embodied in the brush" might possibly mean, whereas in Japan its import is established in the collective memory of the practices of painting. Stephen Davies remarks on the absence of a tradition of aesthetic theory in Bali; Erzen discusses the tension that can emerge between tradition and verbal analysis, and describes a variety of types of theories that have developed in relation to Islamic art, none of which are, unsurprisingly, quite like those of analytic philosophy. James Elkins has boldly claimed that there is no culture outside the West that has developed a *history* of art like that of the West, except under Western influence; the same claim might plausibly be made about a comparable *philosophy* of art or philosophical aesthetics.[3] Such sweeping generalizations, however, threaten to distract attention from the guiding concept here, which is to explicate as clearly as possible a limited number of concepts or practices that may require adjustments in the standard Western theoretical apparatus for discussing the aesthetic and the arts.

This collection makes no claim to comprehensiveness of any sort. Some omissions are glaring; for example, there is nothing on either the indigenous or the colonial arts, art forms, or artistic practices of the Americas, Africa, Australia, or large parts of Asia. Further, as Noël Carroll points out, the arts have adapted when necessary, and borrowed when given the opportunity, within changing networks of ideas and practices throughout history. Variants within traditions can be quite revealing, however, and several papers here provide different perspectives on what one might otherwise be inclined to conceive of as a fairly unified cultural tradition. There are aesthetically very different gamelan traditions in Bali and in Java, perhaps as different as nineteenth-century French Academic painting in France and twentieth-century American abstractionism in the spirit of Franz Kline and Robert Motherwell. Traditional Vietnamese gong music is something else again, and admits of considerable internal variation, as the term 'gong music' is a convenient collective for the musical traditions of numerous ethnic groups. Confucian approaches to calligraphy contrast strikingly with contemporary Chinese avant-garde art.

Two features of the arts and artistic concepts explored by the papers collected here are especially worthy of note. The first, described below in Section II, is the extent to which the arts are portrayed as being a constituent of everyday life, including important events, transitions, and religious attitudes and observances. The second, described in Section III, is the extent to which what in the West are distinguished as different forms of or media for the arts are integrated into a single artistic production or performance, and are endowed with different patterns of artistic and aesthetic relevance. In the final section, I provide summaries of the individual papers, highlighting some of their connections that become more salient when considered serially.

II. ONTOLOGY, ARTISTIC PRACTICES, AND EVERYDAY LIFE

The papers collected here tend to focus on activities and processes, rituals and traditions, rather than on material objects that, in principle, do not change through time, even when it is possible to treat something involved in a process or ritual as an enduring, physical object. This shift in focus can have far-reaching theoretical implications. One is that the aesthetics of process may be overlooked. Numerous visitors to Christo's *Wrapped* *Central Park*, for example, wanted a single viewpoint from which the entire installation could be seen, or at least *the best* viewpoint for seeing the entire installation, instead of taking up the invitation to walk around in and through it. In Yuriko Saito's discussion of the ethics and aesthetics of Japanese packaging, it is the aesthetic and ethical qualities of the activity of wrapping and unwrapping a package that concern her, rather than the visual qualities of the wrapped package itself. Another implication of this shift in focus is the degree to which appreciation of an artwork cannot be abstracted from its context. It is easier—at least for observers of rather than participants in the culture in question—to divorce objects, as opposed to rituals, from their religious and other functions, and hence to divorce their aesthetic or artistic appreciation from their cultural surround. Its being easier does not entail that it is not met with resistance, either in theory or practice, such as in the numerous claims to repatriation of religious and ritual objects that are a constituent of a national heritage or ethnic identity. Eric C. Mullis emphasizes the process of learning calligraphy, and its embeddedness in traditions and a social hierarchy, rather than merely the visual appeal of the calligraphy itself, even in the Chinese context where calligraphy is considered one of the two most important visual arts. In museum displays, it is not uncommon to see scholar-appreciators making imaginary brushstrokes in the air, as if they were writing the calligraphy themselves. Wiseman discusses performances and installations by some contemporary Chinese artists, arguing that they should be understood in part in terms of their "Chinese-ness," as a way of forging one's own national or cultural identity in the face of increasing globalization.

A more finely-tuned ontology of various kinds of actions and practices, along with the necessary and optional components of each, is likely to be needed to understand many of the artistic and cultural traditions discussed. For example, there are rituals, which are cognitively rich in their origins but relatively cognitively depleted in the engagement of them; there are traditions, which extend into the past and the future, beyond the experience of those who participate in them; there are current practices, less formally defined but still likely to extend beyond what any individual practitioner knows. There are skills, sometimes valued and sometimes eschewed; papers by Davies and Susan Pratt Walton provide striking examples of these different valuations. There are skills that are necessarily learned and exercised as members of a group or ensemble, such as described by Alperson, Nguyễn Chí Bén, and To Ngoc Thanh, and also by Mullis, who describes the necessary connection with and responsibility to others in the Confucian attitude towards calligraphy.[4]

Ontological distinctions among different types of processes and activities have not received their due, but neither have all the possibilities been covered with respect to objects that are thought to endure through time. Dominic McIver Lopes raises the matter pointedly with respect to the identity and individuation of buildings in the Japanese tradition of *Shikinen Sengu*, the rebuilding cycle of a temple or shrine, which is relevant to understanding the character of contemporary Japanese commercial and domestic building as well. Erzen describes how Islamic art and architecture reflect the view that no single visual perspective on the world is epistemologically superior to any other, which is in stark contrast with the Italian Renaissance view of painting, for example, where the perspective of the viewer is matched with the perspective in the painting, treating the former as privileged. In the Islamic world, the use of mosaics for picture making is highly prized, in part because the play of light on the colorful chips renders any static, defining perception of them impossible, in contrast with what Richard Wollheim, for example, proposes with respect to pictorial representation.[5] Even if the entire mosaic image falls within one's visual field, appreciation requires looking at it for a period of time to experience its changing qualities. Davies describes the irreplaceable role of candlelight (as opposed to electric lights) for evening performances in Bali, since its flickering creates a constantly changing visual array even if what one views does not move, to ensure that the work remains "alive," which expresses a spiritual concern rather than an epistemological one.

III.   EXPANDING THE CONCEPT OF THE AESTHETIC

For all the discussion of the emergence of the concept of the aesthetic in Europe in, roughly, the eighteenth century, there is no lack of enthusiasm for appropriating it to the arts and reception of the arts in other parts of the globe. 'Aesthetics' or one of its cognates appears in the title of over half of the papers collected here. What emerges, however, is a much more robust sense of the aesthetic,

one that challenges the hegemony that the eye and the ear have enjoyed in Western aesthetic theory for so long. As Walton explains, the Javanese concept of *rasa*, which bears interesting comparison with the concept of aesthetic experience, can refer to the "physical sense of taste and touch and also to emotional feelings." There is also a type of allusiveness, the comprehension of which "engage[s] all one's senses" (p. 31). Kathleen Higgins describes another way in which the concept of *rasa* expands the notion of the aesthetic: the process of achieving an aesthetic "breakthrough," that is, for getting into the frame of mind that will allow one to appreciate the music, the dance, and so on.

What are accepted as standard forms of art elsewhere encourage expansion of the concept in other ways: in relation to morality, also in a somewhat expanded sense; in relation to the body; and in relation to experience in a broad sense and the passage of time. Advocates for the view that morality is internal to the aesthetic and the artistic in some way are not unknown in the West, but the burden of proof, as it were, is clearly on their shoulders. In societies where the arts and their various aesthetic dimensions are incorporated into everyday life and into some of its most important practices and rituals, however, it is reasonable to expect that some attention will be given to how such practices impact others. The Japanese aesthetic tradition, according to Saito, is morally based in that it promotes "respect, care, and consideration for others, both humans and nonhumans" (p. 85). The idea that one should show respect for an *object's* "essential nature" and for the *materials* out of which something is made is virtually unknown in the West, with the most obvious exception being the appreciation of the natural environment. That one should take advantage of the distinctive qualities of the materials used in making art, when using oil paints as opposed to acrylics, for example, may be promoted as an artistic imperative—one that is identifiable in certain strains of modernism— but hardly a moral one. Saito adds that, in various Japanese art forms, caring for *humans* is manifested aesthetically. It is not only the design of objects but also the actions that one performs in relation to those objects that take on moral significance, for example, how in conducting a tea ceremony one's attitudes and intentions are expressed in one's bodily movements.

On Mullis's account, Confucianism supports the view that the arts "should serve the interests of the communities and states that they inhabit," though not merely as a means to the production of something valuable for a community. Using calligraphy as an example, Mullis explains how the development of artistic ability is connected to ritual traditions in general and hence acquires social and moral dimensions. One develops skill by working with a master; improper use of one's skills is a breach of "ritual propriety" and manifests a lack of humility and respect for the traditions that have enabled one to gain that mastery. Improper use of one's skills also misrepresents one's dependence on tradition. Further, since calligraphy involves bodily movement, it is a vehicle for "gestural communication," which is necessarily, on the Confucian view, an expression of one's character.[6]

Western aesthetics rarely recognizes a role for the body in aesthetic theory or in the production or appreciation of the arts, with the concomitant result of a lack of attention to certain art forms, such as dance. On the production side, Davies points out that there is a degree of athleticism in the playing of some instruments in the Balinese gamelan. Richard Shusterman sets out what he characterizes as Western fears of bodily intimacy and sexuality as represented, for example, in paintings, and advocates an aesthetics of sex, where one functions both as the producer and appreciator.[7]

The fact that humans are embodied creatures affects appreciation of the arts in more subtle ways. As Erzen indicates, Islamic architecture generally does not define the way its interior spaces are to be bounded or used in either domestic or commercial architecture. Here, the postmodern idea that the individual completes the work in the act of defining those spaces for one's own use is especially appealing. The defining activity will involve bodily engagement and activity, not just imagining how literally to *see* the building, and makes the relationships between body and space a major component of one's experience. The openness of the architecture, its invitation to walk around in and through its spaces in ways that are not fixated on a main visual target or constrained by a central axis, assumes the participatory activity of an embodied creature. This characteristic of Islamic architecture carries over to buildings designed under its influence, such as in the St. John Co-Cathedral in Valletta, Malta, whose walls are encrusted with patterns of relief, giving the impression of a brocade fabric or screen, and where the bays off the nave are open to each other with multiple avenues of access and a visual openness to match.

An emphasis on corporeal engagement in the activity of aesthetic appreciation provides an opportunity to reconceive the roles of time and process. Time is not merely the mode of presentation of a work, which may or may not have a canonical ordering, but it provides the opportunity for activity, including bodily activity, in ways that infuse what in the West are typically thought of as nontemporal forms of art, such as painting and drawing. Davies discusses the importance of keeping the music alive in gamelan playing by constant movement and visual stimulation. The same is true of images created with mosaics. They are pictures but are not flat and not two-dimensional. Individual tesserae are irregular and hence do not reflect light uniformly across the surface of the image, an effect that is increased by the movements of the viewers. The emphasis on process and change is embedded in a religious view that holds that the perceived world is constantly in flux, as Erzen explains with respect to Sufism and Islamic aesthetics in general. The object is not to transcend the multiple views one has of a building or image, but to embrace change as a necessary part of the process of experiencing them, to emphasize the changing character of one's experience rather than a single, *best* experience.

IV.   SUMMARIES OF THE PAPERS

Philip Alperson, Nguyễn Chí Bến, and To Ngoc Thanh describe traditional gong musical performance of the Tây Nguyên region of the Vietnamese central highlands. Gongs are percussion instruments that may be tonal or nontonal. An important feature is their soundings, "more or less extended durations that decay naturally over time" (p. 13). Rhythms are especially important and, as in salsa music in the West, members of the ensemble "are assigned relatively simple but precisely placed complementary rhythmic parts" (p. 14). Highly trained individuals—gong regulators—are responsible for "bringing each gong into conformity with the tonal array" of the ensemble (p. 15). Though virtuosity is highly prized, the idea that music playing is the personal expression of an individual is alien to the tradition, undermining the relevance of distinctions between art and craft that are so common in the West, for example, as drawn by R. G. Collingwood. Performances of gong music are a component of the recognition of significant transitions or events in the culture and provide opportunities for forging social relationships. Much music in the West is equally embedded in traditions, the authors argue, though war and the pressures of economic globalization have exposed the vulnerability of traditional gong music by disrupting the broader cultural traditions in which it is so deeply embedded.

Stephen Davies focuses on how "the Balinese attitude to the arts is sometimes strangely different from" that in the West, specifically, on the relationships between art and religion, community, competition, and the value placed on novelty and innovation (p. 21). In line with the ontological concerns mentioned above, Davies points out that art "must be infused with life, and that means movement," ensured by oil lamps instead of electric lights, actors' never standing entirely still, and paired instruments tuned slightly apart (p. 22). An abundance of detail exists in the visual arts, music, and dance, accompanied by high esteem for virtuosity, not unlike that discussed by Alperson, Nguyễn Chí Bền, and To Ngoc Thanh. The creation and presentation of art are devotional acts and pervade everyday activities. The gamelan, for example, symbolizes both the cosmological and the social orders, so that the playing of music can never be entirely purged of religious significance (p. 22).[8] Balinese attitudes toward the arts tend to reflect their general tendencies toward both competitiveness and communalism. Gamelan competitions take on some of the trappings of sports, including athleticism, and can be viewed in ways that recall attitudes in the West more toward popular culture than fine art. Paintings and sculptures may be produced jointly by numerous individuals in the community, though recently, under the "influence of Western models," some artists have begun to sign their work (p. 26). Yet, innovation and adaptation have always been highly prized. Davies observes that in Bali "the arts are the lifeblood and pulse of community existence, not merely an accompaniment," raising the question of whether it is possible to separate the appreciation of the arts from their religious and communal role (p. 27–28).

Susan Pratt Walton discusses the gamelan of central Java, the most important function of which "is to accompany dance, theater, and ceremonial occasions, such as weddings, in both ritual and commercial settings" (p. 31). Her concern is with the relationships between gamelan music and mysticism, arguing that the "stated aim of music making, the structure of the music, the leadership

styles, and the creation of melodies have remarkably close parallels in the Javanese mystical world" (p. 31). Based in the Sanskrit theory of *rasa*, in its Javanese application, the structure of music reflects the belief that truth is hidden beneath the surface, and group collaboration is key to uncovering it. As in some of the other papers, Walton addresses one aspect of the contemporary state of the tradition, which continues with solo female singers who perform with the gamelan in central Java today.

Like Walton, Kathleen Marie Higgins examines the concept of *rasa* in the *Nāṭyaśāstra*, which contains an extensive theoretical analysis of the nature, sources, and values of emotions. Higgins's focus, however, is on *rasa* as the *savoring* of one's experience as a response to a dramatic performance, which is a manifestation of sensitivity and cultivation, and she traces some interesting comparisons with Aristotle along the way. But her ultimate objective is to explicate the notion of a "breakthrough" that precipitates aesthetic experience. The eleventh-century philosopher Abhinavagupta provides the definitive analysis of the preconditions for the attainment of *rasa*. On his view, the achievement of *rasa* is possible only with a certain level of moral development, that is, when one is able to transcend concern with one's own self-interest, manifested in one's capacity for empathy, accompanied by the knowledge that one's own emotions are convergent with those of another. In addition, Abhinava holds that *rasa*, though transient and tied to an object, can lead to a sense of tranquility, or "spiritual liberation, the supreme goal of human life" (p. 49).

The theme of Richard Shusterman's paper is "philosophy's persistent pose of resistance to the seductive aesthetics of sex," and it explores how Hindu texts make self-discipline and concern for others as necessary for sexual gratification to be an aesthetic experience (p. 55). He makes the point that, in the West, aesthetic experience is often defined in contrast to sexual experience, a point also made in passing by Arthur Danto (p. 123). Though the philosopher Ronald de Sousa proposes an aesthetics of sex, Shusterman criticizes it as "essentially committed to the idea that sexual performance is aesthetic only in so far that it involves a theatrical fiction or simulation of something else" (p. 58), rather than for the "aesthetic qualities of the sexual performance as a real event that is deeply embedded in . . . the rest of the lives and expectations of the performing lovers" (p. 58). Michel Foucault has also advocated an aesthetics of sex, but Shusterman disagrees with Foucault's claim that pleasure was the most important element for the Chinese, claiming that their recommendations regarding sexual matters had primarily to do with health and medicine. Hindu texts from the third, twelfth, and sixteenth centuries do not see erotic behavior as merely the satisfaction of sensual desire, but as a way of deploying and educating "one's desires in order to cultivate and refine the mastery of one's senses so that one can emerge a more complete and effective person" (p. 62). Aesthetic arts include "an elaborate aesthetics of foreplay and postcoital entertainment" (p. 62), a particular setting, representations in the form of bites and nail markings, analogies to dance, and more. Religious and ritual connections are important: "aesthetic ritualization can artfully transform the most basic functions of life ... and the ordinary practices of living" (p. 64). The *kama* in *Kama Sutra* "concerns the whole domain of sensory cognition," which is enhanced through mastering "a wide range of complex motor coordinations and bodily postures" and using all the senses (p. 65). There is also an ethical dimension in the consideration of others' responses and one's own self-knowledge and self-discipline, a broader field of the ethical that is resonant with Mullis's account of Confucian artistry and with Saito's account of the ethical dimensions of Japanese aesthetics.

Concentrating mainly on the Sufi tradition, Jale Nejdet Erzen describes various Islamic ways of conceiving of and perceiving the world, in particular, with respect to space and time. There is no assumption that the world is fixed or stable; correlatively, a perceiver's vantage point is constantly moving and changing. "[V]isual arrays are designed to reflect the constant movement of the world" and the changing human orientation toward it (p. 70). Mirrors, reflections in water, and lattice screens abound in Islamic architecture, confusing the boundaries between the illusory and the real. Artists express themselves through symbols, rather than through mimesis, which is a way of attaining peace. The world is a manifestation of God, and the artist strives to make something worthy of Him. Erzen also tackles the topic of ethnic identity and makes some suggestions about how more secularized Turkish artists today may nevertheless bring a traditional Islamic aesthetic into their work.

Dominic McIver Lopes looks at a different way that time and change are accommodated in Japanese architecture. He begins his discussion of how cultural variations in art forms and appreciative practices might affect an ontology of art. Variation in art forms, he proposes, are consistent with an ontology of art that is culturally invariant, as in the view defended by David Davies.[9] Yet, he also points out that "cross-cultural studies are relevant to the ontology of art as long as sound practices of art appreciation vary enough that they imply different ontologies" (p. 79). The *shikinen sengu*, or rebuilding cycle, for numerous Japanese shrines—Lopes discusses the shrine at Ise Jingu as an example—is sufficiently different from Western practices of identifying the age of a building and individuating buildings from one another to make it worth "rethinking the ontology of architecture" (p. 77). The sanctified structures of the inner shrine at Ise Jingu have "been rebuilt about every twenty years" on an adjacent lot, and then back again about twenty years later. The rebuilding itself takes about eight years. One can ask of any of these structures: Is it more than one thousand years old, or is it fewer than twenty years old? Japanese appreciative practices seemingly allow for both to be true, which does not seem to be allowed by standard Western views about the ontology of buildings as material objects that persist through time. Even the more recent view that at least some architectural works, such as Tom Sandonato and Martin Wehmann's kitHAUS, are types with multiple instances, Lopes argues, does not accommodate the Japanese case, where the architecture is more like a theatrical production that takes place over time than like a physical object that endures, in principle, unchanging through time.

Yuriko Saito concentrates her discussion on two principles of design that embody a moral dimension in Japanese aesthetics. One involves "respecting the innate characteristics" or "essence of an object, material, or subject matter," and the other involves "honoring and responding to human needs" (p. 85). The former finds expression in what are traditionally called "arts" in the West, such as poetry and painting, and extends to such everyday activities as cooking and packaging. The idea, having its roots in Zen, that each type of food for a dinner should be cooked and presented individually so that "each ingredient retains and expresses its own characteristics" contrasts strikingly with, for example, the constant change that is required to keep Balinese gamelan music "alive" (p. 87). Saito suggests that the practice of respecting any entity for its own essential qualities has a useful pragmatic application in attitudes toward nature, in particular, that not only the magnificent and the beautiful are worth saving, but that "unscenic" natural objects and arrays—bugs and bogs, for example—also deserve our respect. The second principle of design in Japanese aesthetics that involves a moral dimension concerns the expression of caring attitudes toward other humans "through aesthetic means," which include one's actions and bodily movements (p. 89). Once again in relation to food, one's manner of eating shows respect, or disrespect, for the cooking and careful presentation of the food. In general, this aesthetic is other-regarding, as one must imagine the effects on others of what one does, both for what one makes and for how one appreciates something made or done by others.

Eric C. Mullis pursues the idea that "practicing art is necessarily a moral affair as it entails transforming the self, finding a place within a tradition, and otherwise entering into significant relationships with others" (p. 99). Calligraphy as an art developed with the same spirit as religious ritual, seen as instrumental in developing self-cultivation and establishing social stability. 'Practicing calligraphy,' which emphasizes repetitiveness and tradition, is the term that Mullis uses, not 'making an object,' which is more likely to confine attention to the aesthetic qualities of the finished product. To similar effect, a work's organic form is described using "[p]hysiological metaphors [that] ... draw attention to the kinesthetic elements of the characters" (p. 102). These are alleged to be reflective of one's own character and, in turn, one's dependence on society and tradition.

Mary Bittner Wiseman defines 'global' metaphorically and as a matter of degree as "activities or genres that can shake free of their native soil and be transported to almost anywhere" (p. 109). She argues that there are three ways the contemporary Chinese avant-garde does not "shake off" its "Chinese-ness." This is important because the story of art in contemporary China "shows it to be in the service of what is no longer its primary function in the West: the reconstruction of identity of a people and the reinvention of the idea of art itself" (p. 111). There are three distinctive themes in this reconstruction. The first involves the individual's relation to certain social spaces, and whether communism, aided by China's recent turn to exploit the potential of capitalism, provides for a public space that allows for individuals to "be themselves" (p. 111). The second involves the individual's relation to language and utilizes the distinctive, perhaps unique, calligraphic traditions in China to represent the opacity of language and the "loss" of the world because of it. One artist repeats the bodily gestures of writing, destroying meaning in the buildup of ink, another fails to create meaning to begin with, by stamping woodblocks on water. (Need it be pointed out that Confucius would not be pleased?) The third involves the "evisceration" of the self when an individual is ideologically separated from his or her body, with the latter conceived as "a brute and dumb nonsignifying nature" (p. 111).

Arthur C. Danto describes the phenomenon of isotypes, the "International System of Typographic Picture Education," whose function is trans-cultural or global; in Wiseman's sense, they "shake free of their native soil." The Hungarian artist Ágnes Eperjesi transfigures isotypes that appear on the throwaway packaging of ordinary household items into art, and in doing so transforms them into "a portrait of the society in which the products are to be used" (p. 121). It is a very different portrait from that presented by the intensely aesthetic handmade artisanship of wrapping and unwrapping in the Japanese tradition described by Saito. Interestingly, as Danto points out, isotypes representing women mostly depict them as wearing Western clothing, "which has become fairly isotypical" (p. 122). Danto has long proposed that the relationship of aesthetics, with its emphasis on beauty, "was always external and contingent" to art. His main concern here, however, is how Immanuel Kant's notion of aesthetical ideas *does* survive the post-1960s artworld's jest for vernacular imagery and pluralism and is able to accommodate, for example, the dainty and the dumpy and grunge and mess. An interesting juxtaposition is Kant's idea of spirit, "the animating principle of the mind," what gives "life" to a work, and ideas about life and spirit that infuse the arts in other papers included here.[10]

Noël Carroll argues that there has always been global exploration and exploitation and that economic globalization is incomplete, and also that a genuinely new integrated, interconnected, transnational artworld is evolving at the dawn of the twenty-first century. The culture of mass entertainments of film and television is vastly hybridized, but still more regional than global, as we can also see in the history of dance, displaying "poaching and outright assimilation" on many cultural fronts, and "at varying speeds whenever civilizations meet" (p. 135). So what has changed? Carroll begins by looking at the forms of transnational relationships, where new institutions, sets of institutions, and practices arise. What is different about these institutions is that participants in them "share converging or overlapping traditions and practices at the same time that they exhibit and distribute their art on internationally coordinated venues." Contemporary work has "its own preferred idioms" or forms: "video, film, photography, installation pieces ..., conceptual art, and performance art" (p. 138). It is "hard to resist the observation that many of these art forms have been constructed on the basis of some of the very technologies that are transforming the wide world into a small world," technologies that allow us to "overcome" space (p. 139). There are also "shared discourses, both artistic and critical, ... [as] artists find themselves in many of the same contexts with their attendant problematics—including capitalism in particular and modernization in general" (p. 140). More than one paper in this collection has examined the challenges involved in retaining a traditional identity in a more globalized world, and the centrality of art to that mission. But of primary importance, according to Carroll, are the shared themes and shared ways of making sense of art among artists, critics, consumers, and curators. These figure in "a shared tradition and history," "a common art culture," that constructs a transnational and, to some extent, a global artworld.

V.   CONCLUDING REMARKS

A premise of this collection of papers is that the study of the arts and theories about the arts in unfamiliar cultures will provide compelling, specific ways of enriching and enhancing the concepts of the aesthetic and the artistic. Some possibilities raised here have to do with extending the notion of the *aesthetic* to include sense modalities besides vision and hearing, especially to the perception of the body—others' bodies and one's own—in the production and appreciation of art. Oth-

ers call for a more nuanced philosophy of action to understand *art*, one that identifies the relevant features of activities or performances, and their relationship to broader social structures and distinctive characteristics of a culture and community. In some of these cases, participation in and viewing of these activities and performances are deeply embedded in one's sense of self and how one negotiates one's way through the world. A similar claim could be made for those who participate in theorizing about the arts, both within and outside Western traditions of thought and analysis. This collection is one step in the process of taking up the opportunities for knowledge and enrichment in our increasingly global world.

SUSAN L. FEAGIN
Department of Philosophy
Temple University
Philadelphia, PA 19122, USA

INTERNET: Feagin@temple.edu

1. Arthur C. Danto has argued that the metaphysics of many traditions across the globe are so different from that in the West that one should not expect them to provide assistance in moral theory or practice. It is an interesting question whether a similar conclusion would be warranted in aesthetics and philosophy of art. See Arthur C. Danto, *Mysticism and Morality: Oriental Thought and Moral Philosophy* (New York: Basic Books, 1972). See also Denis Dutton, "A Naturalist Definition of Art," *The Journal of Aesthetics and Art Criticism* 64 (2006): 367–377, for a recent defense of a cross-cultural conception of art.

2. On the distinction between choice and influence, see Michael Baxandall, *Patterns of Intention: On the Historical Explanation of Pictures* (Yale University Press, 1985), pp. 105–110.

3. For an examination of this and other related issues, see James Elkins, ed., *Is Art History Global?*, vol. 3 of *The Art Seminar* (New York: Routledge, 2006).

4. Suzanne Langer's controversial *Philosophy in a New Key: A Study in the Symbolism of Reason, Rite, and Art* (Harvard University Press, 1951), situates the arts anthropologically, which might plausibly explain why her work has been more influential outside than inside the philosophical community.

5. Richard Wollheim, *Painting as an Art* (Princeton University Press, 1987), especially ch. 2.

6. The closest Western analogue may be Tolstoy's view about sincerity in the arts, though he does not appeal to the bodily nature of the skills and movements, which ground the Confucian view. See Leo N. Tolstoy, *What Is Art?* trans. Almyer Maude (Indianapolis: Bobbs-Merrill, 1960), ch. 15.

7. John Dewey's *Art as Experience*, especially Chapter 3, "Having an Experience," is especially useful as a canonical

source of such ideas, as is Shusterman's own "Somaesthetics: A Disciplinary Proposal," *The Journal of Aesthetics and Art Criticism* 57 (1999): 299–313.

8. Patrick Maynard has noted the connection between the aesthetic in the sense of the cosmetic, which is derived "from 'cosmos,' denoting a beauty-enhancing order." He makes this point in the "Introduction," with Susan L. Fea-gin, in *Aesthetics*, Susan L. Feagin and Patrick Maynard, ed. (Oxford University Press, 1997), p. 4.

9. David Davies, *Art as Performance* (Malden, MA: Blackwell, 2004).

10. Immanuel Kant, *Critique of Judgment*, translation and introduction by J. H. Bernard (New York: Hafner, 1968), p. 157.

PHILIP ALPERSON, NGUYỄN CHÍ BẾN, AND TO NGOC THANH

The Sounding of the World: Aesthetic Reflections on Traditional Gong Music of Vietnam

For more than three thousand years, members of the more than twenty ethnic minority cultures of the Tây Nguyên region of Vietnam—the central highlands—have practiced gong music.[1] Traditional gong musical performance is so intimately tied to the artistic, religious, and philosophical beliefs and is so closely linked to the affairs of life of these communities, one may say that the cultural identities of the various highland groups are bound up specifically with their individual gong cultures. Unfortunately, the gong music of the Vietnamese uplands has received scant attention from Western scholars, even among ethnomusicologists specializing in the traditional musical cultures of Southeast Asia.[2] Vietnamese gong music has received no attention from aestheticians.

In this paper, we hope to introduce Western readers to this ancient and rich musical tradition and to place that tradition in the context of specifically aesthetic reflection. We shall argue that while traditional Vietnamese gong music may at first seem remote or even inaccessible to the Western ear, it is a musical tradition that has much in common with Western musical practice. At the same time, gong music is a product of its Vietnamese roots and, we shall argue, it can only be fully understood in its Vietnamese cultural context. We shall argue, however, that the importance of placing gong music in its cultural context has a parallel significance for the philosophical understanding of Western musical practices. The aesthetics of traditional Vietnamese gong music thus has something important to say about both Vietnamese and Western musical aesthetics.

A few prefatory points are in order. The terms 'Vietnam' and 'Vietnamese' are here being used as geographical, political designations and do not refer to Vietnamese ethnicity (Việt). When we refer to Vietnamese ethnic groups, we shall do so by naming the groups. There are fifty-five ethnic groups in Vietnam. The largest by far is the Việt group at 85 percent of the population. This paper is concerned solely with the traditional gong music of the minority ethnic groups who live in the central highlands. We recognize that there are many diverse and distinct musical styles and traditions among the various ethnic peoples throughout Vietnam. By "the traditional gong music of the central highlands" we mean the music that is currently being played and that we take to be representative of the musical traditions of the groups in question. We understand that, like all musical traditions, gong music is a cultural practice with its own history and dynamics. What we see and hear today are the distillation and accretion of these thousands-year-old practices.[3]

I. THE AESTHETICS OF GONG MUSIC

Gong music is common to many Southeast Asian and Pacific countries, including Vietnam, Thailand, Cambodia, Laos, Mongolia, the Philippines, and, of course, Indonesia, whose gamelan orchestras are probably most familiar to Western audiences. A defining characteristic of all these practices is the central role of gong playing, that is, the production of sounds on rimmed metal disks by hitting the gongs with implements such as mallets or sticks. Like the gong music of other Asian

FIGURE 1. Ba Na gong ensemble with different size gongs.

and Pacific countries, Vietnamese gongs are of many different sizes and are typically played in ensembles ranging from two to as many as twenty gongs (see Figure 1). Some gongs (*Cồng*) are carried or worn. Others (*Chiêng*) are suspended from the ceiling or a stand.

The traditional gong music of the central highlands of Vietnam has its own characteristics. Vietnamese gong musical performances vary from village to village, but we may start by noting that traditional Vietnamese gong music is a hybrid practice involving one or more associated artistic forms and practices. Gong performers themselves frequently parade or dance while playing. Gong playing may also be accompanied by dancers who move in lines, performing centuries-old hand gestures and steps (see Figure 2). Dancers may carry decorated woven shields and bamboo swords. In some cases, dancers and gong players engage in chanting and vocalizations. Gong performances may involve the sharing of food and drink, including the ceremonial sharing with gods and spirits of the dead. Gong performances may also involve parades or animal sacrifices. Understanding the cultural meaning of gong practice will necessarily involve reference to all these things.

However, the designation "gong" music clearly recognizes the centrality of gong playing itself as the nerve of the practice. The aesthetics of gong playing must begin with this.

Gongs are percussion instruments: they produce their sounds by being percussed or hit.

Vietnamese gong players hit their gongs with a variety of implements, including sticks from the cassava plant, bamboo poles, wooden mallets (which may or may not be covered with cloth, leather, or other padding), and the open or closed hand. Each of the hitting implements has its own characteristic sound. The choice of hitting implements varies from community to community. In some cultures, a bracelet is worn on the wrist of the hitting hand, and the bracelet hits the gong with the hand; the action produces a click at the onset of the ringing of the gong.

Here it is important to bear in mind some basic observations about percussion instruments. Because some percussion instruments such as cymbals and snare drums do not produce sounds that are heard as tonal—that is, as occupying positions in a culturally defined system of definite pitches—it is common to think of percussion instruments as solely rhythmic and nontonal. That is a misconception. Some percussion instruments are tonal: the piano, the xylophone, the vibraphone, the glockenspiel, and the kettledrum being notable examples. It is more accurate to say that gongs are percussive instruments and that all gongs produce sounds but some gongs are nontonal while others are tonal. The musical effects of tonal and nontonal gongs are not the same and their differences are aesthetically significant. In addition, gongs may be flat or they may be "bossed," that is, they may have a raised hub in the center of the disk. Hitting a bossed gong directly on the raised hub produces

FIGURE 2. Ba Na gong players and dancers in procession.

a more bell-like sound; hitting it closer to the perimeter produces more of a crash resonance. The sound is also affected by whether the gong is hit on the outside or the inside of the gong. The instrumentation of traditional Vietnamese gong ensembles may include tonal and nontonal gongs, bossed and flat gongs, drums, cymbals, and bamboo panpipes.

Another aesthetically relevant feature of gongs is that gongs typically produce not just sounds but also "soundings," that is, sounds that have more or less extended durations that decay naturally over time. A gong continues to reverberate after it is hit and gradually softens away into silence. The termination of a gong sound may, however, be imposed on the gong before the natural period of decay. That is, a gong may be stopped or "damped" by the gong player, typically by placing a hand or a mallet on the gong to stop it from ringing.

This is an important point to keep in mind. The stopping of musical sounds is one of the most important, if frequently neglected, aspects of musical performance in the West. Western musical notation can specify the duration of sounds with great precision, but performers do not always pay careful attention to this aspect of musical performance; nor are listeners generally consciously aware of the phenomenon. Still, control over the cessation of sounds can affect the presentation of music in dramatic ways. The style of Glenn Gould, for example, is instantly recognizable even to the rel-

atively untrained ear, especially for the clarity of Gould's presentation of musical lines, both melodically and contrapuntally. This is due in no small measure to Gould's uncanny control over both the onset and the termination of individual tones by means of his keyboard technique and his characteristic use of the foot pedals.

Similarly, Vietnamese gong players pay special attention to the damping of gongs, and this range of discrimination is not something to which most Westerners would attend. For the Vietnamese, however, one means of identifying the characteristic styles of gong playing from different ethnic groups is by means of their respective damping techniques and styles. Differently damped gongs have their own aesthetic qualities. Gongs left to ring interact with other gong sounds. The Chu Ru and Ba Na peoples damp the gongs with the sticks they use to hit the gong. Mạ, Mnông, Kpạ, and Co Ho villagers damp the gongs with the palm of the hand. The Gia Rai damp the gong with various combinations of fingers. Gongs may also be damped by elbows or thighs. Gongs may be damped at the center, toward the perimeter, on the rim, and from the front or the back, each technique resulting in a different effect. Gong sounds may be damped completely, bringing them to a halt, or they may be softly damped, allowing an attenuated sound to continue. A second hit on the same gong also has a damping effect on the first sounding (see Figure 3).

FIGURE 3. Members of the Ma group damping gongs with the left hand.

As a percussive music, Vietnamese gong play-ing places a high premium on its rhythmic ele-ment. One especially interesting feature of Viet-namese gong playing is the high degree to which in-dividual musical elements within musical phrases are assigned to different members of a gong en-semble. We can understand this feature of Viet-namese gong music by contrasting it with the case of a Western jazz drummer playing a rhythmically demanding piece. The drummer has an array of sounding possibilities at his or her disposal: the snare drum, the tom drum, the bass drum, the high hat cymbal, the ride cymbal, the crash cymbal, and other percussion instruments such as shak-ers, chimes, and bells. The drummer might pro-duce a steady underlying beat, say, with the bass drum or the high hat, while simultaneously pro-ducing accents, colorations, and polyrhythms with other parts of the drum kit. Often, one can see the complexity of the rhythm, literally, by watching the drummer's hands and feet ablaze in constant, sometimes furious, motion. (Buddy Rich was fa-mous for such displays.)

Vietnamese gong music may also present dif-fering rhythms, accents, and colorations, but, even in the case of rhythmically sophisticated and com-plex performances, as for example the fast tempo music played by the women of the Bih ethnic group, one is struck by the relative calm of the gong players' hands, as compared with the hands and feet of the jazz drummer. This is so because indi-vidual gong players are assigned particular motifs that, taken together, produce the rhythmic inter-est. The motifs played by individual gong players are not particularly complicated in the sense of consisting of extended rhythmic lines. What mat-ters is rather the placement of the rhythmic accents as the beat is subdivided metrically as well as the precise placement of the individual elements in the rhythmic array of the ensemble. This sort of play-ing requires a highly developed rhythmic sense.

Ensemble rhythmic playing with elements as-signed to different players does occur in West-ern music. Western listeners who would like to get a sense of the particular musical effect of the very highly specialized assignment of rhythmic el-ements in Vietnamese gong music might think of the rhythms of salsa music. One of the great de-lights of salsa music is the overlay of precise syn-copated rhythmic accents on a pulse sometimes stated, sometime implied, always present in the music. As in Vietnamese gong music, the musical effect in salsa is the result of a rhythmic ensemble whose members are assigned relatively simple but precisely placed complementary rhythmic parts. In salsa music, the parts are assigned to the charac-teristic rhythmic instruments of the Latin ensem-ble: the cymbal, the cow bell, the conga, the clave, the maracas, the guiro, the cabasa, and the bass. In an eight-beat phrase, for example, the clave might be hit on the downbeat of 1, the upbeat of 3, and the downbeat of 4, 6, and 7. The conga might be hit on the downbeat of 2 and 4, the upbeat of 5, the downbeat of 6 and 8, and the upbeat of 1. The cowbell might be hit on 1, 2, upbeat of 3, 4, upbeat of 5, and the downbeats of 5, 6, 7, and 8. These patterns are repeated continuously. The challenge for each individual playing this music is in the placement of the musical hits, maintaining not only the precision but the overall rhythmic feel of the music. The combination of these parts gives the rhythmic section its cohesion and salsa its characteristic musical sound and vitality.

And so it is with Vietnamese gong playing. In the tradition of the Brâu people, two players sit facing two gongs hanging between the players. One player beats relatively even eighth notes to establish the meter; the other player punctuates the rhythm by subdividing the beat and hitting accents. Together they produce the complicated and lively rhythm. In other communities, such as the Mạ, Mnông, and Co Ho communities, the gong ensemble may range from six to as many as forty players, where the individual parts are "doubled" (that is, the part is played by more than one player) with as many as five or six players on a part. Players on the same part must sound as a single voice. Since the hits occur at very precise and small metric subdivisions of the beat, the meticulous musical demands of this sort of playing are obvious (see Figure 4).[4]

Gongs must be regulated, which is to say that each gong must be adjusted to produce sounds whose timbral or tonal properties are complementary to the sonorous properties of the other gongs in an ensemble. Typically, each village has a gong regulator who is a master practitioner highly skilled in such matters. One interesting feature of Vietnamese gong music is that while the gongs, which are forged from metal alloys, were previously produced in certain of the highland villages themselves, in recent years, as result of the dislocations and hardships of the Vietnam War (known in Vietnam as the "American War"), they have been manufactured elsewhere by ethnic Việt instrument makers who have a general sense of the individual ethnic musical styles and who sell the gongs to the villages. The gongs must then be finely adjusted and, in the case of tonal gongs, tuned in accordance with the tonal array of the rest of the ensemble. It falls to the gong regulator to make these fine adjustments.

Gong regulation requires another set of musical skills. Regulating the gong is a matter of hammering the gong in spiral or circular patterns on the central disk or along its rimmed edges. The regulator must be sensitive to musical features such as the volume, the timbre, the tone, the overtones (the multiples of fundamental frequencies that give sounding tones their unique colors), and the rate and nature of the onset and durational qualities of the sound of the gong. He (for the regulator is typically a male) must know exactly where and how to hammer the gong to effect the

FIGURE 4. Bih gong players doubling parts in three groups of two.

subtle changes that bring the musical sounds of the gong into adjustment with the ensemble. The existence of gong regulation skills alongside the skills of gong playing brings to mind R. G. Collingwood's observation that, in the case of highly skilled activities, there may be a hierarchical, reciprocating relation between various crafts wherein one craft supplies what another needs.[5]

In the case of gong ensembles in which tonal gongs are used, the gong regulator is responsible for bringing each gong into conformity with the tonal array. The tonal system of traditional Vietnamese gong music is in some ways similar to standard Western tonality. The gongs produce tones or pitches arrayed on a scalar system in which steps can be heard as existing in a system of tones heard as higher and lower in relation to one another. Like Western musical scales, the steps of the scale are heard as fundamentally related to one pitch that is heard as the center of the tonal system. Tonal patterns differ from community to community but, generally speaking, the musical intervals employed are many of the same intervals as we would find in the Western diatonic scalar system (half tones, whole tones, thirds, fourths, fifths, octaves, and so on), with the important exception that in some Vietnamese traditions quarter-tones are employed. Westerners may at first hear the quarter-tones as simply being out of tune. But, as in the case of other micro-tonal musics such as Indian music, these intervals can, with training, be heard by the Western ear as appropriate and functioning within the scalar system. Quarter-tones may also have a subtle trance-inducing effect.[6]

Each tonal gong produces a single pitched sound and each player plays only one gong. So, analogous to the case of the rhythmic patternings discussed above, the melodies (which are typically no longer than four measures long) and the harmonies of traditional Vietnamese music are the product of the assignments of particular pitched tones placed in time so as to produce integrated melodies and harmonies by the ensemble. The same musical demands and musical delights ensue from listening to the melodies and harmonies in rhythmic gestalts emerging from the individualized soundings taken together as a whole.

Traditional Vietnamese gong music has expressive and representational dimensions whose meanings are derived from a combination of purely musical and contextual factors.[7] The relatively slow, uncluttered music played in the context of a funeral is heard as expressive of melancholy.[8] The syncopated music played at the harvest celebration is heard as merry.[9] An Ê Đê piece known as "Ice Rain" represents a hailstorm: a series of hits on a variety of small gongs starts slowly, followed by an increasingly animated and turbulent pattern of sounds involving the full range of gong and drum sounds, much in the way that a hailstorm might begin and develop. In this case the patterning of gong sounds mimics the overall pattern of the growth and development of a hailstorm in general as well as the specific sounds and patterns of sounds that hailstones make as differently sized hailstones hit different surfaces during a storm.[10] In another piece, "Scarecrow," the gongs imitate the rattling made by bamboo scarecrows Ê Đê highlanders use to keep birds away from the fields.[11]

Finally, players may improvise on the fundamental patterns after the patterns have been firmly established in performance. Virtuosity is a prized value. Among the Ê Đê, for example, there are contests in which gong players play variations on fast rhythmic patterns, attempting to throw others in the ensemble off balance, not unlike the "cutting sessions" occasionally had among some jazz musicians in the West.

These observations combine to give us a sense of what we might call the basic aesthetic elements of traditional Vietnamese gong music. They also establish the characteristic features that help us to individuate the styles and artistic creativity of one ethnic group from another and to mark stylistic differences and nuances within the music of particular ethnic cultures. The Ba Na group, for example, typically employs a thirteen-gong ensemble with a nine-step scale, in a homophonic way (that is, having a single melodic line with accompaniment). The Ê Đê group employs an array of six to nine gongs, producing polyphonic music of complex rhythms and fast tempi, with some improvisation.[12] The Mnông use brass gongs in worship ceremonies but bamboo gongs in the funeral ceremony; their music often resembles the dialogue of ordinary speech. Brâu music has a driving feel. Chu Ru is more lilting. The XoĐang music is powerful and stately.

Vietnamese gong players and listeners in the community pay great attention to these temporal, spatial, rhythmic, melodic, harmonic, textural, formal, expressive, representational, improvisatory, and virtuosic musical dimensions. They do so in a way that Western listeners would recognize as having resonance with a common understanding of the aesthetic appreciation of music: they are familiar with the repertoire of the musical culture and they attend to what Western theorists would call purely musical features. Entire villages take enormous pride in the musicianship of the gong players and in the sensibility of the members of the community who attend to this finely nuanced music—we might say—for its own sake. And with good reason: the aesthetic power of this music, its drive, its energy, its sometimes hypnotic force, its expressiveness and rhythmic sophistication, are all there to be heard by Vietnamese and Westerners alike.

II. GONG MUSIC AND ETHNIC TRADITIONS

It would be a mistake, however, to think that the aesthetic qualities and the musical sensibilities and experiences we have so far considered exhaust the meaning of traditional Vietnamese gong music. Nor would this analysis help us to understand the depth of meaning of what is often said of the Tây Nguyên region—that if one visits the region and does not listen to the gong music, one has not been there.

Gong music is very much a part of the traditional cultures of the Tây Nguyên communities, central to the concerns of life. It is not a quotidian music found in everyday activities, in the way that lullabies are. Gong performances are reserved for occasions that mark special meaning in the course of human affairs. In this way, gong music reflects the animistic, agrarian, and ancestral aspects of traditional ethnic life and, as such, has connections with ritual and the sacred, as well as with the mundane. Gong performances signify special points in the cycle of life from birth to the grave, celebrating pregnancy, welcoming newborns into the world, accompanying marriage ceremonies, reminding newlyweds to practice cultural traditions, celebrating the building of a new house, mourning the dead at funerals, and announcing the departure of a dead person's soul for the land of the dead. Performances signal key moments in the planting cycles, with land ceremonies, sowing ceremonies, watering ceremonies, rain ceremonies, and harvest ceremonies.[13] Gong performances provide the opportunity for socialization around a shared set of values. In some cases, the

performances are "performative" in the technical sense of signifying a particular kind of action, such as welcoming a visitor to the village.[14] Gong performances also reflect and instantiate social relationships. Some gong ensembles are entirely male, some female; in others, gender roles are mixed together. The performances speak to ancestors and deities who influence human activities and natural events. In some groups it is thought that gods reside in the gongs.

The gongs themselves may also have a general representative meaning: in some cultures they represent the power and the prestige of the owners. A measure of the importance and power of gongs is that gong sets are considered extremely valuable treasures. A set of gongs among the Gia Rai group may be worth the exchange equivalent of thirty buffaloes. Gong performers typically wear handsome and ornate costumes made specially and worn only for gong performances. Performers frequently wear special facial and bodily decorations.

Clearly, we can begin to grasp the deep cultural meanings and significance of gong performance only when we understand it in the context of the honored place that gong playing holds and the important cultural functions that it serves for the peoples of the Tây Nguyên region. In this light, traditional Vietnamese gong playing can be seen to have affinities with the form of human behavior Ellen Dissanayake calls "making special."[15]

III. ART, CRAFT, AND CULTURE

We can take several lessons from these reflections about Vietnamese gong music that shed light on the musical practices of the Western musical world.

We earlier spoke about Collingwood's observation that one of the characteristics of craft is that a craft may rely on other crafts for what it needs. A craft therefore takes its place in a nested series of interlocking activities. Certainly, when we think of the production and regulation of gongs, of the costumes, decorations, and dances that accompany gong performances, we can see that something of the sort is true of traditional Vietnamese gong practice. These activities involve what the ancient Greeks recognized as the power to produce a preconceived result by means of consciously controlled and directed action.[16] These techniques are certainly taught and passed on from generation to generation by way of example and oral instruction. But Collingwood deployed his analysis of craft as a way of distinguishing craft from art, properly so-called, which, on his view, consists in a certain mode of expressing the emotion of an individual artist.

This is a position that would be totally foreign to the ways of thinking of the ethnic groups of the central highlands we have been examining. Certainly, the subsumption of gong playing under the general rubric of personal emotional expression would strike these Vietnamese as peculiarly narrow. Nor is it clear that these Vietnamese would even recognize the distinction between craft in the Greek sense and art in the sense of activities designed solely or even primarily for the provision of aesthetic enjoyment, much less in Collingwood's sense. As we have seen, the gong players and the members of these societies have a sophisticated aesthetic sense, but gong playing is seen as so closely integrated into the daily lives of people in these societies, that Western categories of art and craft that figure in Western aesthetic discussion would surely strike these Vietnamese as somewhat artificial and narrow. Gong playing is too deeply imbricated in the daily and supernatural meaning of life for these categories to take us very far.

On the other hand, one wonders about the extent to which the same kind of analysis might be given to Western musical practice. Consider the case of one of the great masterworks of Western musical culture, Handel's oratorio, *The Messiah*. *The Messiah* is, of course, a justifiably admired musical achievement of choral composition, notable for its musical eloquence, its harmonic intensity, and monophonic, polyphonic, and homophonic textures. But it also has deep religious significance, celebrating the story of Christ the Redeemer and Savior of the world. It has occasioned philosophical reflections on Hannah Arendt's conceptions of human natality and human possibility.[17] At the same time, *The Messiah* draws on traditional folk music, in particular, themes of the *pifferari*, the wandering musical shepherds of the Abruzzi who went to Rome during the Christmas season to play. It has also become something of an industry. *The Messiah* was already an Easter-time phenomenon in Handel's day. Today, there is hardly a metropolitan area in Europe or North America that cannot boast a tradition of performing the work at Christmas, with hundreds of *Messiah*

groups, societies, and festivals proclaiming their performance as a beloved tradition involving hundreds of voices. Performance of *The Messiah* is an important factor in the economic success of countless concert halls, orchestras, and community choral groups. (In some locales tickets are available through Ticketmaster.) Choir members, including both amateurs and professionals, rehearse for months in preparation for eagerly awaited performances. Participation in these groups evokes a mixture of responses and motivations, from glory in the music itself, to piety, camaraderie, and the self-affirmation and comfort that comes of knowing that one belongs to a particular religious community. *The Messiah* is each of these things and all of these things.

The larger question that our reflections on Vietnamese gong music brings to mind, then, is the extent to which the philosophical understanding of Western music requires an analogously situated inquiry into its human significance. If we were to insist on pushing the Collingwoodian insight about the network of interlocking and reciprocal activities he identified as activities of craft, what we would want to say is that both Vietnamese and Western music must be understood in the context of the larger forms of life that are both presupposed by and that go beyond the musical practices themselves, a suggestion that calls to mind not so much the philosophical views of Collingwood as much as those of John Dewey, Ludwig Wittgenstein, and Bruno Latour. Indeed, understanding musical performance practices in the context of the cultural forms of life out of which they arise may give us some insight into the question of what differentiates the musics of the world as well as what they have in common.[18]

IV. POSTSCRIPT

The gong culture of the Vietnamese central highlands is in danger of dying out. As ethnic communities are increasingly exposed to Western and other outside influences, village youth are becoming less interested in their ancestral music. The responsibility for preserving the traditional patterns, tunes, skills, and lore rests on an older generation. Under the pressure of globalization, traditional rice cultivation is being replaced by other crops such as coffee, black pepper, and cashews, and many of the gong ceremonies based on rice farming seem less vitally connected with the concerns of everyday life.

The supply of musical instruments is also dwindling under the influence of globalization and the ravages of war. Ancestral gongs are being by sold to outsiders by villagers who must cope with the rigors of subsistence farming and the costs of purchasing the necessities of modern life. The gongs are sold by weight. A gong set that had been worth thirty buffaloes to the Gia Rai is now going for eighty-five cents U.S. per pound. In Gia Rai province alone, the number of gong sets has dropped from the tens of thousands in 1980 to about three thousand in 2003. In some villages musicians play damaged gongs because they cannot afford to replace them.

The United Nations Educational, Scientific and Cultural Organization (UNESCO) has recognized gong music as a world heritage music. The Ministry of Culture and Information and the government of Vietnam are taking steps to preserve gong culture through programs of research, conferences, festivals, television broadcasts, and education. Whether traditional Vietnamese gong cultures can survive as a living tradition in the communities of their origin is an open question.[19]

PHILIP ALPERSON
Department of Philosophy
Temple University
Philadelphia, PA 19122, USA

INTERNET: alperson@temple.edu

NGUYỄN CHÍ BẾN
Vietnam Institute of Culture and Information Studies
32 Hao Nam, De La Thanh, O Cho Dua
Hanoi, Vietnam

INTERNET: vncvhnt@fpt.vn

TO NGOC THANH
Vietnam Association of Folklorists
No. 45, Block A, 109 Truong Chinh Street
Hanoi, Vietnam

1. Tây Nguyên is a 26,850-square-mile region of mountains and high plateaus, 90 miles wide east to west, and 280 miles long from north to south, bordering Laos and Cambodia to the west. The Tây Nguyên region comprises the provinces of Lâm Đồng, Gia Lai, Kon Tum, Đắc Lắc, and Đắc Nông.

2. *The New Grove Dictionary of Music and Musicians* has only a few sentences on the subject of Vietnamese gong music. There are recordings of other varieties of traditional Vietnamese music available on CDs in the West where one can hear examples of music featuring the *đàn tranh* (the sixteen-string zither), the *đàn t'rung* (the bamboo xylophone), the *tam thập lục* (the thirty-six-string hammered zither), the *đàn bầu* (the Vietnamese monochord), the *nguyệt cầm* (the moon-shaped lute), and the *sáo* (the bamboo flute), as well as other less familiar musical instruments such as the *pang gu lug u Hmông* (a slide whistle), and the leaf of the blông tree, but few of these recordings include gong music. Exceptions are the CD compilations *Gongs Vietnam—Laos* (Playasound), *Vietnamese Folkmusic 1* (Vietnam Musicology Institute), *Stilling Time: Traditional Musics of Vietnam* (Innova, also available as a download from www.innova.mu), *Music from Vietnam 3: Ethnic Minorities* (Caprice Records), and *Vietnam: Musiques des montagnards* (CNR). The Ministry of Culture and Information of Vietnam has produced a DVD, *The Space of Gong Culture in the Central Highland of Vietnam*, with an accompanying essay, "Cultural Space of Tây Nguyên Gong" (Vietnam Institute of Culture and Information Studies, Hanoi: The Gioi Publishing House, 2006), written by Nguyễn Chí Bến. A portion of the essay appears in To Ngoc Thanh and Nguyễn Chí Bến, "The Space of Gong Culture in the Central Highland of Vietnam," *Vietnam Social Sciences* 112 (2006): 113–126. The current paper is indebted to these materials.

3. For an introduction to the culture of Vietnam as a whole, see Mark W. McLeod and Nguyen Thi Dieu, *Culture and Customs of Vietnam* (Westport: Greenwood Press, 2001); Neil L. Jamieson, *Understanding Vietnam* (University of California Press, 1993); Pierre Huard and Maurice Durand, *Vietnam, Civilization and Culture*, Vũ Thiên Kim, trans. (Paris/Hanoi: Ecole Francaise d'Extrême-Orient, 1998). For background information on the central highlands, see Gerald Hickey, *Kingdom in the Morning Mist: Mayréna in the Highlands of Vietnam* (University of Pennsylvania Press, 1988); Georges Condominas, *We Have Eaten the Forest: The Story of a Montagnard Village in Central Highlands of Vietnam*, Adrienne Foulke, trans. (New York: Hill and Wang, 1977).

4. Listen, for example, to the Jörai Hrap pieces, *Gongs Vietnam—Laos*, tracks 10 and 20, and the Ê Đê music, track 11.

5. R. G. Collingwood, *The Principles of Art* (Oxford University Press, 1938), pp. 16–17.

6. For good examples of quarter-tone gong music, listen to the Thái music, track 7 on *Gongs Vietnam—Laos*, the Ba Na pieces (especially tracks 18, 22, and 25), and the Mnong Rlâm music (track 23).

7. The expressive and representational qualities of Western music have received considerable attention in contemporary Western philosophical aesthetics. For recent overviews, see Philip Alperson, "The Philosophy of Music: Formalism and Beyond," in *The Blackwell Guide to Aesthetics*, Peter Kivy, ed. (Malden: Blackwell Publishing, 2004), pp. 254–275; Stephen Davies, "Music," in *The Oxford Handbook of Aesthetics*, Jerrold Levinson, ed. (Oxford University Press, 2003), pp. 489–515; Mark DiBellis, "Music," in *The Routledge Companion to Aesthetics*, Berys Gaut and Dominic McIver Lopes, ed. (New York: Routledge, 2001), pp. 531–544.

8. For examples, listen to *Gongs Vietnam—Laos*, tracks 14 and 21 (Thái), 15 (Jörai Hrap), 22 and 25 (Ba Na), and 23 (Mnong Rlâm).

9. Listen to the Gié-Triêng harvest music, *Gongs Vietnam—Laos*, track 3.

10. Listen to track 29: "Pliér," on *Music from Vietnam 3*.

11. Listen to track 24: "Kong taár" ("Scarecrow") on *Music from Vietnam 3*. Track 20 is a performance of the same piece on bamboo rods. Comparing these two performances is an excellent way to get a sense of the distinctive characters of gong and bamboo music.

12. For examples of Ê Đê gong music in addition to the performances mentioned in notes 5 and 6 above, listen to track 2: "Dinh tăktàr," track 7: "Ciriria," and track 14: "Nio vit h'gum," on *Music from Vietnam 3*. A gong ensemble accompanying a singer from the Muòng group can be heard on track 18: "Loóng ba," on *Music from Vietnam 3*.

13. The *Gongs Vietnam—Laos* CD has recordings of performance styles from different ethnic communities for similar ritual ceremonies. The disk has music to celebrate the inauguration of a new house from the Mnong Rlâm, Ê Đê, and Ba Na groups, for example, buffalo sacrifice music from the Ba Na and Jörai Hrap, and funeral music from Jörai Hrap, Thái, Ba Na, and Mnong Rlâm villages. In addition, the CD has four separate recordings of performances addressed to the spirit of the communal house by Ba Na players. One can also hear music to summon spirits and to mark the departure of the deceased soul from the grave for the spirit world from the Jörai Hrap, and Gié-Triêng music to celebrate the new year and the end of the harvest.

14. For a discussion of performative utterances, see J. L. Austin, *How to Do Things with Words* (Oxford: Clarendon Press, 1962). For an example of performative gong music, listen to the Ê Đê "Welcome Music" on *Stilling Time*, track 1; six male gong players and a drummer play energetic rhythmic patterns with improvisations while the head woman of the village shares a ceremonial cup of wine with the visitors. Listen also to the Ê Đê welcome music on track 11 of *Gongs Vietnam—Laos*.

15. See Ellen Dissanayake, *What is Art For?* (University of Washington Press, 1988), especially ch. 4. We make this reference without endorsing the specifically sociobiological tenets of Dissanayake's work.

16. Collingwood, *The Principles of Art*, p. 15.

17. Frederick M. Dolan, "An Ambiguous Citation in Hannah Arendt's *The Human Condition*," *The Journal of Politics* 66 (2004): 606–610.

18. These themes are developed in Philip Alperson, *The Philosophy of Music* (Malden: Blackwell Publishing, forthcoming).

19. The authors thank Noël Carroll, Nguyen Thi Dieu, Susan Feagin, Casey Haskins, Mary Hawkesworth, Ngô Thanh Nhàn, and Sophie Quinn-Judge for their helpful comments on earlier versions of this paper. They also thank Bi Hoài Son for his valuable assistance with translation.

STEPHEN DAVIES

Balinese Aesthetics

According to the Balinese expert, Dr. Anak Agung Madé Djelantik, "no writings about aesthetics specifically as a discipline exist in Bali."[1] The arts are discussed in ancient palm leaf texts, but mainly in connection with religion, spirituality, ceremony, and the like. However, there are famous accounts by expatriate Westerners and anthropologists.[2] There have also been collaborations between Balinese and Western scholars.[3] In addition, there is a significant literature written in Indonesian by Balinese experts, beginning in the 1970s.[4] Considerable experience of the culture is necessary to appreciate the full detail of these analyses and to be able to understand the arts from a Balinese perspective. I attempt neither task in this paper.

What I have written is addressed more to the cultural tourist than the anthropologist. Tourists are often captivated by the colorful opulence of Balinese culture and the centrality of art to the daily lives of ordinary Balinese. At the same time, all but the most indifferent or obtuse cannot fail to notice that the Balinese attitude to the arts is sometimes strangely different from our own Western culture. In following sections, I outline what is likely to strike non-Balinese as puzzling or unique in the Balinese attitude to and treatment of the arts. I focus on four areas: the relation between art and religion and between art and community, the competitive aspect of the arts, and the high value placed on novelty, innovation, and adaptation. I begin, though, by discussing notions that are foundational in Balinese aesthetics.

I. BASIC AESTHETIC CONCEPTS

One central concept is that of *taksu*.[5] *Taksu* is the name of a temple shrine at which one can pray for strength, and artists do pray there for success. *Taksu* also refers to the spiritual inspiration and energy within a mask, puppet, character, or ceremonial weapon.[6] Above all, *taksu* denotes the charismatic power of a great performer to please the audience and to become the character or role he or she plays.[7] Alternatively, it refers to the artist's being at one with his or her musical instrument, mask, puppet, or costume.[8] As such, *taksu* is a condition that performers aspire to. Though the term applies primarily to the performing arts, some Balinese extend it to other arts, such as painting, and even to other skilful activities, such as cooking. It is inherited by relics of famous artists from the past, such as antique recordings of famous musicians or old paintings.

The word '*taksu*' is distinctively Balinese.[9] It expresses a notion with which we are very familiar, however. We too attach the highest value to the special ability of great performers to move the audience with the excellence, virtuosity, and conviction of their efforts. We also regard the special qualities that make for greatness in an artistic creator or performer as divine gifts that cannot easily be taught, analyzed, or conveyed. And we too have a special reverence for, say, an old recording of Rachmaninov playing his own compositions or a costume once worn by Nijinsky.

General judgments of what is beautiful (*becik*) in the arts invoke other central concepts in Balinese aesthetics: unity and balance between elements and form, along with technical excellence, and the bond between art and life or nature. All these ideas have a long pedigree in the art of the West and also of other non-Western cultures.[10]

Despite the universality of such aesthetic criteria, their mode of realization in Balinese art is often distinctive. For example, the measurements for a Balinese house are traditionally based on the bodily parts of its occupants in order to ensure mutual harmony and balance between the building and its occupants. The layout of houses and temples pays regard to cosmological principles that are no less vivid to the Balinese than are visible, material aspects of their world.[11] In addition, pairs of drums and gongs in the gamelan [Id.] orchestra are characterized as male and female and the relation between the parts of the ensemble mirror social and cosmological principles of order.[12] Meanwhile, the traditional codes of proportion for human depictions do not come directly from life but from the puppets of the Balinese shadow puppet play.[13] This is not regarded as a departure from verisimilitude, however, because the size, shape, physiognomy, and proportion of many puppets are perceived as relevant to character and spiritual traits that also stand in need of representation. The reflection of the iconography of the shadow puppet play in traditional styles of painting and human depiction is paralleled by mutual reactions between other art forms: the poses of statutes are often modeled on narrative gestures or positions found in old dance and drama genres, for instance.

Art must be infused with life, and that means movement. "In popular Balinese thinking there are three elements: water, fire and air, from which all visible form is composed. Each element moves (typically, water downwards, fire upwards, air laterally or freely) or indeed may change nature. The corollary of this mutability is that composite forms are also continuously transforming (*matemahan*)."[14] Although the voice of the Balinese puppeteer is now electronically amplified, electric lights cannot replace traditional oil lamps because they "kill" the puppets. Electric light is steady, so the puppet characters cannot be seen to breathe. By contrast, their shadows constantly pulse with the flickering of the oil lamp, even when the puppets are stationary. Something similar applies to dancers and actors; they can never be entirely still. They constantly move their fingers (*jeriring*), even when their bodies are otherwise at rest. The effect is also integral to Balinese music. In most Balinese gamelans, the instruments are paired. The pair's members are tuned slightly apart, so that four or five beats a second are heard when the same note is played on both instruments. The result is a seemingly magical, shimmering iridescence in the sound, even through passages of sustained notes.

There is a further way the connection between art and life is forged in Balinese art. The Balinese dislike blank spaces. They fill their artworks with complex, fine, exquisite detail. In the depiction of a forest scene, for instance, every leaf is shown. This predilection acknowledges the fecundity of the tropical environment in which they live. Djelantic makes the connection explicit when he observes: "The compelling desire to be one with nature made the Balinese use his hands to decorate his dwelling with artefacts derived from nature. Flowers and leaves that impressed him by their symmetry, rhythm, and harmony found expression in decorative stone and wood carving in houses, on walls and entrances of compounds. Its practice through the ages has established the general propensity of the Balinese artist towards decorative art, prevailing until the present day."[15]

The same tendency to ornately fill every available space is expressed in music and dance as well. In some Balinese music, one-half of the orchestra plays extremely quickly, yet precisely, and the other half does the same but in syncopation. The air becomes awash with breathtakingly complex passagework that moves twice as fast as seems humanly achievable.[16] A similar delight in intricate detail is shown not only in the elaborateness of Balinese dance costumes but also in the subtle complexity of the movements. I have catalogued the Balinese names of nearly 200 dance positions and attitudes (*agem*), link movements between positions (*abah tangkis*), postures, strides, and foot movements (*tandang*), facial expressions (*tangkep*), movements of the head and neck (*guluwangsul*), and shoulder, hip, hand, finger, and fan movements.[17] The eyes, face, neck, arms, hands, fingers, and fan can be used in dozens of ways.[18] Every cross-accent and drum stroke in the music is echoed by some part of the dancer's body, though often the movements are extremely subtle and small.[19]

Mastery of the complex, decorative detail characteristic of Balinese art obviously provides for the virtuosity the Balinese value so highly. Creating it requires patience, skill, and technique. This is immediately obvious to anyone who views the rococo richness of paintings or of carvings in wood or stone. The same applies to the performing arts, though there the performance can seem so effortless and deadpan that its difficulty could be overlooked. Dancers and musicians train for years, starting as children, to achieve the control, dexterity, strength, and flexibility they need. Consider the fast gamelan playing mentioned above. Most of the instruments have brass keys suspended over resonators. Once struck, these continue to sound until manually damped, which is done as the next key is hit. If the damping is not precise, the sound is either too clipped or one note bleeds into the next, and if the damping is not perfectly coordinated, when twenty-five musicians play in unison the music is turned to mush. Imagine the skill required to play music with perfect clarity at the rate of up to seven notes a second.[20] Yet, the precise coordination of the ensemble is the minimum standard required by Balinese for an adequate performance.

Virtuosity takes other forms, of course. To stay with the musical case, works sometimes contain prolonged passages in free rhythm and with changing tempos and unexpected accents. Like all else in the music, these must be learned by rote and require hours of rehearsal to be played with perfect coordination. Or, to mention woodcarving, great artistry is shown in integrating features of the grain and shape into the scene or depiction that is carved. As in the art of all cultures, a crucial aspect of technique is the skill with which the artist reconciles content and form, subject and medium.

II. ART AS RELIGION

In Bali, the creation and presentation of art is a devotional act. Officially, the Balinese are Hindu, but a strong element of animism shapes religious observances on the island. Along with ancestors, they recognize spirits of the earth and air, many of which are not friendly and must be placated. In general, the goal of Balinese religious practices is to keep the forces of good and evil in balance. Offerings are made on a daily basis at many sites where people live and work, but the most elaborate are reserved for temple ceremonies (*odalan*). Every village and every household compound possesses three temples, and numerous other temples are located in rice fields, intersections, and elsewhere. (It is said there are as many temples as people in Bali.) The anniversary of each temple comes every 210 days according to the Balinese calendar and is the occasion for a ceremony lasting from one

to ten days; the more significant the anniversary, the bigger the ceremony. As well as spectacularly ornate and intricate food, flower, and blood offerings, which are widely regarded as art forms in their own right, temple ceremonies include music, dance, masked dramas, and shadow puppet plays for the gods' delectation.[21] Some temple ceremony dances (for example, *rejang* and *mendet*) are performed by ordinary members of the community and do not involve rehearsal or formal training. Other of the entertainments are presented by trained and practiced groups, though these groups typically draw their membership from the local community. Artists and performers are regularly expected to offer their services free (*ngayar*) for ceremonies at their village's temples.

The Balinese performing arts were classified in 1971 into the religious (*wali*), the intermediate (*bebali*), and the secular (*balih-balihan*).[22] This was done in order to identify those special dances (*tari wali*) that should not be performed for tourists apart from the religious setting with which they are connected. In fact, though, all three types of performance take place at temple ceremonies and all are offerings to the gods. *Wali* performances are reserved for the temple's inner compound, *bebali* ones take place in the temple's outer courtyard, and *balih-balihan* ones occur on stages immediately outside the temple entrance. Art-enriched ceremonies mark other important calendar events as well, such as the Balinese new year of *galungan*, which involves ten days of festivities, and rites of passage and death, such as when the baby is first allowed to touch the ground at the age of 210 days, tooth filing, marriage, and cremation.

The fact that performances at temple ceremonies are intended for the gods is apparent when one comes across a puppet show with musical accompaniment in a corner of the temple's inner courtyard, with not a single member of the busy throng attending to it. Similarly, the pair of instruments played high on the bier for cremations can never be heard above the hubbub of those who carry it. The cacophony of noise at other times indicates that the gods are multitaskers. It is not uncommon in temples for different kinds of gamelans only a few yards apart to play different pieces while from loudspeakers comes the voice of a priest intoning scriptures or describing the entertainments that are to come, all this accompanied by the monotonous pounding of the *kul-kul*, a slit drum used to call people to the temple, the high-pitched ringing of priestly bells, and the constant chatter of the crowd.

Fortunately, most of the Balinese gods partake of the human aesthetic that values beauty and fineness in clothes, decorations, offerings, architecture, drama, music, and dance. However, not all the gods are decorous or friendly. The Balinese world includes witches (*leyak*), nasty spirits (*bhuta* and *kala*), monsters (*raksasa*), and the evil Rangda and her followers. These are also represented and acknowledged in temple and other ceremonies, which contain powerful elements of the bizarre and grotesque as a consequence. Another aspect of Balinese religion that can strike Westerners as strange is the occurrence of trance and the violent forms this can take. Young girls dance standing on the shoulders of men in one form of temple trance dance (*sanghyang bidedari*), while Rangda forces men who attack her to turn their daggers (*keris*) on themselves in another. Trances are often faked for tourists, but not in the temple.

One expects to encounter religious art at temple ceremonies but not when one attends a tourist concert at one's hotel. Nevertheless, the devotional aspect of Balinese art persists in contexts that seem entirely secular to Westerners. At the start of a tourist performance, a priest often says some prayers on stage and splashes performers, costumes, and instruments with holy water. Many tourists think this ritual is bogus, but it is not. The priest will be genuine, and it is important to recall that the gamelan symbolizes both the cosmological and the social orders, so that the playing of music can never be entirely purged of religious significance. Moreover, most performance spaces, including many at tourist venues, are positioned according to the same traditional principles that dictate the alignment of temples.

In summary: "Balinese music in its traditional setting is essentially religious ... Every performance is an offering to the gods or an attempt to placate evil spirits ... Music for entertainment is also religious. Unlike ceremonial music, however, it is a spectator performance. Although the visible audience is composed of Balinese, its primary purpose is to entertain and propitiate an invisible audience: the gods ... However, the same music that is played for the entertainment of the gods is also used on secular occasions when it is performed for tourists or official government guests."[23] And: "Nearly all traditional Balinese performing arts are ultimately rooted in religion and ascribed func-

tions relating to religious practices. The major theater, dance, and musical performances, and even those seemingly nonreligious in character, are frequently presented at festivals to enhance the ritual's power. In addition, arts considered relatively 'secular,' such as *drama gong*, are held in spaces ritually purified, and both performers and performance space are positioned to acknowledge the mountain-sea axis that also informs the positioning of temples."[24]

III. ART AS SPORT

All commentators mention that the Balinese love competitions. Kite clubs battle to have the largest kite and to keep it in the air the longest, for instance. The arts are not exempt from such passions. Djelantik observes: "The inherent tendency in the Balinese people to compete against each other in any kind of public performance stimulates [them to] strive for perfection [in the arts]."[25] Indeed, music and dance are frequently presented in a competitive mode. The word for this is *mabarung* or *mebarung*.

Competitions are also common in Western art, ranging from classical music concerto contests to pub talent quests and paintoffs in shopping malls. Also, audience members sometimes express their support for one artist or group over others. Distinctive to the Balinese context are the pervasiveness of the competitive ethos and the depth of involvement and arousal it provokes in participants and audiences.

Sometimes, Balinese art competitions are relatively informal. *Jegog* is a form of gamelan in which all the instruments are made of bamboo. *Mabarung* between side-by-side *jegog* groups involves the simultaneous playing of different pieces, with each ensemble trying to drown out and outlast the other. "Shortly after one of them begins to play, the music becomes highly animated, and suddenly the other group enters into the midst of the musical argument. Both groups seem to attempt to destroy the music of the other by interfering. The result is something quite at odds with our normal concept of 'music.' Rather than music, this is closer to sports."[26] "As the evening progresses, the groups begin to play simultaneously in a cacophony of short, driving ostinato patterns. The focus then shifts to determining who can play louder, harder and for as long as possible without stopping or losing their place in the melody. Shirts soak through with sweat and fingers get ravaged by blisters as musicians push themselves to the absolute limits of their physical abilities in pursuit of such distinctions. Around 2 a.m., after a trial by a jury of peers, the exhausted players finally disperse."[27]

I should add that the sight of a *jegog* in full flight is truly remarkable. The bass instruments, like the others in the ensemble, are bamboo xylophones, but they are made from bamboo so massive that the player crouches on top of the instrument and strikes the tubes with a heavy rubber mallet. As he bounces around on the frame to reach different tubes, the instrument sways dramatically from side to side, which movement is accentuated by the colorful Balinese umbrellas that bedeck it. Meanwhile, other musicians in the ensemble sway and leap to the rhythm of the music. Viewed from the front, the orchestra seethes and moves like some frenzied machine, energized by the music issuing from it.

More formal competitions usually involve groups taking turns to play the same pieces, or pieces of similar types, before judges. The contest often lasts two or more hours, and the rival groups sit opposite each other on the stage. Island-wide competitions along these lines date back at least to the early years of the twentieth century. Winning such a competition attracts great prestige to the group.[28] "*Gamelans* are extremely competitive, and most groups actively seek to improve their skills and maintain their equipment . . . A Balinese musician loves to tell you about the year he won first prize; a *gamelan* group might tell you that they are striving to be in first place next year."[29]

The most important competition now takes place at the annual arts festival (Pesta Kesenian Bali [Id.]) between *gong kebyar* groups representing the island's eight regencies. Performances in this competition attract an audience of thousands of Balinese. Many people are bused in to support the group representing their region. There is constant catcalling, whistling, and bantering between these claques, even as the music sounds. Despite such behavior, most members of the audience have a deep appreciation of the music and what is required in playing it. "The atmosphere at these events is much more reminiscent of a sporting event than a concert . . . The audience are thoroughly responsive to everything taking place in the music or dance, reacting instantaneously with approving cheers at well-executed passages, or jeering with abandon at the slightest mistake. (At one such concert in Amlapura in 1977, a missed jegogan tone [bass note] brought 3,000 people to their feet in a spontaneous chorus of boos)."[30]

As these remarks suggest, Balinese audience etiquette is more like that for popular than high art in the West. The audience is usually attentive and knowledgeable, but is inclined to mock errors. Positive appreciation is less usual; applause has been adopted from tourists only in the last decade, and is not common at the close of a performance. Indeed, with the first notes of the end-of-show music for shadow puppet plays and other forms of dance or drama, the Balinese audience rises and leaves. The venue is often nearly empty by the time the closing tones sound.

IV. ART AS COMMUNITY

I have already observed that Balinese artists are intimately involved in their community's religious observances. Something similar happens at the political level. The smallest political unit, the *banjar*, is a hamlet or subvillage unit, usually of one hundred or more households, ruled by the heads of these households. It plays a central role in governing and organizing the immediate community. All members are expected to contribute (*gotong-royong* [Id.]) to the *banjar*. This can take the form of labor, money, or other donations. In meeting this obligation, painters and carvers may put their talents at the service of the community, for example, by providing statues and pictures for the shrines at the open-sided meeting/performance space (*balé banjar*) that is the hub of *banjar* life.

Communalism is an aspect of Balinese life in general. Wherever an activity is pursued, a club (*sekaha*) is organized to facilitate it. If kites are flown, there will be a kite-flying club. If a gamelan is played, there will be a club associated with that gamelan of which all players and administrators are members. Sometimes, the members of the *sekaha* all come from the same *banjar*, sometimes not. The musical instruments, costumes, and props of performance groups are rarely owned by individuals. They might belong to the temple, the *banjar*, or the *sekaha* itself.

The same applies to arts thought of as individual in the West, such as painting or sculpture. The Balinese tend to form schools, associations, or communities of painters. As far as I know, it is not common for artists to work jointly on a given painting or sculptural relief—say, with one doing the skies and another the birds—but the members of a group usually share a common style and coordinate their efforts and their resources. As with other clubs, financial revenues and costs are also typically pooled. The signing of paintings is a comparatively recent development and shows the influence of Western models of art creation.

There is also a dynastic tendency within Balinese arts—mask carvers beget mask carvers, dancers spawn dancers, musicians father musicians, and so on. As people sharing the same artistic interests tend to gather together, this has given rise over time to a distinctive sociogeographical distribution of the arts. Particular art forms have become associated with particular villages. The mask carvers of Mas are famous; for silver jewelry, go to Celuk; *geringsing* weaving is associated with Tenganan; the artists of Keramas are renowned as performers of *Arja* (Balinese opera) and those of Batuan for *Gambuh* (a genre of dance drama); for stone carvings, visit Batubulan; Nyuhkuning specializes in frog carvings; the best Balinese carved doors are made in Pujung; Pejaten is the home of traditional ceramics; Saba, Binoh, and Peliatan are known for the quality of their *Legong* dancers.

The Balinese inclination to communalism affects the creation of their artworks. Individual painters, carvers, composers, and choreographers gain renown for the excellence and success of their achievements. They will receive commissions for new works and they will be eagerly sought as teachers. They become famous. But it is also common for all creative artists to draw heavily and explicitly on the creative tradition to which they are the heirs. Creativity often involves the adaptation and arrangement of familiar materials, not radical originality, and what is created, sometimes via group input, is not sacrosanct. It is expected that individual groups will change what they receive from the creator or from another group to suit themselves.

The communalism of the Balinese is also apparent in the content of their artworks. Favorite subjects in the depictive arts are "life of Bali" scenes, showing rice farming, religious rituals, and the activities typically found in the village (along with tourists and their cameras). These representations can be packed with people, none of whom is a primary focus. Or the scene might show only a few

people but make them peripheral to the details of nature that surround them. In other words, depictive works often show sociality or the integration of human life with the natural, rather than accentuating individuality and difference. In music, along with the close cooperation and coordination between players and the pairing of instruments described earlier, the social aspect of the orchestra is apparent in elements of musical form. Similar instruments frequently interlock their parts. This interlocking (*kotekan*) generates an integrated pattern, so that what is heard is the composite, and not the separate, contributions of the individual parts.

Djelantik emphasizes the artist's immersion in his or her wider community, the endemic artistic legacy within which he or she works, and the religious ethos that infuses both of these: "At the aesthetic level this being part of the cosmos and of the community in particular have given the traditional artist the specific Balinese *attitude towards his art*. His aim is not to express in his work his personal concepts or aspirations, but to execute what is expected from him. His satisfaction lies in the devotion which he can put into his activity and to achieve the highest perfection in his product. His aesthetic ideal is not only the conformity with the norms but also the achievement of perfection, in which he aims at the unison with God the Almighty as the symbol of ultimate perfection."[31]

V.   ART AS INNOVATION

Though the arts draw heavily on local traditions, they are not always conservative or static. Special effort is taken to preserve the most sacred forms as they have always existed, along with older dance and drama genres such as *Arja*, *Gambuh*, and *Legong*, but other genres are subject to constant development and innovation. Indeed, Bali is among the most culturally volatile and eclectic places I have visited.

There is a constant demand for new dramas, musical works, and dances (*kreasi baru* [Id.]). Because the tradition is oral (and perhaps also because Indonesian cassettes are fragile at best), the shelf-life of most new performance pieces is brief. They can be lost within months, and this is accepted with equanimity. In this respect, the attitude of the Balinese to their arts is more like that of Westerners to pop culture than to high art.

Paintings and carvings are more permanent, but they wear quickly in the tropics and are often consumed by insects. The stone used traditionally for statues, called *paras*, is so soft that it is easily marked by one's thumbnail. Sculptures made from *paras* weather badly within decades.

The Balinese are innovative in the readiness with which they adopt and adapt new media and technologies in art production. Djelantik records how cement casts and "carvings" first challenged stone in the fields of sculpture and architecture in the 1930s. In the 1970s, production expanded and centered on the village of Kapal. "At present the whole town of Kapal consists of rows and rows of workshops producing traditionally shaped cement casts of every kind, providing a cheap substitute for expensive manually produced carvings of stone or brick."[32] Djelantik observes that, in regard to Balinese aesthetics, the new technology of cement casts did not change anything fundamentally because cement works are assessed in terms of traditional criteria: the artist's skill and the perfection of the work's execution as apparent in the use of the materials and the texture of its surface.

It is in the realm of painting that the most dramatic appropriations and adaptations have taken place. The oldest traditional style draws on the iconography, characters, and themes of the shadow puppet play. (This style is called *kamasan*, after a village where it flourished and still continues.) Balinese painting changed considerably, though, under the influence of Western artists (in particular, Walter Spies and Rudolph Bonnet) who introduced modern materials and Western styles in the 1920s and 1930s. But the Balinese quickly adapted their paintings to local preferences and genres; distinctive regional differences were already apparent in the "modern" paintings of Ubud, Sanur, and Batuan by the late 1920s.[33] The association of artists established in Ubud in 1936, Pita Maha, aimed to preserve the quality of Balinese visual arts, which were to be judged primarily in terms of traditional aesthetic criteria, demanding skillful technique, harmony and balance in colors and design, and so on. Later, the Young Artists of the 1960s (inspired by Arie Smit) adopted a freer style, with strong colors and hard-edged figures, but in time they incorporated finer, more complex decoration, and therefore fell into line with traditional Balinese aesthetic values.[34] Whatever their favored style, the best and most respected artists retain a commitment to the aesthetic virtues listed previously: technical virtuosity, subtlety and complexity of fine detail, balance of form and color, themes from traditional and religious epics, or depictions of communal or natural scenes.

Some indigenous Balinese artists inevitably consider what will appeal to the tourist market and a huge quantity of kitsch paintings and carvings is produced. Indeed, many of the tourist carvings sold across the Pacific as belonging to Polynesia, Micronesia, and so forth are in fact manufactured in Bali, and Balinese tourist shops sell locally made dijeridu and djembe drums, as well as Balinese fare. Balinese artists imitate indigenous Pacific, Australasian, and African styles as effortlessly as they do their traditional ones. Though the influence of religion is surprisingly far reaching in Balinese arts, it does not extend to these products. Yet they also illustrate pervasive aspects of the Balinese aesthetic, such as the supposition that art should be practically useful. Innovation, appropriation, adaptation, and fusion have not been adopted from the postmodern West but are, instead, thoroughly Balinese ways of approaching the arts.

VI. CLOSING COMMENTS

Modern-day anthropologists mock Miguel Covarrubias for writing in 1937: "Everybody in Bali seems to be an artist. Coolies and princes, priests and peasants, men and women alike, can dance, play musical instruments, or carve in wood and stone."[35] His claim does not strike me as ludicrously exaggerated, however. Few Balinese are professional artists, of course, but an extraordinary number are involved in the arts one way or another, especially when one counts among the arts silverwork, weaving, basketwork, and the creation of elaborate food and floral offerings, as well as traditional forms such as the shadow puppet play.

A similar response would apply to the observation that the features I have highlighted as distinctive to the Balinese arts are found in other cultures. It is probably true of most cultures that the arts are involved in religious observances, social ritual, and interpersonal cooperation, that they also foster competition and skill, and that they are often valued for introducing qualities that are novel. What is distinctive to Bali is the degree of intimacy between the arts and these further, important aspects of life. There, the arts are the lifeblood and pulse of community existence, not merely an accompaniment.

And how could it be otherwise? The arts attract and entertain the gods to the religious festivals at which their attendance is crucial if the delicate balance between good and evil is to be maintained in the community and the wider world. The arts are integral to the rites of passage that guide individuals from birth to death and reincarnation. Moreover, through tourism and cultural exports, the contribution of the arts, directly or indirectly, to the Balinese economy is far greater than in most other societies. The Balinese attitude to art (and all else) is pragmatic; there is little of the effete preciousness that goes with high art in the West. But because they are inevitably aware of the value of art to their way of life and what they hold dear, they are masters of its creation and connoisseurs of its appreciation.

STEPHEN DAVIES
Department of Philosophy
University of Auckland
Private Bag 92019
Auckland, New Zealand

INTERNET: sj.davies@auckland.ac.nz

1. Anak Agung Madé Djelantik, "Is There a Shift Taking Place in Balinese Aesthetics?" Paper presented at the Third International Bali Studies Workshop, the University of Sydney, July 3–7, 1995, p. 2.

2. For example, Miguel Covarrubias, *Island of Bali* (Singapore: Periplus Editions; reproduction of the Alfred A Knopf Inc. edition of 1946; first published 1937); Walter Spies and Beryl De Zoete, *Dance and Drama in Bali* (Singapore: Periplus Editions; first published by Faber and Faber in 1938); Margaret Mead, "The Arts in Bali," *Yale Review* 30 (1940): 335–347. More contemporary perspectives are offered in Andrew Duff-Cooper, *An Essay in Balinese Aesthetics*, Centre for South-East Asian Studies, Occasional Papers No. 7 (University of Hull, 1984); Edward Herbst, *Voices in Bali: Energies and Perceptions in Vocal Music and Theater* (Wesleyan University Press, 1997); Mark Hobart, *After Culture: Anthropology as Metaphysical Critique* (http://www.criticalia.org/, 2002; first published in Yogyakarta by Duta Wacana University Press in 2000.).

3. For example, Madé Bandem and Frederik Eugene deBoer, *Balinese Dance in Transition: Kaja and Kelod*, 2nd ed. (Kuala Lumpur: Oxford University Press, 1995); Wayan Dibia and Rucina Ballinger, *Balinese Dance, Drama, and Music* (Singapore: Periplus Editions, 2004).

4. For instance, Madé Bandem, *Ensiklopedi Tari Bali* (Denpasar: ASTI, 1982).

5. Italicized terms are in the Balinese language, unless followed by (Id.), which indicates they are in the Indonesian language.

6. Herbst, *Voices in Bali*, p. 182.

7. Females have always danced in the temple and also in secular dance genres, such as *Legong*, which featured them from early in the twentieth century. Indeed, in the traditional dramatic genres of *Gambuh* and *Arja*, women replaced men in many roles from about the 1930s. Refined male characters are typically performed by women and other kinds of cross-gender roles are fairly common. Many women performers have gone on to become renowned teachers. Nowadays, women are encouraged to play music, though almost always in all-women ensembles. Also in recent times, women have achieved success in painting and literature. Some artistic roles, as in *topeng* (mask) dancing or *dalang* (puppeteer) in the shadow puppet play are more or less the exclusive preserve of men.

8. See Michael Tenzer, *Balinese Music* (Berkeley/Singapore: Periplus Editions, 1991), p. 137; Dibia and Ballinger, *Balinese Dance, Drama, and Music*, p. 108.

9. "The etymology is probably from Sanskrit: *caksu* eye, faculty of sight, look. The *taksu* as a shrine is a derivative, linked to witnessing, which is a key role. Again, there are links to India and the vital role of *saksi*—witnessing—as a quite different relationship here from 'watching,' 'spectating'. There is a distinguished South Asian literature on *saksi*, but nothing on *taksu*, which is pure Balinese" (Mark Hobart, personal communication, November 28, 2005).

10. See Richard L. Anderson, *Calliope's Sisters: A Comparative Study of Philosophies of Art* (Englewood Cliffs, NJ: Prentice Hall, 1990); H. Gene Blocker, *The Aesthetics of Primitive Art* (Lanham, MD: University Press of America, 1993); Denis Dutton, "Aesthetic Universals," in *The Routledge Companion to Aesthetics*, D. Lopes and B. Gaut, ed. (London: Routledge, 2005), pp. 279–291.

11. See L. E. A. Howe, "An Introduction to the Cultural Study of Traditional Balinese Architecture," *Archipel* 25 (1983): 137–158.

12. The Indonesian word 'gamelan' refers to the orchestra and the instruments that comprise it. In Balinese, the term is *gambelan*, though the verb form, *ngambelin*, to play music, is more common than the noun. More often, an orchestra is referred to as a *gong*. Eighteen or more different kinds of *gambelan* occur in Bali. The most common is *gong kebyar*. There are about 1,500 *gong kebyar* groups, each with a membership of thirty or more musicians and dancers. The population of Bali is about 3,000,000. On the way the orchestra echoes the social and cosmological order, see Sue Carole DeVale and I Wayan Dibia, "Sekar Anyar: An Exploration of Meaning in Balinese Gamelan," *The World of Music* 33 (1991): 5–51.

13. Balinese puppets are more lifelike and generally smaller than Javanese ones (where the strictures of Islam require more abstracted characterizations of the human form), but the heads, shoulder span, and arm lengths are exaggerated. Note that the music and other aspects of Balinese shadow puppet plays are also very different from those elsewhere in Indonesia and Southeast Asia.

14. Mark Hobart, *After Culture*, pp. 112–113.

15. Anak Agung Madé Djelantik, "Is There a Shift Taking Place in Balinese Aesthetics?" p. 7.

16. It is useful to contrast Balinese music with that of the courts of central Java. Both involve layers of sound and cyclic, gong-punctuated structures, but they target entirely

different sonic ideals. The Balinese seek explosive energy, contrast, and a degree of controlled rhythmic instability, where the Javanese look for calm, restraint, rhythmic regularity, and evenness of tone. Balinese music includes abrupt tempo changes, whereas gradual acceleration or slowing is preferred in central Javanese court music. And while the Javanese also decorate the music to a high degree, this decoration forms the background texture, whereas it is foregrounded by the Balinese.

17. For descriptions, see Madé Bandem, *Ensiklopedi Tari Bali*; R. M. Moerdowo, *Reflections on Balinese Traditional and Modern Arts* (Jakarta: PN Balai Pustaka, 1983), pp. 87–90; Colin McPhee, "Dance in Bali," *Dance Index* 7–8 (1948): 156–207.

18. To mention only a few neck movements: *ngepik* means to shake the neck right and left without twisting it, *ngelidu* means to look to right and left, *nyulengek* means to look up, *ngetget* means to look down, *kidang but muring* means to shake the neck.

19. Again, the contrast with classical Javanese dancing is instructive. McPhee writes: "Against these two opposing styles [Cambodian and Javanese] the Balinese stands out dramatically in its freedom, its exuberance and almost feverish intensity. Although the ritual dances of the temple and the ancient dance plays of the court have the grave serenity of the Javanese, the trained dancers of today, who appear in plays or by themselves, give theatrical, dynamic performances, wild, moody, filled with sunlight and shade like the rushing, shimmering music of the Balinese *gamelan*. Rhythms are taut and syncopated throughout, and filled with sudden breaks and unexpected accents. Gongs and metal-keyed instruments are struck with small, hard mallets so that tones are bright and incisive. Dance movement is not conceived in a single broad, legato line, but is continually broken by fractional pauses that coincide with the breaks in the music; on these the dancer comes to a sudden stop, and the eyes of the spectators focus momentarily on a motionless, sharply defined pose. These breaks are not endings but phrase accents, like brief 'rests' in music; they last no longer than a flash, and serve as starting points for renewed and vigorous movement. Unlike the almost inaudible drumming in Javanese music, Balinese drums throb continuously in agitated crescendos and diminuendos that forever urge the dancers onward or hold them back" ("Dance in Bali," p. 160).

20. A gamelan from Perean recorded in the 1970s "displays the absolute summit of gamelan speed and virtuosity: [interlocking] played at a rate of 200 beats per minute. At four subdivisions per beat that breaks down to 800 notes per minute, or an average of 400 notes each for [the two interlocking parts], which in turn translates to almost 7 notes per player per second! Can one conceive of 25 people doing *anything* together that fast? All of this was executed with

crystalline clarity and accompanied, one might surmise, by facial expressions of utter nonchalance and boredom [as is the custom] during performance" (Michael Tenzer, *Music in Bali*, p. 80).

21. On these offerings as art forms, see Francine Brinkgreve and David Stuart-Fox, *Offerings, The Ritual Art of Bali* (Sanur: Image Network Indonesia, 1992).

22. Anonymous, *Projek Pemeliharaan dan Pengembangan Kebudajaan daerah Bali: Seminar Seni Sacral dan Seni Profan Bidang Tari* (Denpasar: typescript, 1971).

23. Ruby Sue Ornstein, *Gamelan Gong Kebyar: The Development of a Balinese Musical Tradition* (Los Angeles: University of California; Ph.D. Dissertation, 1971), pp. 8–11; see also pp. 65–66, 369–373.

24. David Harnish, "Balinese Performance as Festival Offerings," *Asian Art* 4 (1991): 9–27; quotation from p. 9.

25. Anak Agung Madé Djelantik, "Is There a Shift Taking Place in Balinese Aesthetics?" p. 8.

26. Minagawa Koichi, Liner Notes (G. Groemer, trans.) for CD *Jegog of Negara* (World Music Library KICC 5157, 1992).

27. Michael Tenzer, *Music in Bali*, p. 92.

28. A further reward went to the famous *gong kebyar* group of Peliatan when it won in 1936: the Dutch exempted the members from universal labor on road building.

29. Margaret Eiseman, "Gamelan Gong: Traditional Balinese Orchestra," in *Bali: Sekala & Niskala*, F. B. Eiseman Jr., ed. (Singapore: Periplus Editions, 1990), pp. 333–342; quotation from p. 339.

30. Michael Tenzer, *Music in Bali*, p. 110.

31. Anak Agung Madé Djelantik, "Is There a Shift Taking Place in Balinese Aesthetics?" pp. 7–8. The Balinese recognize Sang Hyang Whidi Wasa—the unmoved mover of the universe, representing both ordering and disordering forces—as the supreme being.

32. Anak Agung Madé Djelantik, "Is There a Shift Taking Place in Balinese Aesthetics?" pp. 12–13.

33. Representative early twentieth-century Ubud painters include Ida Bagus Kembeng and Anak Agung Gedé Sobrat, Sanur artists include I Sukaria and Ida Bagus Madé Pugug, and Batuan artists include Ida Bagus Madé Togog. Other painters of the time, such as I Gusti Nyoman Lempad and I Gusti Madé Deblog, remained aloof from Western influence while developing distinctive personal styles.

34. For discussion, see Anak Agung Madé Djelantik, *Balinese Painting* (Singapore: Oxford University Press, 1986). Balinese paintings can be viewed via the web, for example, by searching for the names of artists or the sites of ARMA (Agung Rai Museum of Art), Puri Lukisan, the Neka Museum, and the Rudana gallery, all in the Ubud area. A list of the more important art museums is found at http://www.bali-paradise.com/museum.cfm.

35. Miguel Covarrubias, *Island of Bali*, p. 160.

SUSAN PRATT WALTON

Aesthetic and Spiritual Correlations in Javanese Gamelan Music

There are striking similarities and intriguing connections between the tradition of gamelan music in Java and Javanese mystical traditions. A gamelan is an ensemble of gongs, metalophones, drums, bowed lute, xylophone, zither, bamboo flute, and singers. Gamelans of many different types exist in Java, Bali, and Lombok, as well as in Malaysia. Some include only a few gongs; others have up to fifty instruments. The type of ensemble that concerns us is the largest of these ensembles, the gamelan of Central Java. Its most important function is to accompany dance, theater, and ceremonial occasions, such as weddings, in both ritual and commercial settings.

The links between the musical and mystical traditions of Java have not been much noticed or examined in the scholarly literature. The focus of gamelan research has been elsewhere: on the performance styles of particular instruments or musical groups, the history of the tradition, including the effects of Westernization, analysis of mode, musical cognition, and Javanese music theory. Judith Becker, in her fascinating and suggestive *Gamelan Stories: Tantrism, Islam, and Aesthetics in Central Java*, does point out that vestiges of ancient mystical practices can be found in pitch names, the titles of musical pieces, and in the sacred *bedhaya* dance.[1] These observations are symptoms, it seems to me, of more fundamental and more pervasive links between gamelan music and spirituality in Java. I contend that gamelan music mirrors and manifests a central system of thought, experience, and belief in Javanese culture: mysticism. Though waning in recent decades, mysticism has long been a focal point in Javanese culture, so it is not surprising that Java's musical system is organized, at least

in part, to support, manifest, and express that system. The stated aim of music making, the structure of the music, the leadership styles, and the creation of melodies have remarkably close parallels in the Javanese mystical world.[2]

My analysis of the link between Javanese musical and mystical traditions centers on the concept of *rasa*, which is crucial to both traditions. I start with the ancient Sanskrit theory of *rasa*, then move to the central role of *rasa* in contemporary Java musical groups, followed by an analysis of Sumarsam's "inner melody" theory of Javanese music. Finally, I show that *rasa* is not merely an abstract construct accessible to an elite cadre of the most knowledgeable gamelan musicians: it is the basis of music making for many musicians, especially those of the older generation.

Before delving into the links between the mystical and musical traditions of Java, I need to flesh out the concept of *rasa*. The primary meaning is feeling. As 'feeling,' it refers to the physical senses of taste and touch and also to emotional feelings. *Rasa* can also mean 'meaning.' The example Clifford Geertz gives is: "*rasa* is applied to words in a letter, in a poem or even in a speech, to indicate the between-the-lines 'looking north and hitting south' type of allusive suggestion that is so important in Javanese communication."[3] As this example illustrates, *rasa* can mean the essential, often hidden, significance of something obscure. This concept of *rasa* points back to the first notion of *rasa* as feeling and taste. For the Javanese, to fathom something obscure, one has to engage all one's senses, feelings, and intuitions, as if one were tasting the essence of the thing. To use merely one's intellectual capacities is not enough.

Rasa is an integral part of two Javanese mystical traditions: Tantric Shaivism and Mahayana Buddhism on the one hand, and mystical Islam (Sufism) on the other hand.

Sanskrit aesthetic theory constitutes a key element in Java's Tantric Shaivism and Mahayana Buddhist mystical traditions. Sanskrit aesthetic theory was first articulated in the *Natyasastra*, the main Sanskrit treatise on dramaturgy dating somewhere between the second century and eighth century CE, and was further developed in the tenth century by the Tantric Shaivite philosopher, Abhinavagupta, of Kashmir.[4] Java and other parts of Southeast Asia were strongly impacted by Indian culture during the first millennium of this era. The products of this influence include Indian religions, mythology, and, as Laurie Sears posits, Sanskrit aesthetic theory.[5]

A crucial concept in Sanskrit aesthetic theory is the notion of *rasa*. According to this theory, the hallmark of a good drama is its ability to develop a particular *rasa*, which then dominates the work.[6] The *Natyasastra* mentions eight primary *rasa*: the erotic (*srngara*), the comic (*hasya*), the pathetic (*karuna*), the furious (*raudra*), the heroic (*vira*), the terrible (*bhayankara*), the odious (*bibhatsa*), and the marvelous (*adbhuta*). Abhinavagupta added a ninth *rasa*: the *santa rasa*, or tranquil sentiment associated with mystical experience. The exact production of *rasa* is not fully explained in the *Natyasastra* and has thus been interpreted differently by different Indian philosophers. The *Natyasastra* states: "The Sentiment is produced (*rasanispattih*) from a combination (*samyoga*) of Determinants (*vibhava*), Consequents (*anubhava*), and Transitory States (*vyabhicaribhava*)."[7] Determinants are the causes of emotion, such as elements in a drama that might bring forth old memories and rouse the emotions. The consequents are the physical effects (for example, blushing) arising due to the determinants. The *vyabhicaribhava* are secondary, transient emotions, such as weeping with joy. As these three elements work together, the aesthete experiences one of the eight *sthayi bhava*, the primary emotional states. "The welling up of this emotion causes a state of total engrossment, which concomitantly leads to the loss of ego ... The totally unhampered experience of the *sthayi bhava* welling up from within is *rasa*."[8]

The *rasa* magnetizes the viewer, pulling her or him into the dramatic situation so that the viewer can relish the work in an almost gustatory way, experiencing it in mind and body.[9] Enthralled by the *rasa*, the viewer is freed from her or his usual mental chatter, liberated from the ego. Masson and Patwardhan explain:

for the duration of the aesthetic experience, the normal waking "I" is suspended ... all normal emotions are gone ... we experience sheer undifferentiated bliss ... for we have come into direct contact with the deepest recesses of our own unconscious where the memory of a primeval unity between man and the universe is still strong. Inadvertently ... we have arrived at the same inner terrain as that occupied by the mystic.[10]

Thus for Abhinavagupta, aesthetic enjoyment and mystical experience are intimately connected, for through works of art a person reconnects with the fundamental oneness of all things, what some may call the Absolute. But that Absolute resides within oneself. As a person fully experiences an aesthetic work, one merges with the object of contemplation, identifying completely with it, and experiences his or her pure self, or "highest Self." Masson and Patwardhan explain: "We can thus see that all of Abhinava's efforts focus on one important need: to crack the hard shell of the 'I' and allow to flow out the higher Self which automatically identifies with everyone and everything around."[11] This notion of art as a tool for achieving oneness explains a seeming anomaly in this theory: the word 'rasa' refers both to the feelings experienced by the viewers of dramatic works and to the most profound mystical awareness. For Abhinavagupta, the two are the same, for one cannot truly appreciate a work of art without achieving that mystical experience.

However, not everyone is capable of experiencing this level of aesthetic and spiritual bliss. Only a person who can transcend his or her ego, merging completely with the work of art, can do so. Such a person is called *sahrdaya*, "sensitive."[12]

Crucial to this theory of aesthetics is that the essential meaning of a work, its *rasa*, is never stated directly, but only suggested. This is true for two reasons, according to Abhinavagupta. First, a work that makes veiled allusions "carries far greater beauty" than one that bluntly asserts its truths.[13] Second, the very act of unearthing the hidden meaning in an aesthetic work

has spiritual value, for it "impels us to great devotion for another truth, beyond the phenomenal world."[14] The fundamental meaning of an aesthetic work is hidden, just as knowledge of ultimate reality is believed to lie deep within a person.

Several tenets in *rasa* theory touch on key issues of Western aesthetics. Abhinavagupta's focus
on individual experience of intense emotion suggests that for him, aesthetic meaning is located in
the perceiver, not the aesthetic work. For example,
the *rasa* of pathos (*karuna*) resides in the aesthete
and is not an inherent element of the work itself.
Furthermore, for Abhinavagupta, an individual's
response to a work is a product of his or her culture, for the determinants of emotion (*vibhava*)
are, in part, culturally determined. Finally, Abhinavagupta articulates a theory about the location
of the fundamental emotions within the individual.
To access *rasa*, one must free oneself from one's
ego, suggesting that the primary emotions reside
in the unconscious or subconscious.[15]

Rasa theory resonates with some elements of
Arthur Schopenhauer's philosophy. For him, life
is characterized by a continuous striving and crav-
ing. People can escape from that suffering in the
"quiet contemplation of the natural object actually present, whether a landscape, a tree, a moun-
tain."[16] In this reflection, one disassociates oneself from "the principle of sufficient reason"; one
"loses" oneself to such a degree that the person
and the object "become one," and the person becomes a "pure, will-less, painless, timeless subject
of knowledge."[17] In later passages, Schopenhauer
makes clear that artists have a particular ability
to engage in this kind of contemplation, for he
characterizes art as "the way of viewing things independent of the principle of sufficient reason."[18]

Though *rasa* is originally a Sanskrit word, it is
significant not only in Tantric Shaivite and Buddhist texts, but also in Sufi mystic contexts, and in
the syncretic mystical sects that combine elements
of all three religions. Indeed, all these religions
share a belief in the ultimate goal of the union with
the Absolute Being (or Allah in Islamic terms).
According to Mark Woodward:

While this concept [*rasa*] owes much to the Mahayana
Buddhist notion of *sunyata* (S.; void), it will be argued
here that this and other legacies of the Hindu-Javanese
past are interpreted in terms of Islamic assumptions
about the mystical path and the unity (A., *tawhid*) of
Allah.[19]

Both G. W. J. Drewes and Judith Becker stress
that Tantric mysticism and Sufi mysticism in Java
shared so many features that the transition from
the Indian to the Arabic form was probably quite
smooth.[20]

II. *RASA* IN CONTEMPORARY JAVANESE SPIRITUAL CONTEXTS

Moving toward my goal of exploring the similarities between Java's spiritual and musical traditions,
I focus in this section on the central role of *rasa*
in Javanese mystical groups. According to Clifford
Geertz, *rasa* is the "connecting link" between the
three major components of religious life: mystical
practice, art, and etiquette. This is especially true
for the *priyayi* (the aristocratic elite). The person
who truly understands ultimate reality—*rasa sejati*—can express that understanding through gestures in dance, sounds in music, or words in poetry.[21] Such a person is naturally refined (*alus*) in
his or her outer behavior. The concept of *rasa* is important not only to the *priyayi* but to many other
Javanese as well. The popularity of mysticism in
Java may be judged by the presence there of several hundred mystical groups.

One of the most prominent sects is Sumarah.[22]
Established in the mid 1930s, Sumarah includes
elements of Tantric Shaivism, Mahayana Buddhism, and Islam with indigenous mystical practices. The membership, which in 1984 was esti-
mated at 10,000, includes individuals of all ethnic, social, and religious backgrounds.[23] Since the
focus in Sumarah is on individually perceived spiritual experience (though within a group setting),
there is a minimum of dogma. Members meditate
individually and in group meetings, led by a spiritual leader.

According to Sumarah practice, meditation begins with relaxing the body and shifting the attention from thoughts to physical sensations and
to feelings. The purpose is to free oneself from
the usual form of consciousness, which is believed
to center on the obsessive replaying of thoughts
about the future or the past. The practitioner focuses on the feelings experienced in the present:
perhaps a physical sensation or an intense emotion that floats to the surface of the consciousness,
a feeling that is normally hidden by the barrage of
constant thoughts. As stillness and concentration
deepen, one is more able to ignore the thoughts

constantly rushing through one's head, while focusing awareness on a deeper, stiller, nonverbal part of oneself. Gradually, it is thought, the practitioner becomes aware of another level of being, termed *rasa sejati*, which Stange defines as "the absolute or true feeling [or] ... mystical awareness of the fundamental vibration or energy within all life."[24] Most people in Sumarah use the term 'Allah' to refer to *rasa sejati*, though some prefer to avoid the term as too specific. The word '*sumarah*' means surrender, and refers to the process of transcending normal consciousness and becoming aware of *rasa sejati*.

As one frees oneself from a normal form of consciousness, according to Sumarah theory, one becomes aware that one's perception is distorted by one's own experiences and beliefs. Stange describes this process as follows. "Beyond the senses and thought perception there lies a cleaning of internalized subconscious blockages, so that gradually perception is less filtered through subjective structures."[25] When this occurs, according to the members of Sumarah, one is able to perceive a fundamental truth: that all people, even all things, are essentially one.

Since in the phenomenal world, there *appear* to be distinctions between the material and spiritual, the Javanese identify two aspects of reality: *lahir* and *batin*. *Lahir* (from Arabic *zahir*), literally, "outer reality," consists of habits, behaviors, the material world, and surface phenomena. *Batin* (from Arabic *batin*), or "inner reality," is the inner spiritual life of an individual. *Batin* is accorded more value, for whereas surface forms reveal only the appearance of reality, *batin* is the essence.[26] The two are related, for features apparent in the phenomenal world are regarded as manifestations of the inner reality.

Because of the fundamental unity of all things, *lahir* and *batin* are not really opposite, but merely different expressions of reality. They are ultimately identical. According to Javanese thought, a physically beautiful person is necessarily faultless in her or his inner spiritual being, for the exterior is a manifestation of the interior.

These notions of the fundamental identity of *lahir* and *batin* are central to the story of Seh Siti Jenar, a Sufi master of mysticism, as told in the nineteenth-century *Babad Jaka Tingkir*.[27] Siti Jenar was executed for disseminating a secret that the *wali* (Islamic saints) felt should not be made public. Dissemination of that sacred knowledge was threatening to the *walis'* attempts to consolidate their political authority. The "secret" was the knowledge of the means for attaining spiritual empowerment, *sunyata jatimurti*. How does one attain spiritual empowerment? By grasping the essential oneness of all things. That understanding, called *rasa* in the text, is the ultimate reality, the absolute truth. One who has attained that knowledge "has grasped the ultimate of *rasa/Rasa* that is Reality."[28] Such a person has understood that things normally seen as opposites are in fact identical: *lahir* and *batin*, spirit and matter, divine and profane, Being and Nonbeing.[29]

Group meditation is central to Sumarah because of the focus on unity. Absolute truth can be perceived by individuals, but can be "confirmed" only by the group, which comes to a consensus through a process of communal meditation. During periods of group division, members enter deep meditation together. Each person "attunes" himself or herself to the *rasa* of the group. As each one becomes intuitively aware of the feelings of the group, consensus is reached. The group is central in making manifest the underlying truth. The assumption is that the "correct decision ... is implicit in the situation."[30] The absolute truth already exists but has to be discovered by humans. Likewise, in musical terms, as we shall see later, the appropriate choice of a musical pattern is said to be "implicit" in the immediate musical context, and it is the job of the musician to discover that pattern.

III. *RASA* AND GAMELAN MUSIC

Having established the importance of *rasa* and mysticism in Java today, I now turn to the heart of the argument: the remarkable linkages between Javanese spiritual and musical traditions. I will argue that for many Javanese, music has a strong spiritual dimension. In both traditions, *rasa* is central. Furthermore, absolute truth resides beneath surface manifestations. The very structure of the music reflects this belief. Since truth is hidden, the job of the practitioner—whether a mystic or a musician—is to make manifest that spiritual or musical truth. Finally, group collaborative work is key in uncovering those truths in both traditions.

Rasa is fundamental not only to Javanese mystical practice but to Javanese notions of aesthetics as well. According to historian Laurie Sears, *rasa* strongly influenced the development of Java's most important art form: *wayang kulit* (shadow puppet theater), which encompasses drama, classical poetry, epic stories, and gamelan music.[31] Sastrapustaka, a highly respected Javanese musician who was trained in the courts in the 1920s, paints gamelan music in terms reminiscent of Sanskrit theory. He says, "the art [of gamelan]—which is thought to be only for entertainment—is actually important for the physical (*lahir*) and spiritual (*batin*) education of all who study it in depth. Also, art is . . . a device for raising the grandeur of a people's spirit."[32] For Sastrapustaka, music is a guide for spiritual development. In Sanskrit theory, drama also has this function, as aesthetic experience shades imperceptibly into mystical bliss. Sastrapustaka continues: "Indeed it is very clear that this art can only give rise to a radiance or light which is pure, if it resides within a person whose temperament is noble and refined."[33] This statement hints at the Sanskrit notion of the *sahrdaya*, the sensitive aesthete, for only highly spiritually developed individuals can appreciate art, according to Sastrapustaka.[34] Furthermore, his exegesis of the meaning of gamelan pitch names is suggestive of Hindu/Buddhist *chakra*, centers of spiritual energy in the human body, as Judith Becker has argued. The *chakra* were focal points in body-based spiritual techniques of medieval Java.[35]

Sastrapustaka's comments hint at the connections between the musical and mystical traditions; the shared terminology provides tangible proof. In both cases, *rasa* is a crucial concept. For some gamelan musicians, it is "the key to aesthetic understanding."[36] *Rasa* has a wide range of meanings in gamelan music. "Feeling" and "inner meaning" are two common translations. A standard means of categorizing gamelan compositions is by *rasa*, so that there are sad pieces, exuberant pieces, flirtatious pieces, and so forth. This notion of *rasa*, as the primary mood or sentiment of a work, echoes the ancient Sanskrit idea that a poem or drama must convey one primary *rasa*.[37] *Rasa* can also refer to "the ability to express or perceive feeling or inner meaning" or "intuition."[38] This notion of *rasa* is important for musicians who play the gamelan instruments that utilize improvisation. These musicians express the "inner meaning" or *rasa* of a piece by altering standardized melodic patterns or even creating new melodies to fit both the

melodies played by the other musicians and the wider performance context.

One of the basic notions of *rasa*, common to both Sanskrit and Javanese uses of the term, is that the absolute truth resides at a fundamental level. Just as *rasa sejati* is sequestered deep in the *batin* beneath the surface manifestations of the *lahir*, the essence of a piece is thought by some theorists to be hidden beneath surface phenomena. Sumarsam calls this essence the *lagu batin*" or inner melody.[39] This melody is inner not only because it represents the heart of the piece but also because it exists, in complete form, only in the minds of the musicians. It can never be played by just one instrument, but only by the combination of instruments working together. The inner melody that musicians hear inside their heads, then, is a composite—bits of melodies of a variety of instruments. That inner melody represents the essence of the piece, the *batin*, while the melodies actually played on different instruments are akin to the *lahir*, or surface manifestations.

I am making the analogy between the spiritual concept of *batin* and the musical concept of inner melody to point out the shared discourse in the aesthetic and spiritual traditions in Java. The way that many Javanese talk about music and mystical experiences suggests that for them, the experiences of listening to gamelan music and achieving contact with the absolute truth may be akin. In describing both musical and mystical experiences, the Javanese focus on the inner meaning. For example, Sumarsam says:

In a *gamelan* rehearsal or performance, each musician relates the part he plays to the melodies played on the other instruments. This practice is often employed during the learning period. At the same time, it also allows the musicians to gradually absorb the underlying feeling of *gendhing* (composition) as inspired by the melody of the whole ensemble. This underlying feeling of *gendhing* is the essence of Javanese *gamelan* melody—the inner melody as felt by the musicians.[40]

This statement is resonant with Clifford Geertz's informant who stated that the essence of a person resides in the center of four concentric circles—representing (from outer to inner) the body, the five senses, the conscious will, and the unconscious origin of desires. In the center is the essence, which is "fixed and unchanging, it is always good, and it is that which judges and directs our will, or ought to."[41] The progression from outer manifestation to inner absolute reality that the initiate traverses during meditation is described in Sumarah terminology as follows.

"Feeling" in its turn may in the first instance mean awareness of physical sensation within the body, but that gross-level *rasa* becomes progressively more subtle—it shades through inner physical sensation into awareness of the emotions and ultimately into *rasa sejati*, the absolute or true feeling which is itself mystical awareness of the fundamental vibration or energy within all life.[42]

Common to both the inner melody and the absolute truth is an element of concealment. The inner melody is never fully sounded by any one instrument. In Sanskrit aesthetic theory, the *rasa* or true meaning of a work cannot be directly stated, but only suggested. J. Gonda, scholar of Javanese literature, points out that in old Javanese texts, the word *rasa* "often served to translate the Arabic *sirr* 'secret, mystery,' which refers to the most . . . hidden . . . elements in the human heart in which God is said to reside."[43]

This element of concealment pervades other aspects of both gamelan music and Javanese literature.[44] Clara Brakel notes that the texts of the sacred *srimpi* and *bedhaya* dances "are usually wrapped in mystery and symbolizing—indicating the 'magical loadedness' of the situations in which they serve: well-known word-forms are either altered intentionally or replaced by strange, archaic, and foreign sounds."[45] Certain Javanese pieces and Balinese musical instruments are never performed in public. In describing the spiritual power of four unusual *gendhing*, the famous court musician Warsadiningrat states, "our forefathers kept the knowledge of these *gendhing* strictly to themselves, for use in secret. Only a few people had the good fortune to be chosen to receive this knowledge."[46] Sastrapustaka titled his article on gamelan music "*Wedha Pradangga Kawedhar*" ("Knowledge of Gamelan Revealed"). The first section is called "The Cryptic Literature (*Sastra Sinandi*) Concealed in the Tones of the Gamelan."[47]

Because the underlying truth and the inner melody are hidden, it is the task of the practitioner to uncover that truth or to make manifest the inner melody. The process of articulating the inner melody is analogous to the search that Sumarah members undertake in their attempt to find *rasa sejati*. For them, solving a problem is not a matter of creating a solution but of discovering the truth, which is thought to be implicit in the situation. Similarly, the gamelan musician chooses melodic formulas, called *cengkok*, to fit the particular musical situation. Some of those formulas are standard ones, heard in many pieces, but many are contrived for the situation, as variations of the standard ones. Whereas a Western musicologist might regard this task as creating, the Javanese characterize it as *golek*, or searching. R. Anderson Sutton points out that searching differs from innovative creation in that searching implies that the object sought already exists.[48]

Collaboration is a key element in uncovering both the absolute truth and the inner melody. Just as in Sumarah where uncovering the absolute truth is the responsibility of the group, unveiling the inner melody requires the energies of everyone in the ensemble. Although it is theoretically possible for one musician to play his interpretation of the inner melody on a single instrument, no one instrument can play it without breaking rules of style and range. Furthermore, other musicians would not agree with his conception in every detail. The inner melody can be realized only by all the instruments of the ensemble playing the piece together, for the inner melody is a compilation of interpretations of all the musicians present. Although Supanggah's view of the melodic essence of a piece differs in crucial ways from Sumarsam's, Supanggah, like Sumarsam, emphasizes the combinational and holistic aspects of the implicit, unplayed melody. He states: "It is the sound produced by . . . the entire ensemble that is called the *gendhing* or piece. The *gendhing* exists only in the moment of performance."[49] Because of this focus on group rather than individual musical production, there is no tradition of virtuoso solo performers. Gitosaprodjo comments: "The playing of a *gamelan* group must be smooth and harmonious. The situation must be avoided in which one person tries to show off his expertise to the disadvantage of others . . . It must be remembered that *gamelan* playing is a collective activity."[50] Likewise, in Javanese mystical practice, absolute truth (*rasa sejati* or *hakiki*) is manifested only through group experience. According to Stange, "it is understood that Hakiki is only confirmed when it 'meshes' with collected experience during the attunement and achieved through group meditation."[51] People are not encouraged to meditate on their own.[52]

The form that musical leadership takes in gamelan music is reminiscent of the leadership style in the mystical groups. Members of Sumarah stress that the *pamong*, or guide, is not a teacher. Through meditation, the *pamong* becomes intuitively aware of the inner states of the individuals in the group and makes suggestions about their practice based on that knowledge. However, the *pamong* frequently reminds people not to use his or her suggestions without testing them internally for their applicability.[53] If members of the group feel that the *pamong* is not making intuitive contact with them, they replace him or her. Likewise, in gamelan music, leadership is shared and diffuse. There is no conductor. In playing a piece, musicians both follow their own conceptions of the inner melody and listen to the suggestions from other instruments that express it. Sometimes they even ignore it. According to Sutton, unbending fidelity to the inner melody (which he calls *lagu* following his teacher Suhardi) is not aesthetically appropriate. Instead, he says, "instruments should exhibit some aspects of the *lagu* and some pleasing deviations from it."[54] Like Sumarah, the gamelan group has its guide: the *rebab*, a two-stringed bowed lute. Called the *pamurba jatmaka* or "that which controls the soul," the *rebab* is thought to express the main emotion, or *rasa*, of a piece.[55] However, the absence of the *rebab* is not critical: other instruments can take over its role as guide.

All of this suggests a dynamic relationship between individuality and consensus in both the Sumarah group and in the gamelan. Although individual meditators are encouraged to test the validity of suggestions from the *pamong* within themselves, members of a group nonetheless meditate together in order to reach a consensus. The instruments in the gamelan are highly individual in timbre, range, rhythmic density, and style, and the aim in ensemble playing is not a fusion of sounds, but the capacity for each instrument to retain its individuality in a group. Yet, the instruments of the gamelan sound the same pitches at important structural points.

Calmness, harmoniousness, and balance are important features of both Javanese mysticism and gamelan music. Masson and Patwardhan

speak of "the unprecedented mental and emotional calm" achieved in meditation.[56] James L. Peacock describes the mystical experience as follows.

Discovery of the *rasa* is rewarded by an ecstasy comparable to orgasm ... Afterward, one feels at peace and in balance ... By unifying his inner being, he automatically harmonizes his social relations as well. The initiate is now prepared to cope calmly with the struggles of life, and like Arjuna, to carry out his duties with detachment. In fact some of the sects believe that through meditation ... all the Indonesian groups—the entire world—will be brought into harmony.[57]

Certainly not all gamelan pieces are uniformly calm. Nonetheless, it is striking how much of the music does seem to strive for balance and serenity. Musical climaxes are frequently muted. Sutton notes that some melodic patterns suggest the final pitch of a melody several beats before the other instruments arrive at the point of coincidence, "thereby diminishing any jarring sense of surprise, and hence any threat to the equilibrium of the players and listeners."[58] Because of the deeply calming and integrating effect of gamelan music, Javanese occasionally play on a single gamelan instrument at night as a form of meditation.[59]

I have shown how gamelan music and mysticism in Java share many elements of discourse and experience. The Sanskrit scholar says that a work of art can cause transcendent states; some Javanese musicians feel that gamelan music can be spiritually uplifting. The Sanskrit scholar says that only the sensitive aesthete can appreciate a work of art; some Javanese musicians claim that only the spiritually pure can truly understand gamelan music. For Javanese meditators, "ultimate reality" is not overt; in gamelan music, the inner melody is never stated, only suggested. Members of Sumarah believe that solving a problem involves discovering the truth, which is implicit in the situation; gamelan musicians state that all melodic formulas, even ones newly created for the situation, are inherently a part of the music. The Sumarah leader does not control the members of his or her group, but instead guides them; similarly, the gamelan has no conductor in the Western sense. The Javanese mystic emphasizes calmness, balance, and communal experience; so does the Javanese musician.

38 Global Theories of the Arts and Aesthetics

IV. SECRECY IN MYSTICAL AND MUSICAL
TRADITIONS IN JAVA

I suggest that the mystical underpinnings of the
gamelan tradition have not been discussed in detail by scholars of Javanese music because of the
element of concealment associated with mystical traditions. As Warsadiningrat's and Sastrapustaka's statements imply, playing certain *gendhing*
(musical pieces) and discussing the "cryptic" associations and meanings of gamelan music were limited to a select few in times past. Except for giving
a few tantalizing allusions to the hidden spiritual
meaning of gamelan music, Warsadiningrat consciously avoided direct discussion of the subject
in his massive work. He explained his reasons as
follows.

Writings on the history or story of *gamelan* included in
this book only describe *krawitan* [the art of gamelan mu-
sic]; they do not explain the meanings or purposes of
gamelan or *gendhing*. Those things this book does not
explain because the person who truly understands the
meanings and purposes of *gamelan* and *gendhing* must
supply his own interpretation.[60]

His last sentence refers to a reason why the spiritual purposes are not discussed—because coming
to an understanding of the inner meaning of gamelan music is an individual matter, just as gaining
access to one's inner being is an individual matter. In either case, the individual must embark on
an intense inner journey, partly if not wholly spiritual in nature.[61] This is not to say that individuals
achieve these understandings by working entirely
alone; in fact, in both the mystical and musical settings, these understandings are best achieved in
a group context. The doctrines of Sumarah stress
these points about secrecy and individuality: that
mystical traditions are secret not because mystics
want to exclude others but because the task of
uncovering the truth is the responsibility of the
individual.

From the external vantage point it is often assumed that
mystics employ code languages laden with secret meanings designed to exclude outsiders. Even when this is the
case it has little to do with the basis of the esoteric as
gnosis is seen by mystics. In terms of mystical principles
gnosis is fundamentally dependent on an internal journey through meditation or other "opening" procedures.

The "secrets" of mysticism lie *within* rather than being
held by other people. Normal consciousness systemati-
cally blocks individual awareness; the secret is something
which, in mystical terms, we keep from ourselves. In fact
most traditions hold that the gnosis sought by mystics
is readily available to anyone whose internal receptiv-
ity allows it, to anyone who genuinely "wants" it and
regardless of whether they relate to a "mystical" movement.[62]

Stange's last sentence clarifies what may seem
like a paradox to some. On the one hand, gamelan
music is not considered esoteric, abstruse, or in
any way inaccessible to the ordinary person and
yet, on the other hand, the music is associated with
traditions of mysticism. But this is not a paradox,
for in the Sumarah view, each individual has access
to "ultimate reality," though access to it is hidden
by his own limitations. Likewise, in terms of music,
each person can establish for himself the "meaning
or purposes" of gamelan music, as Warsadiningrat
has said.

V. RASA IN THE MUSIC OF SOLO FEMALE SINGERS

Lest the reader conclude that the concept of *rasa*
and the spiritual dimension of gamelan music are
limited to an elite circle of Javanese gamelan the-
oreticians whose venerable status allows them access to secret mystical knowledge, I end with a
discussion of the central position of *rasa* among Javanese gamelan performers. I will use *pesindhen*,
solo female singers who perform with the gamelan, as an example.

Nyi Gitotenoyo (born 1919; died around 1995)
was one of the most influential *pesindhen* of her
generation. She was a pivotal figure in the history of solo female singing in the central Javanese
city of Solo, for she popularized the style associated with the main palace, the *kraton*, the style
that prevails even today.[63] Several younger singers
told me that they modeled their singing after Nyi
Gitotenoyo's.

In a personal communication in 1992, Gitotenoyo stressed to me the central role of *rasa* in
her music making. "I must say that I, well, *pesindhen* in the past, did not understand writing and
did not go to school. So, we could only practice
... *rasa*. With *rasa*, wherever the music went, I
could enter in. I could sing just by listening to the

sound of the *gamelan*." The understanding of *rasa* among *pesindhen* in Nyi Gitotenoyo's generation allowed them to sing pieces they had never even heard before, though they could not read notation.

Nyi Gitotenoyo explained that *pesindhen* of her time were trained to discover what they should sing by listening to the melodies played on the softer sounding instruments, particularly the *rebab*, the bowed instrument. In her words, *pesindhen* "sang by using *rasa*"; for they felt or sensed where the melody was going before it went there. Embedded in the *rebab* melody are clues about the identity of the goal tone for the next phrase. The *pesindhen* should sing a *cengkok*, or melodic formula, whose last pitch matches the pitch of the goal tone. As soon as the *rebab* melody hints what the next goal tone is, the *pesindhen* chooses a *cengkok*.

Nyi Gitotenoyo told me that to deepen her engagement with the music, she closed her eyes when she sang. Her voluntary sightlessness did not separate her from her fellow musicians, but intensified her awareness of their veiled musical suggestions. The image of Nyi Gitotenoyo immersing herself in musical sounds and interweaving her *cengkok* with them is strikingly akin to the subtle harmonizing of individual feelings to the *rasa* of the group in Sumarah meditations. In both cases, practitioners direct their inner reception to the *rasa* of the group so that their contributions could be attuned to that communal *rasa* or to that collective musical expression.

The spiritual dimension in Nyi Gitotenoyo's singing is also evident in her stated focus on starting her melodic patterns approximately when the instruments begin theirs. This allowed her to sing her patterns slowly, stretching them out before finally resting on the goal tone. Most *pesindhen* nowadays start their *cengkok* so late that have to rush through them to end at the appropriate time. She told me proudly that another musician had said of her singing: "Singing like that can make a person feel calm." According to her most prominent student, her deliberately slow style creates a feeling of *sumeleh*. "*Sumeleh* is a good feeling, like surrendering all problems to God, a feeling of tranquility."[64] Again, it is noteworthy that the language of spirituality has been invoked to describe a musical phenomenon.

I am not suggesting that Nyi Gitotneoyo was consciously using her singing to communicate spiritual feelings (though she may have), but that her stated musical goals are strikingly resonant with Javanese spiritual practices. Those goals are discovering the hidden inner truth (*rasa*) and working collaboratively with others to create harmoniousness and tranquility.[65]

My main point in this paper has been to show the striking similarities and remarkable connections between the musical and mystical traditions of Java. Perhaps for some Javanese, especially the older generation, the aesthetic and spiritual experiences are inseparable, as they seem to have been for the early twentieth-century nationalist, Raden Ajeng Kartini, who described her feelings listening to gamelan music: "And my soul soars with the murmuring pure silver tones on high, on high, to the isles of blue light, to the fleecy clouds, and to the shining stars—deep low tones are rising now and the music leads me through dark dales, down steep ravines, through somber woods on into dense wildernesses, and my soul shivers and trembles within me with anguish and pain and sorrow."[66]

The strong link between musical and mystical traditions in Java that I have suggested throughout this paper is shifting, especially among young *pesindhen*. They no longer talk about *rasa* as crucial to their music. However, instrumental musicians still do regard *rasa* as the centerpiece of their musical experience. True, the explicit spiritual associations of *rasa* have receded, to be replaced by more worldly interpretation of the word as feeling, as Marc Benamou has noted.[67] I speculate that the spiritual links are still there, just below the surface, and those links are part of the deep attraction many Javanese musicians feel for their music. The Javanese term, '*lango*,' which is frequently associated with gamelan music, captures best the Javanese sense of the "spiritual." Echoing Abhinavagupta, Zoetmulder says of *lango*: "It is a kind of swooning sensation, in which the subject is completely absorbed by and becomes lost in its object, the appeal of which is so overwhelming that everything else sinks into nothingness and oblivion." It seems to me that emotions of this kind—which we can term *rasa*—are a prominent feature of the passion for gamelan music of many people in Java. Many musicians play gamelan music all night several times a week, even when there is no audience and no remuneration. Entranced by beautiful *pesindhen* and copious alcohol, these musicians seem to be surrendering themselves completely to the scene, totally immersed in *lango*, a luscious feast of sensuality, pleasure, and mystical/musical bliss.

SUSAN PRATT WALTON
University of Michigan
Ann Arbor, MI 48104, USA

INTERNET: swalton@umich.edu

1. Judith Becker, *Gamelan Stories: Tantrism, Islam, and Aesthetics in Central Java* (Arizona State University, 1993).

2. Mangkunegara VII explores the mystical meaning of the *wayang kulit* (shadow puppet theater) and touches briefly on the link between gamelan music and mysticism. See "On the Wayang Kulit (Purwa) and Its Symbolic and Mystical Elements," in *Data Paper Cornell University Southeast Asia Program* No. 27, trans. Claire Holt (Southeast Asia Program, Dept. of Far Eastern Studies, Cornell University, 1957), original text published in *Djawa* xiii (1933). See also Benedictus Suharto, *Dance Power: The Concept of Mataya in Yogyakarta Dance* (Bandung: Sastrataya, Masyarakat Seni Pertunjukan Indonesia, 1998).

3. Clifford Geertz, *The Religion of Java* (University of Chicago Press, 1976, first printed 1960), p. 238.

4. Bharata Muni, *The Natyasastra: A Treatise on Hindu Dramaturgy and Histrionics Ascribed to Bharata Muni*, trans. Manomohan Ghosh (Calcutta: The Asiatic Society, 1950); Laurie Jo Sears, *Text and Performance in Javanese Shadow Theatre: Changing Authorities in an Oral Tradition* (Ph.D. dissertation, University of Wisconsin at Madison, 1986), p. 25.

5. Sears, *Text and Performance*, pp. 24–25.

6. Sears, *Text and Performance*, p. 35.

7. Manomohan Ghosh, *The Natyasastra of Bharata Muni* (Calcutta: The Asiatic Society, 1950), p. 105, as quoted in Sears, *Text and Performance*, pp. 35–36.

8. Stephen Slawek, "Engrossed Minds, Embodied Moods and Liberated Spirits in Two Musical Traditions of India," *Bansuri* 13 (1996): 31–35, quote is from p. 35.

9. I use feminine pronouns to indicate that women were probably not excluded from aesthetic experience in Abhinavagupta's time. Stephen Slawek points out (in personal communication) that the word for an individual who experiences *rasa*, '*rasik*,' is gender neutral and that numerous sculptures from pre-Islamic times and paintings from the Mughal period depict women playing musical instruments. He concludes, "it would appear that women were viewed as capable of creating an aesthetic experience."

10. J. L. Masson and M. V. Patwardhan, *Santarasa and Abhinavagupta's Philosophy of Aesthetics* (Poona: Bhandarkar Oriental Research Institute, 1969), pp. vii–viii.

11. Masson and Patwardhan, *Santarasa*, p. 89.

12. Masson and Patwardhan, *Santarasa*, pp. 49–50.

13. Masson and Patwardhan, *Santarasa*, p. 108.

14. Masson and Patwardhan, *Santarasa*, p. 107.

15. Slawek, "Engrossed Minds," pp. 33–35.

16. Arthur Schopenhauer, *The World as Will and Idea (Die Welt als Wille und Vorstellung)*, trans. R. B. Haldane and J. Kemp (London: Routledge and Kegan Hall Broadway House, 1964), Vol. I, p. 231.

17. Ibid.

18. Schopenhauer, *The World as Will and Idea*, p. 239.

19. Mark R. Woodward, *Islam in Java: Normative Piety and Mysticism in the Sultanate of Yogyakarta* (The University of Arizona Press, 1989), p. 68.

20. G. W. J. Drewes, "Indonesia: Mysticism and Activism," in *Unity and Variety in Muslim Civilization*, ed. Gustave E. von Grunebaum (University of Chicago Press, 1967), p. 287; Becker, *Gamelan Stories*, p. 3. As *rasa* moved from ancient India to Java, it changed. Javanese aesthetic theory conflates *rasa* and the various forms of *bhava*, referring to both as *rasa*.

21. Clifford Geertz, *The Religion of Java* (University of Chicago Press, 1976, first printed 1960), pp. 238–239.

22. Paul Denison Stange, *The Sumarah Movement in Javanese Mysticism* (Ph.D. dissertation, University of Wisconsin at Madison, 1980); David Howe, *Sumarah: A Study of the Art of Living* (Ph.D. dissertation, University of North Carolina at Chapel Hill, 1980).

23. Paul Denison Stange, "The Logic of Rasa in Java," *Indonesia* 38 (1984): 116–121, quote is from p. 116.

24. Stange "The Logic of Rasa," p. 119.

25. Stange, "The Logic of Rasa," p. 121.

26. Howe, "Sumarah," p. 116.

27. See the translation by Nancy K. Florida, *Writing the Past, Inscribing the Future: History as Prophecy in Colonial Java* (Duke University Press, 1995), p. 78.

28. Florida, *Writing the Past*, p. 190.

29. Florida, *Writing the Past*, p. 361.

30. Stange, "The Logic of Rasa," p. 123.

31. Sears, *Text and Performance*, pp. 19–35.

32. Sastrapustaka, "Wedha Pradangga Kawedhar" ("Knowledge of *Gamelan* Revealed"), in *Karawitan: Source Readings in Javanese Gamelan and Vocal Music*, ed. Judith Becker and Alan Feinstein; trans. R. Anderson Sutton (Ann Arbor: Center for South and Southeast Asian Studies, 1984), Vol. 1, p. 310.

33. Sastrapustaka, "Wedha Pradangga Kawedhar," p. 310.

34. Why would gamelan be necessary as an aid to spiritual development if people were already noble and refined? In Javanese thought, gamelan can enhance spiritual development, but only for people who already have the seed of nobility and refinement in them.

35. Becker, *Gamelan Stories*.

36. Marc Benamou, *Rasa in Javanese Musical Aesthetics* (Ph.D. dissertation, University of Michigan, 1998), p. 63.

37. This is generally true, but some pieces do mix *rasa* either sequentially or simultaneously. See Benamou, *Rasa in Javanese Musical Aesthetics*, p. 141.

38. Benamou, *Rasa in Javanese Musical Aesthetics*, p. 63.

39. Sumarsam, "Inner Melody in Javanese Music," in *Karawitan: Source Readings in Javanese Gamelan and Vocal Music*, ed. Judith Becker and Alan Feinstein (Ann Arbor: Center for South and Southeast Asian Studies, 1984), Vol. 1. Two other Javanese theorists, Supanggah and Suhardi, have articulated slightly different conceptions of this phenomenon. Calling these melodies "implicit" or "unplayed" melodies, Marc Perlman discusses all three theories in *Unplayed Melodies: Javanese Gamelan and the Genesis of Music Theory* (University of California Press, 2004). See also Perlman "The Social Meanings of Modal Practices: Status, Gender, History and Pathet in Central Javanese Music," *Ethnomusicology* 42 (1998): 45–80.

40. Sumarsam, "Inner Melody," p. 303.

41. Geertz, *The Religion of Java*, p. 315.

42. Stange, "The Logic of Rasa, p. 119.

43. J. Gonda, *Sanskrit in Indonesia*, 2nd ed. (New Delhi: International Academy of Indian Culture, 1973), p. 256, as quoted in Stange, "The Logic of Rasa," p. 127.

44. The Javanese even have a word for this kind of deliberate concealment: *semu*. See Florida, *Writing the Past*, p. 275. She defines it as "the merely glimpsed perceptible dimension of the concealed."

45. Clara Brakel, "Traditional Javanese Poetry and the Problem of Interpretation," *Indonesia Circle* 26 (1981): 13-24, quote from p. 21.

46. R. T. Warsadiningrat (R. Ng. Prjapangrawit), "Wedha Pradangga," in *Karawitan: Source Readings in Javanese Music*, ed. Judith Becker; trans. Susan Pratt Walton (Ann Arbor: Center for South and Southeast Asian Studies, 1987), Vol. 2, p. 65.

47. Sastrapustaka, "Wedha Pradangga Kawedhar," pp. 305–309.

48. Sutton, *Variation in Javanese Gamelan Music: Dynamics of a Steady State, Monograph Series on Southeast Asia, Special Report No. 28* (Center for Southeast Asian Studies, Northern Illinois University, 1998), p. 199.

49. See Rahayu Supanggah, "Balungan," *Balungan* 3 (1988): 4 (trans. Marc Perlman).

50. Sulaiman Gitosaprodjo, "Ichtisar Teori Gamelan dan Teknik Menabuh Gamelan," in *Karawitan: Source Readings in Javanese Gamelan and Vocal Music*, ed. Judith Becker and Alan Feinstein; trans. Judith Becker (Ann Arbor: Center for South and Southeast Asian Studies, 1984), Vol. 1, p. 384.

51. Stange, "The Logic of Rasa," p. 123.

52. Geertz, *The Religion of Java*, p. 309.

53. Stange, "The Logic of Rasa," pp. 117–118.

54. Sutton, *The Javanese Gambang and Its Music* (unpublished masters thesis, University of Hawaii, 1975) p. 207.

55. Sastrapustaka, "Wedha Pradangga Kawedhar," p. 315.

56. Masson and Patwardhan, *Santarasa*, p. vii.

57. James L. Peacock, *Indonesia: An Anthropological Perspective* (Pacific Palisades, CA: Goodyear Publishing Co., 1973), p. 149.

58. Sutton, *Variation in Javanese Gamelan Music*, p. 120.

59. Geertz, *The Religion of Java*, p. 289.

60. Warsadiningrat, "Wedha Pradangga," p. 31.

61. In contrast, most Western theorists do not hold that appreciating art involves a spiritual journey.

62. Stange, "The Sumarah Movement," p. 10.

63. The crucial position that Nyi Gitotenoyo holds in the history of classical Javanese singing was first pointed out to me by Alexander Dea (personal communication).

64. Supadmi, personal communication, 1992.

65. This is not to deny that occasionally agonistic elements enter into gamelan playing.

66. Raden Adjeng Kartini, *Letters of a Javanese Princess* (New York: W. W. Norton, 1964), p. 50.

67. Benamou, *Rasa in Javanese Musical Aesthetics*, pp. 78–79.

KATHLEEN MARIE HIGGINS

An Alchemy of Emotion: *Rasa* and Aesthetic Breakthroughs

"*Now* they're cookin'!" my companion announced. This was the first live jazz performance I had ever witnessed and I was intrigued by his comment. Something had changed for him just then. Lacking much exposure to jazz before this, I was not certain *what* had changed, but I wanted to know.

The Western aesthetic tradition, for all it says about aesthetic experience, says little about the breakthrough that precipitates it. The case of Friedrich Nietzsche, a notable exception, is instructive. In *The Birth of Tragedy* he describes the experience of music as provoking a sense of transformed identity, in which awareness of one's ordinary roles drops away. He describes the way in which this transformation rendered the spectator of Athenian tragedy a veritable Dionysian votary, suddenly able to see through the actor to the character, and through the character to the god.[1] Nietzsche's emphasis on these magical transformations, however, is not generally picked up by later Western philosophy.

By contrast, we find a great deal on these matters in traditional Indian aesthetics, which focuses on aesthetic breakthrough to a far greater extent than the aesthetics of our own tradition. (Significantly, Arthur Schopenhauer's account of spiritual transformation, which influenced Nietzsche's analysis of Greek tragedy, draws directly on Indian thought.[2]) The Indian tradition analyzes the psychology of aesthetic breakthroughs and situates them in the broader context of human aspirations. The work of Abhinavagupta (eleventh century), in particular, also analyzes the relationship between aesthetic experience and other breakthroughs within human experience.[3] Indian investigation of breakthroughs both within and beyond aesthetics challenges Western philosophy to investigate further art's connections with the ethical and spiritual dimensions of life.

I consider these Indian analyses of aesthetic breakthrough, beginning in Section I with a discussion of the concept of *rasa*, the emotional flavor of an aesthetic experience. In Section II, I consider the mechanisms involved in the production of *rasa* in the context of a dramatic performance and show that the experience of *rasa* is itself an indication of a breakthrough on the part of an audience member. The spectator optimally moves from awareness of the emotional content of a performance (which is evident to virtually any member of the audience of a competently performed drama) to a state of savoring the drama's emotional character in a universalized manner (something that depends on the particular spectator's degree of spiritual development, as we shall see). I proceed in Section III to consider Abhinavagupta's authoritative interpretation of *rasa* theory. Abhinava explicates a number of stages involved in the experience. He also suggests that the experience of *rasa* has a trajectory of development toward another breakthrough, this one into a state of tranquility, which I discuss in Section IV. Abhinava compares attaining the latter condition to achieving the most important breakthrough possible in a human life, that of spiritual liberation, or *mokṣa*. Thus, the breakthroughs involved in aesthetic experience facilitate spiritual aspiration by offering a taste of the achieved aim.[4]

The key to any analysis of aesthetic transformations in the Indian tradition is the theory of *rasa*,
the emotional flavor of aesthetic experience. In
this section, I discuss the basic terms *bhāva* and
rasa, which are discussed in the oldest surviving
Indian text on aesthetics, the *Nātyaśāstra*. The
terms are not always kept distinct in this text, but I
follow the interpretation of Abhinavagupta, who
uses these terms to make a basic distinction between emotion as it is rendered in dramatic performance and aesthetic experience of an emotional
state, which is an achievement on the part of the
spectator.[5]

The *Nātyaśāstra*, attributed to Bharata (200–
500 CE), is a detailed compendium of technical
knowledge about the performing arts.[6] A practical
manual for the production of successful dramati-
cal works, which included music and dance as well
as acting, the *Nātyaśāstra* articulates *rasa* theory
in light of the dramatist's pragmatic goal of conveying emotional states to the audience. Specifically, it is concerned with the practical means for
creating a distinct mood through the performance
that can be transformed into a *rasa*, aesthetic relish of the emotional tone, in the suitably cultivated
audience member.[7] (Bharata assumes that only
the more cultured and discerning theatergoers will
have this optimum experience, a matter that I consider later in more detail.) Everything within the
drama should be subordinate to the aim of producing *rasa*, including the construction of the plot.[8]
Already we can observe the contrast between this
Indian conception of aesthetic experience, which
emphasizes the audience savoring particular emotional tones, and various Western notions, such as
Immanuel Kant's cognitive "free play of imagination and understanding" or David Hume's generic
aesthetic "sentiment."

The status of the *Nātyaśāstra* is akin to that of
Aristotle's *Poetics*. Both offer detailed accounts of
what it takes to write a good play (albeit the *Poetics*
is restricted to such a discussion of tragedy), and
each provides its respective tradition with basic
criteria of artistic success not only for theater, but
for other arts as well. Yet there are some revealing contrasts. Both focus on action, but with very
different emphases. Aristotle stresses the plot, the
actions of the character within the drama, while
Bharata does not. This is appropriate, for Indian

drama is less focused on decisive events than is
Western drama, and the convention is to idealize
characters' actions by presenting them as according with *dharma* (the moral law). The actions that
Bharata emphasizes are those of the person playing the role of a character. Specifically, Bharata
analyzes in detail the physical movements and gestures of the actor, a topic ignored by Aristotle.

Similarly, although both thinkers take unity to
be a criterion of success for the work, the unity that
Bharata considers stems from the achievement of
a dominant mood or emotional tone, while Aristotle seeks unity primarily in the plot (through its
focus on a single action, its constrained length, and
so forth).[9] Moreover, both Aristotle and Bharata
contend that the aim in drama is to convey certain
emotions to the audience. However, Aristotle con-
fines his discussion of the arousal of emotion by
tragedy to a few remarks (for example, his con-
tention that tragedy should arouse pity and fear
for the purpose of catharsis and his claim that even
hearing the basic plot outline should arouse these
emotions). Bharata, on the other hand, develops a
detailed taxonomy of emotion and emotional expression, the topic to which I now turn.

The central importance of affective transformation in the *Nātyaśāstra* is underscored by the distinction, suggested by the text, between *bhāvas*
and *rasas*.[10] The dramatist's goal is to facilitate
the transformation of a *bhāva*, an emotion represented in the drama and recognized by the audience member, to a *rasa*, an experience of the
spectator. The term *bhāva* means both "existence"
and "mental state," and in aesthetic contexts it
has been variously translated as "feelings," "psychological states," and "emotions."[11] *Bhāvas* are
emotions or affective states as they typically occur
in ordinary life. In the context of the drama, they
are the emotions represented in the performance.
According to the *Nātyaśāstra*, "*Bhāva* is so called
because of its representing (*bhāvayan*) the inner
feeling of the play-wright by means of an expression coming from speech, limbs, face and Sattva"
[that is, involuntary emotional expression, such as
shuddering or becoming pale].[12] Bharata proposes
that the playwright has experienced an emotion, a
bhāva, which is then expressed through the play;
actors represent this emotion through their performance.

Rasas, by contrast, are aesthetically transformed emotional states experienced with

enjoyment by audience members. The term *rasa* is not restricted to aesthetic contexts. Arindam Chakrabarti observes that the term has many uses, all of which inflect its aesthetic meaning: "a fluid that tends to spill, a taste such as sour, sweet or salty, the soul or quintessence of something, a desire, a power, a chemical agent used in changing one metal into another, the life-giving sap in plants, and even poison!"[13] In its aesthetic employment, the word *rasa* has been translated as "mood," "emotional tone," or "sentiment," or more literally, as "flavor," "taste," or "juice."[14] The gustatory character of the term resembles that of the Western aesthetic term "taste." However, *rasa* is not a faculty, as is Western "taste"; it is literally the activity of savoring an emotion in its full flavor.[15]

In a dramatic production, the *sthāyibhāva* (durable emotion) is the overarching emotional tone of a play as a whole. Table 1 shows the *Nāṭyaśāstra's* lists of the *sthāyibhāvas* and the *rasas*.[16]

Only certain emotional flavors are counted as *rasas*.[17] The list of *rasas* comprises an inventory of emotions as objects of aesthetic relish. Significantly, they are characterized impersonally, as emotions in themselves, a matter to which I shall return. Each of the *rasas* listed in Table 1 corresponds to a *sthāyibhāva*, an emotion that can serve as the basic affective tone of an entire play. Inclusion of emotions on the list of *sthāyibhāvas* is determined, according to scholars A. K. Ramanujan and Edwin Gerow, by the fact that they are "so basic, so universal, so fundamental in human experience as to serve as the organizing principle of a sustained dramatic production."[18] These basic emotions were taken to be inherent possibilities for all human beings and thus easily recognizable in a drama.[19]

Table 1

Durable Emotions (*sthāyibhāvas*)	*Rasas*
Erotic love (*rati*)	The erotic (*śṛṅgāra*)
Mirth (*hāsya*)	The comic (*hāsya*)
Sorrow (*śoka*)	The pathetic, or sorrowful (*karuṇa*)
Anger (*krodha*)	The furious (*raudra*)
Energy (*utsāha*)	The heroic (*vīra*)
Fear (*bhaya*)	The terrible (*bhayānaka*)
Disgust (*jugupsā*)	The odious (*bībhatsa*)
Astonishment (*vismaya*)	The marvelous (*adbhuta*)

II.

The *Nāṭyaśāstra* considers several affective dimensions, all of which play a role in the production of both the *sthāyibhāva* and the *rasa*. In this section, I describe these, pointing out that they are insufficient for the achievement of *rasa* without the audience member's transcendence of narrow personal interest. The aesthetic breakthrough of *rasa*, accordingly, depends on the moral cultivation of the spectator as well as on features of the aesthetic object.

How does the presentation of a *sthāyibhāva* lead to the experience of *rasa*? The *Nāṭyaśāstra* states: "*Rasa* is produced from a combination of determinants (*vibhāvas*), consequents (*anubhāvas*), and complementary psychological states (*vyabicāri-bhāvas*)."[20] The *vibhāvas* (literally the "causes" of "emotions") are the conditions, the objects, and "other exciting circumstances" that produce the emotional state in the characters.[21] For example, in *Hamlet*, the determinants of the emotion within the play (and hence of a spectator's specific *rasa*) are the circumstances of Hamlet's mother's remarriage to his uncle, his encounter with his father's ghost, the suspicions this encounter leads him to harbor, and so on.

The *anubāvas*, translated "consequents" or "resultant manifestations," include the performer's gestures and other means of expressing emotional states.[22] Some of these may be involuntary, for example, sweating, horripilation, and shivering. Others are voluntary, including patterns of action and deliberate gestures. Hamlet's pale aspect, his demeanor, his raving remarks in conversation, his arranging for the production of *The Murder of Gonzago*, his accusations toward his mother, his killing Polonius, and so forth, are all among the consequents.

The *vyabicāribhāvas* are the complementary psychological states, also translated "transient emotions." These are those relatively brief conditions that, although fleeting, contribute to the basic emotional tone of the play. The *Nāṭyaśāstra* cites thirty-three of these transient emotions, including "discouragement, weakness, apprehension, envy, intoxication, weariness, indolence, depression, anxiety, distraction, recollection, contentment, shame, inconstancy, joy, agitation, stupor, arrogance, despair, impatience, sleep, epilepsy, dreaming, awakening, indignation, dissimulation, cruelty, assurance, sickness, insanity, death, fright and deliberation."[23]

This list includes many things that we in the West would not consider to be emotions at all, such as sleep, epilepsy, death, and deliberation. These may, however, occur as side effects or consequences of an emotional state, and that is enough for Bharata to classify them as *vyabicāribhāvas*. In the drama, these and the other *vyabicāribhāvas* are represented only in passing, but they strengthen and provide shadings for the durable emotions they accompany, though they are of brief duration. In *Hamlet*, for example, Hamlet's fear of the ghost, his wistful recollection of Yorick, his sarcastic attitude in speaking to the king, his wrathful outburst toward his mother, are all among the temporary emotional states that Hamlet undergoes and that contribute to the impression of his avenging anger as the prevailing emotional tone of the play.

In addition to the *vyabicāribhāvas*, other *sthāyibhāvas* can sometimes serve as transient affects that contribute to the formation of a *sthāyibhāva*. For example, in *Romeo and Juliet*, the relatively enduring *sthāyibhāva rati* (erotic love) contributes to the *sthāyibhāva śoka* (sorrow), which is the overarching emotional tone of the play.

The transformation that precipitates aesthetic experience is the conversion of a *sthāyibhāva* (that is, a durable emotion) into a *rasa*. How does this happen? The *Nātyaśāstra* compares the production of a *rasa* to the preparation of a dish from its various ingredients. "As a (spicy) flavour is created from many substances (*dravya*) of different kinds, in the same way the *bhāvas* along with (various kinds of) acting, create *rasas*."[24] Bharata elaborates the gustatory metaphor in a way that emphasizes the impact of well-combined elements of the drama on the sensitive member of the audience.

As gourmets (*sumanas*) are able to savor the flavour of food prepared with many spices, and attain pleasure etc., so sensitive spectators (*sumanas*) savor the primary emotions suggested … by the acting out of the various *bhāvas* and presented with the appropriate modulation of the voice, movements of the body and display of involuntary reactions, and attain pleasure etc. Therefore they are called … *nātyarasas* (dramatic flavours). On this same subject there are the following two traditional … verses: As gourmets … savor food prepared with many tasty ingredients (*dravya*) and many spices. So

sensitive people (*budha*) enjoy in their minds the permanent emotions presented with different kinds of the acting out of (transient) emotions (and presentation of their causes). This is why (these primary emotions) are known as *nātyarasas*.[25]

The ingredients—a combination of *vibhāvas* (determinants), *anubhāvas* (consequents), and *vyabicāribhāvas* (transient psychological states)—are conjoined and altered through the chemistry of acting into a form that can be aesthetically relished by the audience. This passage is one in which the *Nātyaśāstra* equates the *bhāvas* (that is, *sthāyibhāvas*) with *rasas*.

However, the *Nātya śāstra* makes it clear that even though a play competently conveys a durable *bhāva*, every audience member does not automatically experience *rasa*. Bharata emphasizes that the people who experience *rasa* are (according to various translations) "sensitive," "cultured," or "learned." He compares them to connoisseurs or gourmets. The tastes and understanding of people varies depending on age, sex, and class. The cultivation necessary for *rasa* according to the *Nātyaśāstra* involves general cultural sophistication (high social status and the education that attends it, as well as awareness of cultural conventions) and also knowledge of the dramatic arts and their conventions. Bharata sets the bar for the ideal spectator much higher than the requirements Hume sets for the true judge of taste. Bharata stipulates that ideal spectators are:

possessed of [good] character, high birth, quiet behaviour and learning, are desirous of fame, virtue, are impartial, advanced in age, proficient in drama in all its six limbs, alert, honest, unaffected by passion, expert in playing the four kinds of musical instrument, very virtuous, acquainted with the Costumes and Make-up, the rules of dialects, the four kinds of Histrionic Representation, grammar, prosody, and various [other] Śāstras, are experts in different arts and crafts, and have fine sense of the Sentiments and the Psychological States.

Moreover, the ideal spectator should be a paragon of "unruffled sense, … honest, expert in the discussion of pros and cons, detector of faults and appreciator [of merits]" and also experience "gladness on seeing a person glad, and sorrow on seeing him sorry," and be one who "feels miserable on seeing him miserable." Bharata acknowledges that "[a]ll these various qualities are not known to exist in one single spectator." He concludes that in a general audience "the inferior common persons . . . cannot be expected to appreciate the performance of the superior ones."[26] Only superior individuals are likely to experience *rasa*.

Of Bharata's prerequisites for the ideal spectator, later interpreters emphasize the requirement of being capable of empathetic response to the emotions of others as indispensable to the spectator's ability to experience *rasa*. The capacity to take joy in the joys of others and feel sorrow in response to the sorrows of others is crucial to the spectator's ability to thoroughly imbibe the emotional aspects of the drama and thereby take them as objects of aesthetic savoring. In this sense, the *rasika* (the connoisseur who experiences *rasa*) is characterized by a superiority of moral character, not just eminence within society.

Practical details of performance and play construction are subordinated in the *Nāṭyaśāstra* to the goal of the presenting a *sthāyibhāva* and facilitating the experience of *rasa*. In this endeavor, the text details the optimal way to sequence episodes within a plot. It also elaborates on the way the actor should represent the unfolding of emotional expression, on the basis of how such expression occurs in ordinary life. For example, Bharata lists the stages of erotic love: longing, anxiety, recollection, enumerations of the beloved's merits, distress, lamentation, insanity, sickness, stupor, and death.[27] He proceeds to itemize the nature of each of these and how one indicates them on stage. For example: "When a woman introduces topic about him (i.e. the beloved) on all occasions and hates all [other] males, it is a case of Insanity. To represent Insanity one should sometime look with a steadfast gaze, sometimes heave a deep sigh, sometimes be absorbed within oneself and sometimes weep at the [usual] time for recreation."[28] Properly presented, the various gestures and behaviors of the actors will replicate the real sequence of stages experienced by a person undergoing a particular emotion. The sensitive audience member, by empathetically attending to this affective trajectory, experiences the taste of the emotion in its essence, that is, *rasa*.

III.

The *Nāṭyaśāstra* remains vague on the details of what happens when the spectator's recognition of a *sthāyibhāva* gives way to an experience of *rasa*. Later interpreters elaborate various accounts, but the definitive analysis is provided by Abhinavagupta (eleventh century).[29] Abhinavagupta is one of the giants of Indian thought. A theologian and mystic as well as a philosopher, he explicates the psychological preconditions for the attainment of *rasa*. I consider his analysis in this section.

Although Abhinava, like Bharata, took the *rasa* produced by drama to be paradigmatic, he also acknowledged the production of *rasa* in purely literary works. In this he follows the *dhvani* theorists (in particular Ānandavardhana of the ninth century), who claimed that poetry conveys *rasa* by means of suggestion (*dhvani*). *Dhvani* (also termed '*vyañjanā*') was proposed as a third power of language, in addition to *abhidhā* (denotation) and *lakṣanā* (secondary meaning, or metonymy).[30] While these other two powers convey meaning conceptually, *dhvani* conveys affective meaning. Abhinava, endorsing the idea of this third linguistic power, claims that *rasa* can be communicated only through *dhvani*. Describing *rasa* as it is produced in poetry, Abhinava asserts that "*rasa* is . . . of a form that must be tasted by an act of blissful relishing on the part of a delicate mind through the stimulation . . . of previously deposited memory elements which are in keeping with the *vibhāvas* and *anubhāvas*, beautiful because of their appeal to the heart, which are transmitted by [suggestive] words [of the poet]."[31]

In this statement, Abhinava postulates the role of unconscious memory traces (*samskāras*) in the arousal of *rasa*. He spells this out in greater detail in his discussion of a vignette from the *Ramayana*, in which the sage Vālmīki, the epic's traditional author, describes his coming to write the epic. Vālmīki was bathing and enjoying the sight and song of mating birds, a pair of curlews. Suddenly, he saw an arrow kill one of the birds. Vālmīki's response to this scene was to curse the hunter, and as he did so, his words came out in the form of a verse (*śloka*). Afterward, he was remorseful at having cursed the hunter, but also amazed by the poetic form that his curse had taken. Brahma, the Lord of Creation, appeared to Vālmīki and said that the *śloka* had come through his intention. He tells Vālmīki to write the *Ramayana* in *ślokas*, which he does. Vālmīki's power to write poetry, according to this legend, sprang forth as a consequence of a powerful emotional experience. Indeed, in that Vālmīki is considered the first poet, the suggestion is that poetry itself came into being in his manner.

Characterizing Vālmīki's experience as *rasa*, Abhinava explains:

The grief which arose from the separation of the pair of curlews, that is, from the destruction of the mating arising from the killing of the bird's mate, a grief which was a basic emotion different, because of its hopelessness, from the basic emotion of love found in love-in-separation: that grief, by the poet's ruminating upon its [*ālambana-*] *vibhāvas* [i.e., the birds] in their [unhappy] state and on the *anubhāvas* arising therefrom, such as the wailing [of the surviving bird], met with a response from his heart and with his identifying [of the bird's grief with the grief in his own memory] and so transformed itself into a process of relishing.[32]

Abhinava describes the poet's *rasa* as arising from his response to the emotion expressed by the surviving bird.[33] The stages involved in Vālmīki's experience of *rasa*, then, include:

1. His recognition of the emotion expressed by the surviving bird, through witnessing the emotion's *vibhāvas* (the circumstances causing it) and *anubhāvas* (the bird's involuntary emotional expressions).
2. His rumination on this emotion.
3. His feeling response, predicated on his sense of sharing the emotion expressed by the bird.
4. His aesthetic relishing of his continued rumination on the emotion, which is now felt to be intersubjective.

Why should the poet relish what would seem to be a very painful experience? Abhinava goes on to explain that grief is transformed into the *rasa* of compassion. To explain how this differs from ordinary grief, he compares the emotion transformed into *rasa* to "the spilling over of a jar filled with liquid."[34] Where Plato uses an image of iron rings being joined together through magnetism, Abhinava uses the image of overflowing liquid to describe the *rasa* giving shape to the form of the poem, and the further communication of *rasa* from the poet to the receptive reader or listener.[35]

The poet's own experience of *rasa* depends on empathy with the bird. According to Abhinava, the poet was experiencing *rasa*, however, not the *bhāva* of grief. According to Abhinava, this empathy arises because the poet has latent impressions of grief in his own memory, which are stimu-

lated, and he identifies this remembered grief with that of the bird.[36] However, he does not wallow in memory of his own experience. Daniel H. H. Ingalls interprets Abhinava as implying that when the poet relishes the grief of others, "he has lost his own griefs within them."[37] As Abhinava himself puts it:

Grief is the basic emotion of the *rasa* of compassion, for compassion consists of relishing (or aesthetically enjoying) grief. That is to say, where we have the basic emotion grief, a thought-trend that fits with the *vibhāvas* and *anubhāvas* of this grief, if it is relished (literally, if it is chewed over and over), becomes a *rasa* and so from its aptitude [toward this end] one speaks of [any] basic emotion as becoming a *rasa*. For the basic emotion is put to use in the process of relishing: through a succession of memory elements it adds together a thought-trend which one has already experienced in one's own life to one which one infers in another's life, and so establishes a correspondence in one's heart.[38]

The elements of resuscitated memory enable one who experiences an artwork or other affect-producing stimuli to recognize the convergence of one's own experience and the emotion one encounters in another.[39] This recognition of common emotional experience depends on moving beyond a narrowly egoistic outlook to a more generalized, transpersonal sense of the emotion.[40] One interprets the perceived emotion as an instance of a type and recognizes its common character with one's own remembered emotion, thereby undercutting one's sense of personally owning one's emotion. This breakthrough is essential for *rasa* to occur.

An everyday example might help illuminate the delight one experiences in *rasa*. An older adult, observing the emotional expressions of a small child, is often reminded of his or her own juvenile emotional experiences, particularly at times when the adult is not called on to control the child's behavior. The grandparent, for example, who finds virtually all the grandchild's responses charming might well find the child's emotion familiar from his or her old childhood (or that of the child's parents). Or a parent at a nonconfrontational moment might feel a certain delight in the sense that the adolescent child's emotions and responses are steps along a well-traveled trail that the parent has also navigated. Although these reactions may be limited to a sense of sharing between oneself and a close family member, they might also prompt reflection on the emotional repertoire and trajectory of human beings generally. If the adult moves on to this more general reflection, he or she is close to the type of contemplation that precipitates *rasa*.

The breakthrough that initiates the experience of *rasa* can be impeded by various obstacles. Abhinava identifies seven.

1. Inability to find the drama convincing.
2. Overly personal identification.
3. Absorption in one's own feelings.
4. Incapacity of the appropriate sense organ.
5. Lack of clarity within the play.
6. Lack of a dominant mental state.
7. Doubt about what emotion particular expressions are meant to convey.[41]

The elimination of these obstacles makes room for the experience of *rasa*. Several of these (Nos. 1, 5, and 7) depend primarily on the play and its performance; even No. 6 can be considered a consequence of the play's inept focus. One (No. 4) concerns the fact that sound sensory organs are necessary for artistic enjoyment. The remaining impediments (Nos. 2 and 3) are psychological; they are forms of inability to overcome narrow self-absorption.

The transformation of a *bhāva* to a *rasa* depends on transcendence of the narrowly personal sense of self. Accordingly, any experience of *rasa* requires the overcoming of egoism. This breakthrough enables the artistic audience member to achieve *rasa*, a condition of pleasure, or rapture.

IV.

Beyond analyzing the breakthrough involved in the attainment of *rasa*, Abhinava also discusses the possible development of the experience into a further breakthrough. In this section, I consider his suggestion that *rasa* involves an inherent tendency toward tranquility, a condition that he sees as resembling that of ultimate spiritual liberation.

Abhinava considers the delight of *rasa* to be basic to the value of drama, and he considers this as antecedent to any instruction that drama might offer.

[T]he purpose (of the drama) for those who are unhappy (is threefold): it calms the pain of those who are grieved,

it gives immediate pleasure, and it gives happiness later (through instruction, which if followed leads to happiness). As for those who are not in sorrow, but are almost always happy, such as princes, etc., even for them the drama provides instruction in the ways of the world and in the means leading to the (four) goals of life, such as *dharma*, etc. ... Question: does the drama instruct the way a teacher (or an elderly person) does? (Answer:) No. Rather it causes one's wisdom to grow.[42]

Valuable as enhanced wisdom is, aesthetic pleasure is the primary purpose of drama, according to Abhinava. Indeed, aesthetic pleasure is the means to the wisdom available through art. "Even of instruction in the four goals of life delight is the final and major result." Abhinava continues, "Nor are pleasure and instruction really different things, for they both have the same object," that is, happiness.[43]

The kind of happiness Abhinava has in mind is "mental repose."[44] The detachment and profound pleasure involved in *rasa* produce a sense of tranquility, or equanimity, in the person who experiences it. Tranquility, or *śāntarasa*, is the putative ninth *rasa* defended by some later interpreters of the *Nātyaśāstra*, including Ānandavardhana and Abhinava.[45] The legitimacy of this ninth *rasa* is not a minor issue for Abhinava. He argues that all other *rasas* guide one toward tranquility and that this is their ultimate goal.

The idea that all *rasas* tend toward tranquility suggests a further breakthrough that is possible within aesthetic experience. Relative to the other *rasas*, which correspond to emotions that are in some sense driven toward an end, *śāntarasa* is the most placid.[46] The other *rasas* are more transitory in character than is *śāntarasa*, and *śāntarasa* is the aim of the others. Abhinava compares this supreme *rasa* to the experience of *moksa*, or spiritual liberation, the supreme goal of human life.

Abhinava's interpretation of *moksa* is based on his religious views as a Śaivite (a devotee of Śiva). His monistic theological vision has become the canonical view of Kashmiri Śaivism. Abhinava's system holds that the only ultimate reality is the consciousness of Śiva. The world is a manifestion of Śiva, literally a play of Śiva's consciousness. The spiritual goal of the human being is to overcome the misconception that one has a distinct individual being and to recognize one's identity (and the identity of the whole world) with Śiva, one's true Self. This recognition involves seeing one's individual consciousness as a play of the universal consciousness. Compared with many other Indian systems, Kashmiri Śaivism is highly life-affirmative, for it considers the world a manifestation of the supreme reality and holds that realization of one's true Self and the liberation, *mokṣa*, that comes with it are possible within this life.[47]

The experience of *rasa* borders on the experience of *mokṣa*. Lifting one to a transpersonal perspective on the emotion one tastes, *rasa* moves one past the limitations of ego-identification and closer to liberation. The kinship of *rasa* and *mokṣa* becomes evident in Abhinava's analysis of the durable emotion correlating with *śāntarasa*. The debate about the legitimacy of including *śānta* as a *rasa* led to consideration of what *sthāyibhāva* would correspond to *śāntarasa*. The reasoning was that if *śāntarasa* were really a *rasa*, it should correlate with a *sthāyibhāva*, as does every other *rasa*. Abhinava contended that this *sthāyibhāva*, the stable basis for a *rasa*, would be the state of mind that is conducive to *mokṣa*. This state of mind would be recognition of the Self, and the *rasa* associated with it involves the blissful taste of knowledge of the Self. As in the case of other *rasas*, the content of the *sthāyibhāva* carries over into *śāntarasa*. Knowledge of the Self is the basis for the tranquility that becomes *śāntarasa* when aesthetically enjoyed. However, this *sthāyibhāva* is much more stable than the others, just as *śāntarasa* is the most stable of the *rasas*.

(The other states) such as sexual passion, whose mode of existence (ever) is to be (either) facilitated or obstructed, in accordance with the appearance or disappearance of various causal factors, are said to be "stable" relatively [*āpekṣikatayā*], to the extent that they attach themselves for a time to the wall of the Self, whose nature it is to be "stable." Knowledge of the truth, however, represents the wall itself (on which are displayed) all the other emotions [*bhāvāntara*], and is (thus), among all the stable (emotive states), the most stable. ... Before the stable (affective state), knowledge of the truth, the entire group of mental states, both mundane and transcendental, becomes "transitory."[48]

Śāntarasa, however, is not identical to *mokṣa*. Like all the other *rasas*, it is premised on the artwork or other aesthetic phenomenon as its condition, for in *rasa* one aesthetically relishes an object (for example, an emotion presented through a play). *Rasa* is also transient. In the case of the performing arts, *rasa* continues while the performance continues but does not persist beyond it.[49] *Mokṣa*, by contrast, endures. It is not dependent on a play or any other aesthetic phenomenon. Instead, it is the blissful state of identification with universal consciousness. The experience of *mokṣa* is thus the most stable of all possible states of mind. All other emotional conditions are transient in relation to it, even *śāntarasa*.

Nevertheless, Abhinava takes *śāntarasa* to be both a foretaste of *mokṣa* (liberation) and a means to understand it.[50] Although similar to *mokṣa*, *śāntarasa* is a response to the separate "world" of the artistic performance, whereas *mokṣa* pertains to reality.[51] However, we tend to be deluded about our real situation, and Abhinava considers the experience of *rasa* through drama to be an ideal metaphor for our actual status. As a Śaivite, Abhinava believes that Śiva expresses himself through our consciousness and action. In our world, Śiva in effect takes on the role of individuals in a play that he produces for his own delight. Śiva identifies with all the characters in the drama of our world. Through *rasa* in response to drama we begin to approximate Śiva's impersonal identification with every conscious being and all the actions of our world. *Rasa* thus gives us a taste of the impersonal identification that, sustained, would be liberation itself.

The Western reader might wonder whether Abhinava's theory has much relevance to someone who does not share his spiritual vision or the Indian conviction that *mokṣa* is the supreme end of human life. Abhinava's suggestions that aesthetic experience leads to tranquility, and that this has some significant but complex relationship to equanimity in "real" life are, however, transposable to Western formulation, regardless of whether we want to consider the possibility of a universal consciousness. In secular Western terms, Abhinava's analysis also prompts the question of whether aesthetic experience is a generic thing, or whether different kinds of aesthetic experience have different preconditions and trajectories. Of interest, too, is Abhinava's view that pleasure, not moral message, is the means by which the aesthetic dimension elevates the soul and improves the character, a position that somewhat resembles Friedrich Schiller's but is largely foreign to Western aesthetics.

More generally, the Indian aesthetic tradition builds its account of aesthetic experience from a psychology of emotions, and this serves as the basis for analyzing aesthetic breakthroughs. *Rasa* theory offers an explanation for the power and intersubjectivity of aesthetic experience that serves as an alternative to both the Kantian interplay of intellectual faculties and Hume's generic sentiment of taste. The psychological emphasis of Indian aesthetics also contrasts strikingly with recent Western aesthetics. Since the mid-twentieth century, anglophone Western philosophy has for the most part resisted discussing inner states, with the result that the spiritual aspects of art (and of other phenomena) are approached only obliquely. Traditional Indian aesthetics reminds us of how much more there is (whether on heaven or on earth) than contemporary Western philosophy is willing to dream of. [52]

KATHLEEN MARIE HIGGINS
Department of Philosophy
The University of Texas at Austin
Austin, TX 78712, USA

INTERNET: kmhiggins@mail.utexas.edu

1. See Friedrich Nietzsche, *The Birth of Tragedy* (with *The Case of Wagner*), trans. Walter Kaufmann (New York: Vintage, 1966), § 8, pp. 61–67.

2. See Arthur Schopenhauer, *The World as Will and Representation*, in 2 vols., trans. E. F. J. Payne (New York: Dover, (vol. I) 1969 and (vol. II) 1958), vol. I, § 68, pp. 378–398, especially pp. 388–389. Nietzsche was later critical of Schopenhauer, but his thought remained profoundly influenced by the latter.

3. Abhinavagupta, who lived from the middle of the tenth century into the eleventh century CE, was prolific. He wrote numerous philosophical works, including commentaries and surveys on Tantra and the *pratyabhijñā* (recognition) school of Śaivism, literary critical works, and religious poetry. Abhinava's contributions to aesthetics are multiple. He is noteworthy for elaborating a theory of the philosophical foundations of aesthetics in two important commentaries, the *Locana* (on Ānandavardhana's *Dhvanyāloka*) and the *Abhinavabhāratī* (on the *Nātyaśāstra*). These commentaries present a number of innovations, such as the strict distinction between the emotion of the character on stage and *rasa*, and an analysis linking *rasa* with religion. (These innovations will be discussed below.) Despite his relative lack of interest in history as such, Abhinava is also the primary source through which we know the aesthetic views of other important aesthetic theorists, such as Bhaṭṭa Lollaṭa, who contended that *rasa* was just an intensified form of a durable *bhāva*, and Bhaṭṭanāyaka, who sought to undermine the concept of *dhvani*, or poetic suggestion. See Daniel H. H. Ingalls, "Introduction," in *The Dhvanyāloka of Ānandavardhana with the Locana of Abhinavagupta*, ed. Daniel H. H. Ingalls; trans. Daniel H. H. Ingalls, Jeffrey Moussaieff Masson, and M. V. Patwardhan (Harvard University Press, 1990), p. 17n and pp. 30–32.

Abhinavagupta is not the only Indian aesthetician to analyze aesthetic breakthroughs. A school of Bengali Vaiṣṇavites (devotees of Vishnu) in the sixteenth century, among them Rūpagisvāmin, offer an alternative account. For them, the supreme *rasa* was *śṛṅgāra* (the erotic), which they considered to reach its pinnacle in devotion to the god (*bhakti*). They interpreted *śṛṅgāra* as encompassing not only many other kinds of love beyond the erotic, but indeed all emotion. I will not, however, consider this school here, given the restrictions of space. For a more extended summation of their views, see Edwin Gerow, "Indian Aesthetics: A Philosophical Survey," in *A Companion to World Philosophies*, ed. Eliot Deutsch and Ron Bontekoe (Malden, MA: Blackwell, 1997), pp. 319–321.

4. This point is made by Edwin Gerow. See Edwin Gerow, "Abhinavagupta's Aesthetics as a Speculative Paradigm," *Journal of the American Oriental Society* 114(2) (1994): 191.

5. The exclusion of *rasa* from the emotion that was presented on stage was an innovation of Abhinava. See Ingalls, "Introduction," p. 35.

6. I follow the customary practice of referring to the positions taken in the *Nātyaśāstra* as Bharata's, despite the fact that modern scholars do not believe that this work was written by a single author. See Edwin Gerow, *A Glossary of Indian Figures of Speech* (The Hague: Mouton, 1971), p. 75. See also Gerow, "Indian Aesthetics: A Philosophical Survey," p. 315. There, Gerow points out that "the properly aesthetic portions of the treatise are thought to be among the latest matters added to the collection, perhaps in or by the sixth century CE."

7. "Aesthetic relish" is V. K. Chari's characterization of *rasa*. See V. K. Chari, *Sanskrit Criticism* (University of Hawaii Press, 1990), p. 9. Gerow characterizes *rasa* as "emotional 'tone.'" See Gerow, "Indian Aesthetics: A Philosophical Survey," p. 306.

8. See Bharata-muni (ascribed), *The Nātyaśāstra*, vol. I, chs. I–XXVII, rev. 2nd ed., ed. and trans. Manomohan Ghosh (Calcutta: Granthalaya, 1967) [hereafter *N.S.*], XXI.104, p. 396.

9. See Gerow, *A Glossary of Indian Figures of Speech*, p. 76.

10. Again, this distinction is sharp in Abhinavagupta's interpretation, which I follow here. The meanings of these terms are not consistently distinct in the *Nātyaśāstra* itself. Nevertheless, the terms are differentiated. Gerow notes that even in the *Nātyaśāstra*, *rasa* has "elements of the contemplative, the platonic, and the vicarious," and he emphasizes the universal character of *rasa*. See Gerow, "Indian Aesthetics: A Philosophical Survey," p. 316.

11. Richard A. Shweder and Jonathan Haidt, "The Cultural Psychology of the Emotions: Ancient and New," in *Handbook of the Emotions*, 2nd ed., ed. Michael Lewis and Jeannette M. Haviland-Jones (New York: The Guilford Press, 2000), p. 399; A. K. Ramanujan and Edwin Gerow, "Indian Poetics," in *The Literatures of India: an Introduction*, ed. Edward C. Dimock, Jr. (University of Chicago Press, 1974), p. 117; *N.S.*, I.2, p. 100 and VI.15, p. 102; Arthur Berriedale Keith, *The Sanskrit Drama in its Origin, Development, Theory, and Practice* (Oxford University Press, 1924), p. 319; Bharata-Muni, *Aesthetic Rapture: The Rasādhyāya of the Nādyaśāstra*, ed. and trans. J. L. Masson and M.V. Patwardhan (Poona: Deccan College, 1970), p. 43.

12. *N.S.*, XXIV.8, p. 443.

13. Arindam Chakrabarti, "Disgust and the Ugly in Indian Aesthetics," in *La Pluralità Estetica: Lasciti e irradiazioni oltre il Novecento, Associazione Italiana Studi di Estetica, Annali 2000–2001* (Torino: Trauben, 2002), p. 352.

14. Ramanujan and Gerow, "Indian Poetics," p. 117; Gerow, "Indian Aesthetics: A Philosophical Survey," p. 306.

15. This follows Abhinavagupta's account, which emphasizes that *rasa* is a type of perception. See J. Moussaieff Masson and M. V. Patwardhan, *Śāntarasa and Abhinavagupta's Philosophy of Aesthetics* (Poona: Bhandarkar Oriental Research Institute, 1969), pp. 73 and 73n [hereafter *Śāntarasa*].

16. The translations given are those in the translation of the *Nātyaśāstra* by Manomohan Ghosh. See *N.S.*, VI.15, p. 102. See also B. N. Goswamy, "Rasa: Delight of the Reason," in *Essence of Indian Art* (San Francisco: Asian Art Museum of San Francisco, 1986), pp. 17–30; Gerow, "Abhinavagupta's Aesthetics as a Speculative Paradigm," p. 193n. Gerow points out that it is appropriate that the names of the *rasas* are formulated as "descriptive adjectives . . . or their appropriate abstractions." Interestingly, Bharata divides the *rasas* into four that are more basic and four that are outgrowths of them. He describes the Erotic, the Furious, the Heroic, and the Odious as the "four [original] Sentiments," and goes on to say, "the Comic [Sentiment] arises from the Erotic, the Pathetic from the Furious, the Marvellous from the Heroic, and the Terrible from the Odious." More specifically, he says that "a mimicry of the Erotic [Sentiment] is called the Comic," while in the other cases, the second *rasa* results from the first (*N.S.*, VI.38–41, p. 107).

17. Later Indian thought debated whether Bharata's list should be considered as exhaustive. Some later thinkers accepted a ninth *rasa*, *śāntarasa* (tranquility), as we shall see. *Śāntarasa* was also added to the list in a probably spurious edition of the *Nātyaśāstra*.

18. Ramanujan and Gerow, "Indian Poetics," p. 135. See also Manomohan Ghosh, "Introduction," in *The Nātyaśāstra*, rev. 2nd ed., p. xxxvii.

19. So characterized, the list of *sthāyibhāvas* bears some resemblance to proposed lists of "basic emotions" that are the topic of cont emporary debate in psychology and philosophy. See, for example, Paul Ekman, "An Argument for Basic Emotions," *Cognition and Emotion* 6 (1992): 169–200; Robert C. Solomon, "Back to Basics: On the Very Idea of 'Basic Emotions'" (1993, rev. 2001), in *Not Passion's Slave: Emotions and Choice* (Oxford University Press, 2003), pp. 115–142. However, Richard Shweder and Jonathan Haidt have pointed out many divergences between the list of *rasas* and Ekman's list of basic emotions. See Shweder and Haidt, "The Cultural Psychology of the Emotions: Ancient and New," pp. 397–414.

20. *N.S.*, VI.31, p. 105.

21. See Ghosh, "Introduction," in *The Nātyaśāstra*, p. xxxviiin; Gerow, "Abhinavagupta's Aesthetics as a Speculative Paradigm," p. 194n; V. K. Chari, *Sanskrit Criticism* (University of Hawaii Press, 1990), p. 17.

22. See Gerow, "Abhinavagupta's Aesthetics as a Speculative Paradigm," p. 194n.

23. *N.S.*, VI.18, p. 102. The first term on this list is *nirveda*, which is often translated as "world-weariness." An argument was sometimes made that because this was the first term on the list of *vyabicāribhāvas*, it might also be read as the last in the list of durable emotions (*sthāyibhāvas*). See

Masson and Patwardhan, *Śāntarasa*, p. 123n; Gerow, "Abhinavagupta's Aesthetics as a Speculative Paradigm," p. 195n. Alexander Catlin points out that while the argument was in circulation by the time Abhinava wrote his commentary on Bharata, Abhinava rejected it. It was not demolished by Abhinava's argumentation, however, for the later figure Mammaṭa (active mid-late eleventh century) repeated this argument. See Alexander Havemeyer Catlin, "The Elucidation of Poetry: A Translation of Chapters One through Six of Mammaṭa's Kāvyaprakāśa with Comments and Notes" (unpublished dissertation, The University of Texas at Austin, 2005), ch. 4.

24. The *Nātyaśāstra*, VI.35, as translated in Masson and Patwardhan, in *Aesthetic Rapture*, pp. 46–47.

25. The *Nātyaśāstra*, VI.37, as translated in *Aesthetic Rapture*, pp. 46–47. Ghosh translates the passage as follows.

[A]s taste (*rasa*) results from a combination of various spices, vegetables and other articles, and as six tastes are produced by articles such as, raw sugar or spices or vegetables, so the Durable Psychological States, when they come together with various other Psychological States . . ., attain the quality of a Sentiment [*rasa*] [that is, become Sentiment (*rasa*)] . . . it is said that just as well disposed persons while eating food cooked with many kinds of spice, enjoy . . . its tastes, and attain pleasure and satisfaction, so the cultured people taste the Durable Psychological States [*bhāvas*] while they see them represented by an expression of the various Psychological States with Words, Gestures and the Sattva [involuntary emotional responses], and derive pleasure and satisfaction . . . For in this connnexion there are two traditional couplets:

Just as a connoisseur of cooked food while eating food . . . which has been prepared from various spices and other articles taste it, so the learned people taste in their heart (*manas*) the Durable Psychological States (such as love, sorrow etc.) when they are represented by an expression of the Psychological States with Gestures. Hence these Durable Psychological States in a drama are called Sentiments [*rasas*]. (*N.S.*, VI.31–33, pp. 105–106)

'*Dravya*' is the basic term for "substance." '*Budha*,' like the term 'Buddha,' comes from the root "*budh*," which Heinrich Zimmer translates as meaning "to wake, to rise from sleep, to come to one's senses or regain consciousness; to perceive, to notice, to recognize, to mark; to know understand, or comprehend; to deem, consider; to regard, esteem; to think, to reflect." See Heinrich Zimmer, *Philosophies of India*, ed. Joseph Campbell, Bollingen Series XXVI (Princeton University Press, 1951), p. 320. This also the root for "*buddhi*," the intellect or faculty of (intuitive) awareness, which is understood to be independent of the ego, the ego being dependent on it. It is the source of the insights of the conscious mind, but the conscious mind does not control it.

Manas is the thinking faculty, or mind. Sometimes the term *manas* is used to refer to the *buddhi*, but sometimes (as, for example, in the *Sāṅkhya* system) it is used for the mental faculty as it is mediated by the ego (that is, the individuated sense of self).

26. *N.S.*, XXVII.50–58, pp. 523–524. Bharata characterizes the way different types of people respond to drama in *N.S.*, XXVII.60–62, p. 524. His various accounts of the different types of emotional display in persons of superior, middling, and inferior quality also illuminate his conception of

these different social strata. See, for example, *N.S.*, VII.14, p. 123, and *N.S.*, VII.40–44, p. 130.

27. *N.S.*, XXIV.169–171, p. 465.

28. *N.S.*, XXIV.184–185, p. 468.

29. Abhinava is our only source of knowledge of many other contemporaneous interpretations of *rasa* theory. See Navjivan Rastogi, "Re-Accessing Abhinavagupta," in *The Variegated Plumage: Encounters with Indian Philosophy (A Commemoration Volume in Honour of Pandit Jankinath Kaul "Kamal")*, ed. N. B. Patil and Mrinal Kaul "Martand" (Delhi: Motilal Banarsidass and Sant Samagam Research Institute, Jammu, 2003), p. 144.

30. "Metonomy" is Gerow's translation. See Gerow, "Indian Aesthetics," p. 313. *Lakṣaṅā* sometimes is translated as "metaphor," but it has particular characteristics that make this translation too broad. *Lakṇaṣā* involves those alternate meanings that make sense of a locution when the obvious denotation is blocked for some reason. Without a blockage of the most obvious denotation, however, *lakṣaṅā* does not occur. A classical example of *lakṣaṅā* is: "The village is on the Ganges." The "on" in Sanskrit has a very strong locative force, meaning "placed on top of." Since the village is not literally built on top of the waters of the Ganges, the statement is construed to mean that it is alongside the Ganges. See K. Kunjunni Raja, *Indian Theories of Meaning* (Chennai: Adyar Library and Researc Centre, 1969), pp. 232–233. Raja does, however, translate *lakṣaṇā* as "metaphor."

31. Abhinavagupta, *Locana*, in *The Dhvanyāloka of Ānandavardhana with the Locana of Abhinavagupta*, 1.4aL, p. 81.

32. Abhinavagupta, *Locana*, 1.5, p. 115.

33. Whether poets or actors experience *rasa* is the subject of serious debate. See Masson and Patwardhan, *Śāntarasa*, p. 84; Gerow, "Abhinavagupta's Aesthetics as a Speculative Paradigm," p. 188. Abhinava himself indicates various views on this topic, noting the difference between Lollata, who contended that the actor felt *rasa*, and *Śaṅkuka*, who denied this. See Masson and Patwardhan, *Śāntarasa*, pp. 68–69. See also Goswamy, "*Rasa*: Delight of the Reason," p. 25. Goswamy points out that many commentators argue that the actor can experience *rasa* only if he or she imaginatively takes on the point of view of a spectator. The Bengali Vaiṣnavites of the sixteenth century also held that the actor experiences *rasa*. Their analysis, which emphasizes the role-playing aspect of the human being within the cosmic drama, largely eliminated the distinction between the actor and the audience. See Rūpagisvāmin, "Bahktirasāmṛta," trans. José Pereira, in *Hindu Theology: A Reader*, José Pereira, ed. (Garden City, NY: Image Books, 1976), p. 339; David L. Habermas, *Acting as a Way of Salvation: A Study of Rāgānugā Bhakti Sādhana* (Oxford University Press, 1988), pp. 7–11 and 30–39.

34. Abhinavagupta, *Locana*, 1.5L, p. 115.

35. Abhinava characterizes the experience of the receptive spectator as a "melting of the mind," a state that Masson and Patwardhan describe as "a state when the mind is exceedingly receptive." See Masson and Patwardhan, *Śāntarasa*, p. 83n.

36. Abhinavagupta, *Locana*, 1.5L, pp. 115–116. Masson and Patwardhan contend that even if the poet ever does feel grief, he or she must take some distance on this immediate emotional response in order to be able to compose poetry. See Masson and Patwardhan, *Śāntarasa*, p. 84.

37. Abhinavagupta, *Locana*, 1.5L, p. 118n.

38. Abhinavagupta, *Locana*, 1.5L, pp. 116–117. Although the translation refers here to inferring in another person the same thought-trend one has experienced oneself, we should not conclude that Abhinavagupta considers *rasa* to be a matter of inference. Indeed, he devotes a considerable portion of the *Locana* to refuting this idea.

39. For Abhinava, *saṃskāras*, or latent memory traces, include karmic latencies from previous lives as well as from the present one.

40. Abhinava attributes the view that all representations within a play were generalized to Bhaṭa Nārāṅaya, a thinker with whom he agreed on many points. See Gerow, "Indian Aesthetics: A Philosophical Survey," pp. 316–317.

41. Masson and Patwardhan, *Śāntarasa*, pp. 47–48.

42. Abhinavagupta, *Abhinavabhāratī*, on the *Nāṭyaśāstra*, I.108–110, as translated in Masson and Patwardhan, *Śāntarasa*, p. 57. See also *Śāntarasa*, pp. 54–57; Gerow, "Abhinavagupta's Aesthetics as a Speculative Paradigm," p. 188. Traditional Indian thought postulates four basic goals for human life: *kama* (sensual pleasure), *artha* (material well-being), *dharma* (moral and religious duties), and *mokṣa* (spiritual liberation). Patankar contends that the durable emotions on which the *rasas* are built are dominant within the psyche precisely because they do promote these ultimate goals. R. B. Patankar, "Does the *Rasa* Theory Have Any Modern Relevance?" *Philosophy East and West* 30 (1980): 301–302. Masson and Patwardhan point out that Abhinava considers four mental states, which correlate with the four basic goals of life, to be most important. Abhinava's correlations are as follows: erotic love (*rati*) corresponds to the goal of *kama*; anger (*krodha*) corresponds to *artha*; energy (*utsaha*) corresponds to *kama, artha*, and *dharma*; and a fourth, which Masson and Patwardhan identify as *nirveda* (world-weariness), corresponds to *mokṣa*. See Masson and Patwardhan, *Śāntarasa*, pp. 47–48. Gerow's notes to his translation of the Abhinavabhāratī (Abhinava's Commentary on the *Nāṭyaśāstra*) characterizes *nirveda* as "that sense of futility following upon the recognition of the transiency of all attainments, and leading to the desire for liberation." See Gerow, "Abhinavagupta's Aesthetics as a Speculative Paradigm," p. 195n. In his translation, Gerow challenges Masson and Patwardhan's identification of *nirveda* as the *sthāyibhāva* of *mokṣa*. See pp. 196–197nn and p. 198n. I follow Gerow's reading here.

43. Abhinavagupta, *Locana*, as translated in Masson and Patwardhan, *Śāntarasa*, p. 55.

44. See Masson and Patwardhan, *Śāntarasa*, p. 56.

45. Masson and Patwardhan propose as its translation "the imaginative experience of tranquility." See *Aesthetic Rapture*, vol. I, p. III. The origins of this proposed addition to Bharata's list of *rasas* are obscure; Masson and Patwardhan estimate that this idea may have been formulated sometime around the eighth century CE. See Masson and Patwardhan, *Śāntarasa*, p. 35. Although Abhinava seems to acknowledge that Bharata's list included only eight *rasas*, he considers *śāntarasa* to be consonant with the *Nāṭyaśāstra*. The appropriateness of this addition continues to be debated.

46. Contemporary psychologist Nico Frijda analyzes all emotions as involving action-tendencies. See Nico Frijda, *The Emotions* (Cambridge University Press, and Paris:

Editions de la Maison des Sciences de l'Homme, 1986), pp. 69–90. Aesthetic emotions might seem to be counterexamples, but action-tendencies need not be geared to energetic activity. Aesthetic emotion has a tendency to seek the continuation of savoring, as Frijda argued in Nico Frijda, "Refined Emotions," presented at the general meeting of the International Society for Research on the Emotions, University of Bari, July 12, 2005.

47. See Dr. Kapila Vatsyayan, "Śaivism and Vaiṣṇavism," in *The Variegated Plumage: Encounters with Indian Philosophy*, pp. 124–125.

48. Abhinavagupta, *Abhinavabhāratī*, as translated in Gerow, "Abhinavagupta's Aesthetics as a Speculative Paradigm," pp. 200–201.

49. Indeed, the *rasas'* dependence on conditions is what differentiates them. My thanks to Alexander Catlin for pointing out that this is how Abhinava avoids collapsing experience of *rasa* into a homogenous notion of aesthetic experience. See Catlin, *The Elucidation of Poetry*, ch. 4.

50. Contemporary scholars disagree about whether Abhinava's theological commitments shape his aesthetics or the other way around. Masson and Patwardhan, *Aesthetic Rapture*, pp. 32–33, contend that Kashmiri Śaivism is the basis for Abhinava's aesthetic theory. Gerow suggests that Abhinava's aesthetics came first, and that his aesthetic thought helped him articulate his theological and metaphysical views. See Gerow, "Abhinavagupta's Aesthetics as a Speculative Paradigm," pp. 186–192. On this point I follow Gerow.

51. This distinction between the theatrical and ordinary worlds is denied by Rūpagisvāmin and other sixteenth-century Bengali Vaiṣṇavites. See Gerow, "Indian Aesthetics: A Philosophical Survey," pp. 318–321.

52. My thanks to Stephen Phillips and his aesthetics seminar for their insights on this topic.

RICHARD SHUSTERMAN

Asian *Ars Erotica* and the Question of Sexual Aesthetics

Faire l'amour n'est pas moderne, pourtant c'est encore ce que j'aime le mieux.

There's nothing modern about making love, yet it's still what I like best.

                                        Francis Picabia

I

On a recent visit to Vienna's opulent Kunsthistorisches Museum, I unexpectedly encountered a genre painting that expressed, with art's most powerful immediacy, a central theme of this paper. The theme is philosophy's persistent pose of resistance to the seductive aesthetics of sex, and the painting, *The Steadfast Philosopher* by Gerrit van Honthorst (1592–1656), depicts the attempted seduction of a diligent philosopher by a lovely young woman with fully exposed breasts (Figure 1).

The philosopher in the painting is a manly, moustached figure in the prime of life, seated at his desk with a pile of books to his right and an open book directly in front of him. He has apparently been interrupted in the act of writing, since his right hand holds a feathered-quill pen, while his left arm is raised forward with its fingers spread in a gesture of "stop," as if to ward off both physically and symbolically the advances and attractions of the seductress who stands near the desk and seems to be removing the wrap covering his left shoulder and tugging gently on the upper sleeve of his shirt. The woman's blue dress and undergarments hang about her waist, while under a matching blue cap (whose feather corresponds nicely to the philosopher's quill) her open-mouthed smile and intent eyes are invitingly directed toward the philoso-

pher, whose gaze is turned away, his lips pursed, and his face flushed red (whether from mere embarrassment or other passions). In the chiaroscuro style of the painting, the woman's confident, open, naked posture is bathed in painterly light, while the philosopher's figure contrastingly shrinks defensively toward the shadows. Not only uninterested in engaging in the pleasurable beauties of sexual seduction, he also seems, with his averted gaze, resolutely unwilling to face up to the reality of their attractions—personifying philosophy's willful, fearful blindness to the aesthetics of erotic experience, a blindness that the painter van Honthorst seems to portray with some critical irony.[1]

If the painting reminds us of the familiar ancient quarrel between philosophy and the mimetic arts, it should also recall philosophy's traditional hostility and neglect regarding erotic arts, extending back to Socrates's condemnation of sex as "a savage and tyrannical master" and despite his provocative self-definition as "a master of erotics."[2] Making a case for the aesthetic potential of lovemaking means confronting the problem that modern Western philosophy has tended to define aesthetic experience by contrast to sexual experience.[3] Consider this history in brief summary.

Shaftesbury defined the contemplation of beauty as disinterested and distanced by explicitly contrasting it to sexual feelings aroused by (and in) human bodies—"a set of eager desires, wishes and hopes, no way suitable ... to your rational and refined contemplation of beauty." Though "wonderful as they are," sexually attractive bodies "inspire nothing of a studious or contemplative kind. The more they are viewed, the further they are from satisfying by mere view."[4] Kant made this notion

FIGURE 1. Gerrit van Honthorst, *Der Standhafte Philosoph [The Steadfast Philosopher]*, first half of 17th Century. Private property, currently on display at Kunsthistorisches Museum, Vienna.

of contemplative disinterestedness a cornerstone for defining aesthetic pleasure (and judgment) in opposition to the agreeable feelings of sensuality and the satisfactions of appetite that also give pleasure. Refining still further the notion of aesthetic disinterestedness and linking it to the perception of Platonic Ideas, Arthur Schopenhauer draws the contrast of sexual and aesthetic experience still more sharply and explicitly. In "aesthetic pleasure" we enjoy the disinterested experience of "delight in the mere knowledge of perception as such, in contrast to the will"; "aesthetic contemplation" is "pure will-less knowing and with the knowledge, which necessarily appears therewith, of the Ideas." Sexual experience, instead, involves the "strongest" of life's interests—"the will-to-live"—and is cognitively deficient and distorted by this insistent will. For Schopenhauer, "the genitals are the real *focus* of the will, and are therefore the opposite pole to the brain, the representative of knowledge."[5]

Deriding the prudishness of this anti-sexual aesthetic tradition, Friedrich Nietzsche remarks: "When our estheticians tirelessly rehearse, in support of Kant's view, that the spell of beauty enables us to view even *nude* female statues 'disinterestedly' we may be allowed to laugh a little at their expense. The experiences of artists in this delicate matter are rather more 'interesting'; certainly Pyg-

malion was not entirely devoid of esthetic feeling." But even if Nietzsche astutely admits "the possibility that the peculiar sweetness and richness proper to the esthetic condition may involve a sexual ingredient," he still refuses to affirm that erotic experience of sexual activity can be aesthetic. Insisting that the "emergence of the esthetic condition transmutes [sexual feeling] in a way that it is no longer experienced as a sexual incentive," Nietzsche follows the anti-sexual aesthetic tradition by warning that actual sexual activity is detrimental for aesthetic creation and recommending "sexual continence" for artists and philosophers. "Every artist is familiar with the adverse effect which sexual intercourse has during times of great intellectual tension and preparation. The strongest and instinctually strongest among them do not need to learn this by experience, since their 'maternal' instinct has from the start made its strict dispositions, putting all animal instincts at the service of that one great end, so that the lesser energy is absorbed by the greater dangers of such activity."[6] The erotic play of human sexual behavior is thus relegated to the realm of mere animal instincts and deprived of aesthetic recognition.

Contrasting sexual and aesthetic experience has become so deeply entrenched in our Western philosophical tradition that the authoritative *Oxford Companion to Aesthetics* even insists that one of the four major desiderata for a theory of aesthetic experience is explaining the difference between such experience and the experience of sex and drugs.[7] A careful analysis of the concept of aesthetic experience, however, reveals that the most crucial features attributed to such experience seem also attributable to certain sexual experiences. If we put aside philosophical prejudice and recall our most gratifying sexual performances, do we not recognize that some such experiences can be truly aesthetic? Many of us, I sincerely hope, have had experiences of lovemaking that are rich in beauty, intensity, pleasure, and meaning, that display harmonies of structure and developing form, and that deeply engage both thought and feeling, stimulating body, mind, and soul.

If human sexual performance can be significantly aesthetic, then we can think of the erotic arts as arts in a truly aesthetic sense rather than simply in the general (nonaesthetic) meaning of the word 'art' as any organized expertise, skill, or branch of learning. Such a reorientation not only has value in expanding our theoretical perspectives on aesthetics and erotics while challenging the presumption that art must be distinguished from performances in "real life," but it could also enrich, in a most practical and pleasurable way, the actual aesthetic experience of our lives by enhancing the artistry and appreciation of our erotic activity. This in turn could deepen our appreciation of the aesthetic potential of other somatic practices, thus promoting further explorations in the emerging field of somaesthetics.[8] Since our Western intellectual tradition seems to offer very little guidance or encouragement in sexual aesthetics, it seems worth exploring the Asian traditions of *ars erotica*.

II

The erotic arts of ancient China and (especially) India form the core of my study, but their distinctive character can be brought into sharper focus by examining them against the background of two interesting contemporary exceptions to Western philosophy's resistance to the aesthetics of sex, which I first briefly discuss. One is a short article by the distinguished Anglo-American analytic philosopher Ronald de Sousa, who "argue[s] for the rehabilitation of certain forms of imaginative rehearsals of love in 'casual,' 'uncommitted,' or

even commercial sex."[9] His provocative claim is motivated by an equally bold assertion that "the project of romantic love is in essence incoherent or impossible" because such love involves conflicting commitments to both consummation and the impossibility of possession, to Platonic idealization of what is loved and anti-Platonic affirmation that it is a concrete particular, to unique novelty and the desire for permanence that instead involves repetition of consummation with the beloved.

Given the alleged impossibility of realizing such romantic love, de Sousa argues that individuals committed to its ideal (and seeking consolation for its perceived impossibility) can seek satisfaction in what he calls "the theater of love" that "mixes real sex and aesthetic imagination." In contrast to the theatrical traditions of marriage ceremonies (which de Sousa claims are essentially opposed to erotic love because they highlight social and family relations), "the theatrical ceremonies" he recommends are sexual encounters that "consist in *staging the erotic gestures of love* with a view to pleasure and an *aesthetic* creation or re-creation of the poignancy of love, of the impossibility of possession and the irreplaceability of time." "Such ceremonies," he insists, "require some of the same qualities of art and of the best kinds of nonerotic love—integrity, honesty, intense attention, generosity, imagination, and a capacity to take pleasure in the pleasure of the other. It can therefore be demanding in the sense in which all aesthetic experiences can be demanding. Nevertheless it can remain primarily an aesthetic experience, a piece of theater, a form of play, because both parties agree to keep the experience of romantic love confined inside a kind of frame isolated from the rest of their lives and expectations."

Unfortunately, de Sousa does not adequately elucidate the dimensions in which such sexual experiences are aesthetic. The required qualities he mentions clearly refer to qualities demanded of the persons engaged in the ceremonies rather than aesthetic qualities of the experience of such ceremonies. His assertion of the aesthetic status of these sexual engagements seems to rest wholly on their theatrical nature, and their theatrical nature seems to rests almost entirely on the idea of some sort of fictionality of simulation and separation from life. The aesthetics of his theater of love is constituted by "the self-conscious *playing out* of an emotion relatively insulated from the rest of reality." Though such theater is not explicitly and fictionally "scripted" as most plays are, de Sousa argues that it is implicitly scripted by our past performances—and, one could add, by our fantasies. Further, its fictional, simulational essence, he assumes, is already established by the fact that the romantic love it expresses cannot be real. With an obliging nod "to the aesthetics and ethics of prostitution," de Sousa concludes: "If the conscious simulation of love bolstered by the power of sex is a valuable form of theater, why should some people not make a profession of it?"

I shall not pause here to examine the contested reality of romantic love as de Sousa defines it, nor to insist that there are other notions of romantic love worth exploring that do not seem caught in the web of contradictions that make him think the whole notion is incoherent. Nor shall I belabor the point that reality need not imply permanence and consistency, so that romantic love can be real even if transient and conflicted. Instead, I wish to underline how his defense of the aesthetics of sex is essentially committed to the idea that sexual performance is aesthetic only in so far that it involves a theatrical fiction or simulation of something else (that is, an impossible ideal or feeling of romantic love). It is not aesthetic because (or in terms) of the intentional and appreciated aesthetic qualities of the sexual performance as a real event that is deeply embedded in (rather than "isolated from") the rest of the lives and expectations of the performing lovers. This sexual aesthetics, with its double commitment to fictionality and isolation, reflects the old philosophical dogmas of contrasting art to reality and dividing aesthetics from the affairs of real life—whether practical, political, or sexual. In contesting these dogmas, pragmatist aesthetics not only makes a case for the robust role of the arts and aesthetics in the diverse currents of real life, but also argues that the very doctrine that relegates them to the realm of fictional simulations implies the regrettable counterpart and consequence that real life is robbed of artistry and beauty.[10]

A post-Puritan pragmatism should recognize that sexual performance provides a realm of human artistry and aesthetic experience to be practiced and enjoyed in real life and real love (marital or extramarital) without invoking the need for theatrical fictions.[11] The possibility of practicing and theorizing such real-life sexual aesthetics is shown in the Asian *ars erotica*, which Michel Foucault, the second contemporary West-

ern exception I shall consider, highlights and opposes to the *scientia sexualis* of modern Western culture.

Unlike de Sousa's, Foucault's advocacy of sexual aesthetics has been extremely influential. His most prominent advocatory theorizing of sexual artistry concerns gay sex and, more particularly, consensual homosexual S/M, which Foucault celebrates as "a whole new art of sexual practice which tries to explore all the internal possibilities of sexual conduct." This art, a "mixture of rules and openness," combines consensual codes (that significantly script sexual behavior) with experiments "to innovate and create variations that will enhance the pleasure of the act" by introducing novelty, variety, and uncertainty that otherwise would be lacking in the sexual act.[12] Moreover, despite its use of scripting and special fictional frames of performance (for example, the sexual dungeon), this sexual activity is not portrayed by Foucault as isolated from the rest of one's life and subjectivity. One's formation as a sexual subject is an important part of one's thoughtful shaping of one's self in terms of one's "aesthetics of existence."[13]

Foucault's sexual theorizing was not principally inspired by the Asian erotic arts but rather by his study of ancient Greek and Roman literature on the erotic and by his own erotic desires and activity. However, he does enlist the Asian erotic arts to demonstrate the valuable importance of an alternative to our modern Western "*scientia sexualis*."[14] In contrast to our sexual science, whose discourse of truth combines the ancient tool of confession with the modern "imperative of medicalization" (*HS*, p. 68) of sexual behavior and function, the erotic arts draw their truth "from pleasure itself, understood as a practice and accumulated as experience" (*HS*, p. 57). In these arts, the pleasure of erotic practice, Foucault explains:

is not considered in relation to an absolute law of the permitted and the forbidden, nor by reference to a criterion of utility, but first and foremost in relation to itself; it is experienced as pleasure, evaluated in terms of its intensity, its specific quality, its duration, its reverberations in the body and the soul. Moreover, this knowledge must be deflected back into the sexual practice itself in order to shape it as though from within and amplify its effects. In this way, there is formed a knowledge that must remain secret, not because of an element of infamy that might attach to its object, but because of the need to hold it in the greatest reserve, since, according to tradition, it would lose its effectiveness and its virtue by being divulged. Consequently, the relationship to the master who holds the secrets is of paramount importance; only he, working alone, can transmit this art in an esoteric manner and as the culmination of an initiation in which he guides the disciple's progress with unfailing skill and severity. The effects of this masterful art, which are considerably more generous than the sparseness of its prescriptions would lead one to imagine, are said to transfigure the one fortunate enough to receive its privileges: an absolute mastery of the body, singular bliss, obliviousness to time and limits, the elixir of life, the exile of death and its threats. (*HS*, p. 57)

Refining, in a later interview, his views on *ars erotica* and summarizing the differences between Greek, Christian, and Chinese cultural attitudes to sexual practice in terms of the three factors of "act, pleasure, and desire," Foucault claims that in contrast to the Greeks, who focused on the act and its control as "the important element" by defining the quantity, rhythm, occasion, and circumstances of its performance, but also in contrast to the Christians, who focused on desire in terms of how to fight it and extirpate its slightest roots while limiting or even avoiding pleasure when performing the act, the Chinese elevated pleasure as the highest, most valuable factor in sex. "In Chinese erotics, if one believes van Gulik, the important element was pleasure, which it was necessary to increase, intensify, prolong as much as possible in delaying the act itself, and to the limit of abstaining from it."[15]

As this interview indicates, Foucault's understanding of the Asian *ars erotica* rests largely on Chinese sources, particularly those compiled, translated, and analyzed by Robert van Gulik in his groundbreaking classic *Sexual Life in Ancient China*.[16] Unfortunately, Foucault seems to have misconstrued the texts and gloss that van Gulik provides in some important ways, which I shall presently demonstrate.

III

First, it is very misleading to characterize the classical Chinese texts of *ars erotica* in sharp contrast to sexual science and the medical approach to sex.[17] These writings (which the Chinese often described

as treating "the Art of the Bedchamber" or as "handbooks of sex") were instead very much concerned and largely motivated by health issues; so much so that when they are listed in the bibliographical sections of the ancient written histories of the various dynasties, they often appear under the heading of medical books or, when listed separately, after the medical books (*SL*, pp. 71, 121, 193). Van Gulik himself repeatedly affirms that the "handbooks of sex . . . constituted a special branch of medical literature" because their two primary goals of sexual intercourse were focused on promoting health—that of the husband, his wife, and the child to be conceived (*SL*, p. 72).[18] "Primarily," he argues, "the sexual act was to achieve the woman's conceiving" (preferably a male child) so as to perpetuate the family. "Secondly, the sexual act was to strengthen the man's vitality by making him absorb the woman's *yin* essence [held to be an invigorating power], while at the same time the woman would derive physical benefit from the stirring of her latent *yin* nature" (*SL*, p. 46).

This suggested the following twofold sexual economy. Since "a man's semen [where his *yang* force is concentrated] is his most precious possession, the source not only of his health but of his very life[,] every emission of semen will diminish this vital force, unless compensated by the acquiring of an equivalent amount of *yin* essence from the woman" (*SL*, p. 47). Therefore, a man's sexual activity should seek to ensure that his female partners be given full satisfaction so that he can absorb the *yin* essence that will flow from their multiple orgasms, "but he should allow himself to reach orgasm only on certain specified occasions," notably those most suitable for conceiving a child with his wife (*SL*, p. 47). A plurality of wives and concubines was accordingly recommended to provide this abundance of *yin*, since relying on a single woman for multiple orgasms would eventually drain her of the *yin* essence needed both to maintain her own health (and consequent power to conceive) and to increase the health of her male partner.[19] By copulating with many women each night without reaching orgasm and saving his semen only for occasional ejaculations, the man not only increased his vitality and *yang* (that is, male) essence, but in doing so raised the chances of conceiving a male child to perpetuate the family name.

These principles of sexual logic, explains van Gulik, "implied that the man had to learn to prolong the coitus as much as possible without reaching orgasm; for the longer the member stays inside, the more *yin* essence the man will absorb, thereby augmenting and strengthening his vital force" (*SL*, p. 46). The sex handbooks therefore advise the man of methods to "prevent ejaculation either by mental discipline or by such physical means as compressing the seminal duct with his fingers. Then his *yang*-essence, intensified by its contact with the woman's *yin* will flow upwards along the spinal column and fortify his brain and his entire system. If therefore the man limits his emissions to the days when the woman is liable to conceive, his loss of Yang essence [sic] on those occasions will be compensated by the obtaining of children perfect in body and mind" (*SL*, p. 47).[20]

Moreover, according to some of the radical Taoist-inspired texts, a man who thus preserves his semen through such *coitus reservatus* while absorbing the *yin* of the many women he brings to orgasm will not only sustain his health but also become more youthful and age-resistant, even to the point of achieving immortality.[21] To quote one of the Tang Dynasty texts that van Gulik supplies (whose title *Fang-nei-pu-i* is "freely translated as 'Healthy Sex Life'"): "If one can copulate with twelve women without once emitting semen, one will remain young and handsome for ever. If a man can copulate with 93 women and still control himself, he will attain immortality" (*SL*, p. 194). Though most potent in the woman's genitalia, the invigorating flows of *yin* could also be drawn from the secretions of her mouth and breasts, both in erotic foreplay and in the act of coitus itself. These secretions were often referred to as the "Medicine of the Three Peaks" (*SL*, pp. 96, 283).

Coitus reservatus served another health-related function—the emotional stability and peace of mind that depends on a harmoniously managed and satisfied household of women. Already in the ancient Confucian *Book of Rites* (*Li-chi*), a man's sexual duty to both his wives and concubines was firmly asserted and even inscribed in strict protocols of sequence and frequency of intercourse, the violation of which was "a grave offense." As the *Li-chi* states: "Even if a concubine is growing older, as long as she has not yet reached the age of fifty, the husband shall copulate with her once every five days. She on her part shall, when she is led to his couch, be cleanly washed, neatly attired, have her hair combed and properly done up, and wear a long robe and properly fastened house shoes" (*SL*, p. 60). These duties (apart from brief

respites in periods of mourning) only ceased when the husband "reached the age of seventy" (*SL*, p. 60). Without saving his *yang* through *coitus reservatus* and without the erotic ability to consistently give his wives and concubines real sexual (and emotional) gratification, a husband with a large household of women could easily exhaust himself without satisfying his females, thus creating a disgruntled, disorderly home whose ill-repute as mismanaged "could ruin a man's reputation and break his career" (*SL*, p. 109).

It should already be clear from this brief account (and there is an overwhelming wealth of further evidence in van Gulik) that, *pace* Foucault, the Chinese *ars erotica* were very deeply motivated by health issues and very much concerned with medical matters and sexual science (albeit not in the dominant forms of modern Western medical science). Foucault thus is wrong in highlighting pleasure as the most important aspect of China's erotic arts, since matters of health clearly trump it.[22] He also is confused in thinking that pleasure, for them, is more important than the sexual act because it is pleasure that they seek to prolong by delaying and even abstaining from the act. Instead, it is the act itself that the Chinese male seeks to prolong so as to magnify his *yin* and *yang* powers and the salutary benefits these bring. Pleasure is indeed significant for Chinese sexual theory but it is integrally bound up in the act and cannot be increased by being separated from it. Foucault's error seems to be in identifying the sexual act with the act of orgasm rather than the act of coitus or the broader act that we could call the entire erotic performance and that would include foreplay, coitus, and (when present) also postcoital play.

Though sometimes celebrating sexual pleasure as "the supreme joy" and "climax of human emotions" and affirming its embodiment of "the Supreme Way" (*SL*, pp. 70, 203), classical Chinese sexual theory embedded its importance into the larger goals of health and good management (of self and household). The view was that sexual pleasure should be used to regulate and refine one's body, mind, and character through the ritual shaping of the rules of *ars erotica*. As one Former Han Dynasty document puts it: "'The ancients created sexual pleasure thereby to regulate all human affairs.' If one regulates his sexual pleasure he will feel at peace and attain a high age. If, on the other hand, one abandons himself to its pleasure disregarding the rules set forth in the abovementioned treatises [i.e., the sex handbooks] one will fall ill and harm one's very life" (*SL*, pp. 70–71).

If the classical Chinese erotic arts were largely aimed to promote practical matters such as health, does it then follow that we cannot speak of them as having aesthetic character? That misguided inference rests on the common error of assuming (because of the dogma of disinterestedness) that functionality and aesthetic quality are incompatible. The fact that religious paintings and sculptures have spiritual functions and that protest songs have political goals does not rob them of having aesthetic value and of being appreciated for their aesthetic qualities even while we appreciate their other functions. Such appreciation of functionality can even feed back into our aesthetic appreciation by adding dimensions of meaning to aesthetic experience of these works. Intrinsic value is not inconsistent with instrumental value. We can appreciate the intrinsic taste of a meal we are eating even if we know that the meal is also nourishing us; likewise our intrinsic enjoyment of good sex is no less in knowing that it is also good for us.

One can indeed make a case for the presence of aesthetic dimensions in the classic Chinese erotic arts, as these are described in the texts presented by van Gulik. These aesthetic elements can be discerned in certain remarks relating to the cosmic meanings of the sexual relations between man and woman, to issues of harmonizing the couple's energies through foreplay, to the aesthetic arrangement of "the bedstead" as the stage of the erotic encounter, and to the blending of different erotic movements and pleasures, including the orchestration of different styles, depths, speeds, and rhythms of the penetrating strokes of the penis. But since discussion of the aesthetic aspect of these elements is rather limited and is overwhelmingly overshadowed by the emphasis on health issues, the case for the aesthetic character of the erotic arts can be much better made by moving from Chinese to Indian sexual theory.

IV

My discussion of Indian *ars erotica* is based on three classic texts from three different periods: the *Kama Sutra*, the *Koka Shastra*, and the *Ananga Ranga*, from around the third, twelfth, and six-

teenth centuries, respectively.[23] The founding and most influential work of this tradition, the *Kama Sutra*, was written in prose by a religious student, Vatsyayana, on the basis of more ancient texts (now lost) that, according to legend, stretch back to the God Shiva who, after falling in love with his own female emanation, discovered sexual intercourse and then celebrated its pleasures in many thousands of books. In contrast, the *Koka Shastra* and *Ananga Ranga* are shorter works composed in poetry and, because they were written in much later times when Indian society was increasingly more chaste and morally restrictive, they also differ from the *Kama Sutra* in some of their sexual attitudes or emphases. While the *Kama Sutra* was directed to a more promiscuous and wide-ranging population of lovers intent on engaging with multiple partners in both marital and extramarital sex, the *Koka Shastra* and *Ananga Ranga* were essentially addressed to husbands and their wives, primarily aiming to promote the couple's conjugal satisfaction so as to enable them to avoid the temptations of extramarital erotics; they therefore contain far more sexual prohibitions (relating to partners, times, and places) than the *Kama Sutra*.[24] Nonetheless, because these later works were substantially derived from the *Kama Sutra*, they essentially agree with its fundamental principles, including the aesthetic character of erotic arts as necessary for the proper realization of *kama*—a term that signifies not only sexual love but sensuality in general, and that together with *dharma* (duty or right conduct) and *artha* (practical activity) constitute the traditionally requisite three-part way of life leading to the goal of *moksha* or liberation (*KS*, p. 102).

In making a case for the aesthetic character of Indian erotic arts, the first point to underline is that expertise in sexual artistry implies proficiency in the arts more generally. Though recognizing that brute animals have sex and that humans can also engage in it at this brute level, the *Kama Sutra* insists that human sexuality is motivated primarily by attractiveness and pleasures rather than dictated by the seasonal instincts of animals in heat, and that human sexual performance therefore can and should be rendered more enjoyable and rewarding through the application of knowledge, methods, and refinements introduced by learning, thought, and aesthetic sensitivity— exactly the sort of mastery "of proper means" that the erotic texts aim to promote (*KS*, p. 103).

Unfortunately, as the *Ananga Ranga* laments, men typically neither give their wives "plenary contentment nor do they themselves thoroughly enjoy their charms" because "they are purely ignorant" of the erotic arts "and, despising the difference between the several kinds of women [elaborated with colorful detail in the texts of erotic theory], they regard them only in an animal point of view" (*AR*, p. 1).

The artistic training considered essential for mastering the erotic arts and perfecting sexual performance emphatically includes and highlights those arts Western culture distinctively denotes as fine arts, though it ranges far wider. In urging that both men and women "should study the *Kama Sutra* and the arts and sciences subordinate thereto," Vatsyana insists on the study of sixty-four arts from which the book's erotic artistry draws its skills. "Singing, playing on musical instruments, dancing, union of dancing, singing, and playing instrumental music, writing and drawing" are the first to be mentioned, but the list also includes other practices central to the Western fine arts tradition, such as "picture making," "scenic representation" (or "stage playing"), "architecture," "composing poems," and "making figures and images in clay." Other arts among the sixty-four also clearly have aesthetic character—from tattooing, working in stained glass, bed and flower arrangement and the making of artificial flowers, to the fashioning of jewelry and other ornaments and further to various cosmetic and culinary arts (*KS*, pp. 108–111).

To regard these diverse arts as contributing to *ars erotica* is not, however, to assert that their highest purpose is sexual, for the expressed goal of even the *Kama Sutra* itself is not merely the satisfaction of erotic or more broadly sensual desire. It is rather to deploy and educate one's desires in order to cultivate and refine the mastery of one's senses so that one can emerge a more complete and effective person. Vatsyana concludes his book by insisting that it "is not intended to be used merely as an instrument for satisfying our desires" but to enable a person "to obtain the mastery over his senses" and thus obtain "success in everything that he may undertake" (*KS*, p. 292).

Aesthetic arts are not only included in the recommended training for Indian erotics; they also contribute significantly to the erotic performance itself. This performance is not limited to the act of coitus but includes an elaborate aesthetics of foreplay and postcoital entertainment. As described by Vatsyana, "the beginning of sexual union" involves the gentleman receiving his lady love in an aesthetically arranged "pleasure room, decorated with flowers and fragrant with perfumes," where he and his lover are "attended by his friends and servants." "He should then seat her on his left side, and holding her hair, and touching also the end and knot of her garment, he should gently embrace her with his right arm. . . . They may then sing . . . and play on musical instruments, talk about the arts, and persuade each other to drink" until her loving feelings and desire for coitus are strongly aroused (*KS*, p. 167).

Then, when the other people are dismissed, more intimate foreplay ensues that leads to the consummation of "congress." The end of coitus, however, does not terminate the sexual performance, which instead continues into postcoital embraces, massage, sweet refreshments, and entertaining conversation, including the gentleman's pointing out the different celestial beauties of the night sky that his lady contemplates, lying "in his lap, with her face towards the moon." Only at this point does Vatsyana demarcate "the end of sexual union" (*KS*, p. 168). The clear sense of a staged, choreographed structure with a beginning, middle, and end in the sexual performance suggests a dramatic, stylized *mis-en-scene* with aesthetic intent.

The aesthetically designed stage for the erotic event is reaffirmed in the *Koka Shastra* and elaborated most fully in the *Ananga Ranga*, whose recommended artistic furnishings include not only musical instruments but "books containing amorous songs" and "illustrations of love-postures" for "gladdening the glance," and "spacious and beautiful walls" decorated "with pictures and other objects upon which the eye may dwell with delight," such aesthetic delights enhancing those of sex by quickening our sensory imagination and pleasures (*AR*, pp. 96–97).[25]

The staging of the sexual performance does not confine itself to aesthetic considerations of artfully organized space and artistic activities; temporal factors also need to be harmonized into the performance. According to the type of woman and the day of the (lunar) month, the woman lover will be best aroused in different parts of her body and by different forms of foreplay; in the same way, different kinds of women will enjoy sex at different times of the day. These different times, days, body parts, and modes of foreplay (involving different styles of embracing, kissing, biting, scratching, rubbing, sucking, stroking, squeezing, and the making of certain erotic sounds) are articulated in great detail, and the lover is instructed that "by varying the site of your caresses with [the calendar] you will see her light up in successive places like a figure cut in moonstone when the moon strikes on it." In short, not only the setting and acts of sexual arousal, but also the display of arousal itself is clearly aestheticized (*AR*, pp. 6–14; *KKS*, pp. 105–110, citation p. 107).

Music, choreographed movement, artistic decorations of the erotic stage, and the lovers' aesthetic discourse form part of India's extended notion of sexual performance; there are also distinctly aesthetic dimensions in its aims, methods, and principles of sexual foreplay and coitus.[26] Many of these methods and principles aim at both stimulating and harmonizing the energies of the lovers and ensuring that coitus brings fullness of pleasure to both man and woman. Hence the intense concern with classifying male and female types in terms of size (and sometimes also texture) of the genitals, force of desire, and time required for its satisfaction, so that disparities between the lovers regarding these dimensions can be identified and then remedied through appropriate foreplay and coital positions, which overcome such disproportions that impinge on the aesthetic harmony, graceful balance, and pleasurable ease of the union. Proportionate unions are deemed best, and the optimum desire cannot be the most intense, since extreme intensity could so captivate the lovers that they would neither notice nor oblige the needs of each other nor have the patient presence of mind to stylize their sexual performance so as to maximize its beauties and draw out its pleasures to the fullest (*AR*, pp. 21–24; *KS*, pp. 127–130).[27]

Aesthetic intent is clearly displayed in the making of certain representational forms on the body of the lover through bites and nail markings, so that the sexual performance also becomes a performance of figurative art. Besides the tactile pleasures they give the lovers, these erotic figurations are aesthetically appreciated as artful representations.[28] One variety of nail marks made on the neck and breasts "resembles a half-moon" (*AR*, p. 105; cf. *KS*, p. 143), another "made on the breast by means of the five nails … is called the peacock's foot" and "is made with the object of being praised, for it requires a great deal of skill to make it properly" (*KS*, p. 143). The varieties of bite marks include a special cluster of impressions

on the woman's brow, cheek, neck, and breast that together form "the mouth-shaped oblong" of the mandala summarizing the different forms of biting, and, we are told, "it will add greatly to her beauty" (*AR*, p. 108). Such nail and bite markings also serve as symbols of affection that endure beyond the sexual performance and aesthetically document it, serving as a comforting "token of remembrance" that also rekindles love and desire between the lovers (*AR*, p. 106; *KS*, p. 144).[29] Such markings are also appreciated by strangers who, when noticing them (on either the man or the woman), are "filled with love and respect" for the lovers (*AR*, p. 144).[30]

Complementing the various styles of biting and use of the nails are varieties of embraces, kisses, love sounds, modes of erotic striking of the body, and ways of holding the hair. Indian *ars erotica* is, however, probably most famous for its detailed articulation, classification, and colorful naming of a wide variety of coital positions. Variety here, as elsewhere, derives from the aesthetic impulse for the richness of diversity that renews interest, compounds pleasure, and so prevents the boredom of monotony. As Vatsyayana argues, "if variety is sought in all the arts and amusements, … how much more should it be sought in the present case," that is, erotic arts; for just "as variety is necessary in love, so love is to be produced by means of variety" (*KS*, p. 144).

That many of these coital positions (or *bandhas*) seem somewhat to overlap or blend into each other suggests that this variety is to be deployed within one act of coitus, rather than limiting the coital act to a single posture. In other words, in any particular coital event, a number of diverse *bandhas* can be aesthetically arranged as sequenced dance steps into a choreography of sexual performance. These postural changes not only add variety and can help prolong the act by delaying the male's ejaculation, but they also can have special symbolic significance in terms of the names and associations they bear. Thus, for example, "by adopting successively the 'fish,' 'tortoise,' 'wheel,' and 'sea-shell' position (*mātsya, kaurma, cakra, śankhabanda*) one identifies oneself with the first four avatars of Vishnu."[31] Moreover, in such animal-named positions, the lover is encouraged to dramatize "the characteristics of these different animals … by acting like them," thus adding a further dimension of artistic representation to the sexual performance (*KS*, p. 152).

The analogy of sexual performance to dance, though present in other cultures, is especially salient in the Indian tradition. Close affinities exist, for example, between its erotic texts and the twenty-fourth chapter of the *Bharata Natya Sastra* (the classic ancient text on drama, dance, and aesthetics), which, as one commentator notes, treats "the practice of harlotry ... as part of the technique of dance. Not only did the virtuosi of one art practice the other, but judging from sculptural representations [often found in holy temples] it was in the spirit of a dance that ritual [notably Tantric], and possibly also secular, coition was undertaken."[32] In this cultural context, sexual union with its taste of heavenly pleasures and god-like feelings of radiating fulfillment could be seen both as an analogue and an instrument to the higher mystical union with God.[33]

Well beyond the sexually intense framework of Tantrism, Indian tradition regarded the proper pursuit of erotic arts as divinely inspired and leading toward religious progress. Vatsyayana insisted that his *Kama Sutra* was "composed according to the precepts of Holy Writ ... while leading the life of a religious student and wholly engaged in the contemplation of the Deity" (*KS*, p. 222), and the *Ananga Ranga* argues that having carefully studied the arts of carnal knowledge and being fulfilled and refined through their pleasures, a man "as advancing age cooleth his passions, ... learneth to think of his Creator, to study religious subjects, and to acquire divine knowledge" (*AR*, p. 223).

The religious significance of the sexual union—whether symbolized in terms of copulating deities (such as Shakti and Shiva) or in the more abstract terms of basic gender-related principles (such as Purusha and Prakriti or, in Chinese theory, *yin* and *yang*)—adds further richness of symbolic meaning to the erotic arts and encourages their ritualized aestheticization even in contexts that are not explicitly religious.[34] Recognition that such aesthetic ritualization can artfully transform the most basic functions of life is a crucial insight of Asian culture that could be therapeutic for our dominantly Platonic-Kantian aesthetic tradition grounded on the art/reality and aesthetic/functional dichotomies. Art's transfiguration of the commonplace need not require the production of fictional counterparts to the real world, but simply a more intensified experience and mindfully stylized performance of the ordinary practices of living (whether having sex or taking tea) that ren-

ders those practices replete with special beauty, vividness, and meaning. Such transfigured practices of the real can in turn inspire art's fictional figurations.

It is therefore not enough to insist that India's erotic arts deploy the objects and practices of fine art; we must acknowledge that its fine arts reciprocally draw on its *ars erotica*. The positions outlined in the *Kama Sutra* clearly helped inspire the sculptural depictions of sexual union in medieval Hindu temples, most notably in Konarak, Khajuraho, Belur, and Halebid, and also in Buddhist centers, such as Nagarjunikonda, where many statues of sexual congress "could be identified as sculptural versions of Vatsyayana's sutras—sometimes as interpreted by poets."[35] His seminal text of *ars erotica* indeed became the main paradigm for literary depictions of love (and the characters of lovers) in Sanskrit poetry. Its influence was especially strong in epics and dramatic works (which traditionally included also dance and music) and extended also to lyrics of love and even some religious poetry (for example, the *Gita Govinda*, which treats of the love of a girl cowherder for the god Krishna as analogical to the human soul's thirst for the ecstasy of union with the divine). This central role in literature and sculpture helped the *ars erotica* further its influence also in other Indian fine arts.[36]

Unity in variety is among the most prominent of our traditional definitions of beauty. In Indian erotic arts, the richness of variety is found not only in the diversity of embraces, kisses, scratchings, bitings, strikings, hair fondlings, temporalities, love noises, coital positions (which include oral and anal sex[37]), and even different ways of moving the penis inside the vagina, but also in the ways these several modes of variety are combined into an aesthetic unity, achieving, in the words of one commentator, "the creation of an elaborate sexual sensation as a positive work of art."[38] Sexual performance is heightened and harmonized by paying careful attention to which elements of these various modes fit most successfully together so as to both stimulate and satisfy desire. An entire chapter of the *Kama Sutra*, for example, treats of "the various modes of striking, and of the sounds appropriate to them," which should also appropriately vary according to whether the man or woman is striking or being struck, and according to the stage of foreplay or coitus in which the lovers find themselves (*KS*, pp. 154–156). Guiding this aesthetic of a dynamically harmonizing mixture is the recognition that these rules of art are not absolutely fixed prescriptions, but rather need to be applied with a sense also to the varieties of context, ranging from the contingencies of the individual lovers (their bodily condition, social status, habitual inclinations, and current feelings) to circumstances of time, place, and culture. "The various modes of enjoyment are not for all times or for all persons, but they should only be used at the proper time, and in the proper countries and places" (*KS*, p. 157).

In drawing on so many varieties of sensorial, formal, cognitive, cosmic, sociocultural, and ethical aspects, the aesthetic variety of Indian *ars erotica* self-consciously served a variety of purposes. One purpose that became increasingly important was the sustaining of sexual attraction and sexual love between the married couple in order to preserve domestic harmony and through it social stability. "The chief reason for the separation between the married couple and the cause, which drives the husband to the embraces of strange women, and the wife to the arms of strange men, is the want of varied pleasures and the monotony which follows possession," concludes the *Ananga Ranga*. "There is no doubt about it. Monotony begets satiety, and satiety distaste for congress, especially in one or the other; malicious feelings are engendered, the husband or the wife yield to temptation, and the other follows being driven by jealousy." From such monotony and discord "result polygamy, adulteries, abortions, and every manner of vice" that even "drag down the names of deceased ancestors." The book's study of erotic arts is thus dedicated to showing "how the husband, by varying the enjoyment of his wife, may live with her as with thirty-two different women, ever varying the enjoyment of her, and rendering satiety impossible" while also teaching the wife "all manner of useful arts and mysteries, by which she may render herself pure, beautiful, and pleasing in his eyes" (*AR*, pp. 128–129).

If Indian erotic arts strive both to give women "plenary contentment" and to "thoroughly enjoy their charms," such satisfactions are characterized in clearly aesthetic terms of the participatory enjoyment of sensorial harmonies of pleasurable perceptions and movements, replete with representational forms and complex meanings, and carefully structured with dramatic self-consciousness and performative stylization. The aesthetic goal of artfully creating harmony and pleasure through skill in playing variations on an instrument of beauty is stated most explicitly in the *Ananga Ranga*: "all you who read this book shall know how delicious an instrument is woman, when artfully played upon; how capable she is of producing the most exquisite harmony; of executing the most complicated variations and of giving the divinest pleasures" (*AR*, p. xxiii). One might understandably balk at objectifying woman as an aesthetic instrument for man's pleasure, but the sting is somewhat mitigated by Indian eroticism's insistent advocacy that women reciprocally play on male instruments, and sometimes even play the male by taking on his actions and coital positions. Here, in the different forms of Purushayita, the wife mounts the prostrate man, effects the penetration, initiates the rhythmic coital movement, and thus "enjoys her husband and thoroughly satisfies herself" (*AR*, p. 126).

Besides the aims of conjugal happiness through the pleasures of love and the bonds of intimate friendship they can create, the aesthetic variety of the Indian erotic tradition has broader cognitive and ethical aims. Extending well beyond matters of sexual and sensual pleasure, *kama* concerns the whole domain of sensory cognition. *Ars erotica*'s rich stimulation and sophistication of the senses, together with its mastery and refinement of a wide range of complex motor coordinations and bodily postures, cannot help but bring significant cognitive enhancement to both sensory and motor abilities. Its cultivation of perception includes an education in recognizing the enduring dispositions but also the changing thoughts and feelings of others, so that the lover can properly respond to them. Considerable attention is paid to discerning the movements and expressions that indicate a woman's character, erotic accessibility, interest, inclinations, changing moods, sexual passions, and the means and degrees to which her interests and passions are satisfied. Such perceptual training develops ethical sensitivity to others and to their diversity (reflected in the complex, multiple classifications of different types of lovers but also of go-betweens and courtesans).[39] Conversely, ethical self-knowledge and self-discipline are similarly deepened and honed through erotic practices that probe our desires and inhibitions as they reshape them, while also testing and refining our self-control, through artful, pleasurable mastery of our senses and sensuality. As "Kama is the enjoyment of appropriate objects by the five senses of hearing, feeling, seeing, tasting and smelling, assisted by the mind together with the soul," so its practice in the *ars erotica* aims at a varied "mastery of [one's] senses" (*KS*, pp. 102–103, 222). These aims of masterful sensuous enjoyment remain aesthetic despite their practical value.

To conclude, ancient India (even more than ancient China) has much to teach the West about the aesthetic powers and possibilities of sexual activity. Because our culture is dominated by the model of *scientia sexualis* and the Cartesian notion of body as machine, it is obsessively preoccupied with improving sex through mechanical, nonperceptual means (such as pills, lubricants, penis enlargements), thus neglecting the artistic techniques of enhancing erotic experience. Although Indian erotic theory (including the three exemplary texts here discussed) likewise offers an abundance of mechanical devices (pharmacological, prosthetic, and even magical) for enhancing sexual performance and desirability, its dominant emphasis is on cultivating erotic artistry through aesthetic expertise and its perfection of sensorimotor skills relating to lovemaking. For the nascent discipline of somaesthetics, a field of theory and practice devoted to the study and cultivation of our bodies as loci of aesthetic perception and self-fashioning, the Asian erotic arts, especially as theorized and practiced in classical Indian culture, constitute an exemplary resource and an invaluable inspiration.[40]

RICHARD SHUSTERMAN
Department of Philosophy
Florida Atlantic University
Boca Raton, FL 33431, USA

INTERNET: shuster1@fau.edu

[1.] The resistance of philosophers to the beauties of erotic seduction is a classic theme in the arts, exemplified by Keats's famous poem "Lamia," in which the philosopher seeks to rescue his student from the wiles of a beautiful woman who is actually a lamia (a creature with the head and breast of a woman and the lower body of a serpent and that is said to suck the blood of those it seduces). The female figure depicted by Honthorst, with her head and breast exposed but her lower body concealed, could represent such a creature.

2. See Plato's *Republic* 329c, where Socrates confirms this condemnation, originally attributed to Sophocles. See also *Symposium* 198D for his self-description as erotic master and 203C–212B for his account of the philosophical quest in the erotic terms of seeking and giving birth in beauty.

3. See Richard Shusterman, "Aesthetic Experience: From Analysis to Eros," *The Journal of Aesthetics and Art Criticism* 64 (2006): 217–229.

4. Anthony Ashley Cooper (Third Earl of Shaftesbury), *Characteristics of Men, Manners, Opinions, Times*, ed. Lawrence Klein (Cambridge University Press, 1999), p. 319.

5. Arthur Schopenhauer, *The World as Will and Representation*, trans. E. F. J. Payne (New York: Dover, 1958), vol. 1, pp. 200–202, 330–331.

6. Friedrich Nietzsche, "The Genealogy of Morals," in *The Birth of Tragedy and The Genealogy of Morals*, trans. Francis Golffing (New York: Doubleday, 1956), pp. 238–240.

7. Gary Iseminger, "Aesthetic Experience," in *The Oxford Handbook of Aesthetics*, ed. Jerrold Levinson (Oxford University Press, 2003), pp. 99–116.

8. For my account of somaesthetics, see, for example, Richard Shusterman, "Somaesthetics: A Disciplinary Proposal," *The Journal of Aesthetics and Art Criticism* 57 (1999): 299–313; *Practicing Philosophy* (New York: Routledge, 1997), chs. 4, 6; *Performing Live* (Cornell University Press, 2000), chs. 7–8. For further discussions of somaesthetics, see, for example, the essays of Martin Jay, Gustavo Guerra, Kathleen Higgins, Casey Haskins, and my response in *The Journal of Aesthetic Education* 36 (2002): 55–115; and the symposium on *Pragmatist Aesthetics*, 2nd ed., with contributions by Antonia Soulez, Paul Taylor, and Thomas Leddy (and my response) in *Journal of Speculative Philosophy* 16 (2002): 1–38. See also Peter Arnold, "Somaesthetics, Education, and the Art of Dance," *The Journal of Aesthetic Education* 39 (2005): 48–64; Eric Mullis, "Peformative Somaesthetics," *The Journal of Aesthetic Education* 40 (2006): 104–117.

9. Ronald de Sousa, "Love as Theater," in *The Philosophy of (Erotic) Love*, ed. Robert Solomon and Kathleen Higgins (University of Kansas Press, 1991), pp. 477–491, citations on pp. 478, 479, 483, 489, 485, 486, 488.

10. See, for example, John Dewey, *Art as Experience* (Southern Illinois University Press, 1987); Richard Shusterman, *Pragmatist Aesthetics* (Oxford: Blackwell, 1992).

11. There is not much emphasis on the erotic in the classical pragmatists, and William James even affirms, in his famous *Principles of Psychology*, the role of an "anti-sexual instinct" (Harvard University Press, 1983), pp. 1053–1054. Noting Dewey's neglect of the erotic, Paul Taylor argues that Du Bois's frank recognition of sexual dimensions of self-realization usefully enriches the classical pragmatist notion of perfectionism. See Paul C. Taylor, "What's the Use of Calling Du Bois a Pragmatist?" in *The Range of Pragmatism and the Limits of Philosophy*, ed. Richard Shusterman (Oxford: Blackwell, 2004), pp. 95–111.

12. Michel Foucault, "Sexual Choice, Sexual Act," in *Essential Works of Michel Foucault* (New York: New Press, 1997), vol. 1, pp. 151–152. In making his case for "aesthetic appreciation of the sexual act as such," Foucault praises gay S/M because "all the energy and imagination, which in the heterosexual relationship were channeled into courtship, now become devoted to *intensifying* the act of sex itself. A whole new art of sexual practice develops which tries to explore all the internal possibilities of sexual conduct." Likening the gay leather scenes in San Francisco and New York to "laboratories of sexual experimentation," Foucault claims such experimentation is strictly controlled by consensual codes, as in the medieval chivalric courts "where strict rules of proprietary courtship were defined." Experimentation

is necessary," explains Foucault, "because the sexual act has become so easy and available … that it runs the risk of quickly becoming boring, so that every effort has to be made to innovate and create variations that will enhance the pleasure of the act." "This mixture of rules and openness," Foucault concludes, "has the effect of intensifying sexual relations by introducing a perpetual novelty, a perpetual tension and a perpetual uncertainty which the simple consummation of the act lacks. The idea is also to make use of every part of the body as a sexual instrument" (Foucault, "Sexual Choice, Sexual Act," pp. 149, 151–152). For a critical study of Foucault's somaesthetics of sex as part of his idea of philosophy as an art of living, see Richard Shusterman, "Somaesthetics and Care of the Self: The Case of Foucault," *Monist* 83 (2000): 530–551.

13. Michel Foucault, *History of Sexuality* (New York: Pantheon, 1986), vol. 2, pp. 12, 89–93.

14. Michel Foucault, *History of Sexuality* (New York: Pantheon, 1980), vol. 1, pp. 57–71 [hereafter *HS*].

15. A version of this interview, "On the Genealogy of Ethics: An Overview of Work in Progress," was first published in English in *Michel Foucault: Beyond Structuralism and Hermeneutics*, ed. Herbert Dreyfus and Paul Rabinow (University of Chicago Press, 1983), but I am citing (and translating) from the more complete French version that was revised by Foucault and published in his *Dits et Ecrits*, vol. 2 (Paris: Gallimard, 2001), pp. 1428–1450, quotations on p. 1441. In this interview, Foucault acknowledges that the ancient Greeks and Romans did not really have an elaborate *ars erotica* comparable to that of the Chinese (see p. 1434).

16. R. H. van Gulik, *Sexual Life in Ancient China: A Preliminary Survey of Chinese Sex and Society from ca. 1500 B.C. till 1644 A.D.* (Leiden: Brill, 2003) [hereafter *SL*].

17. It is also worth noting that Chinese texts on the erotic arts are not a monolithic unity but rather display some variety in different historical periods and according to the different dominant philosophical ideologies that inspired their authors (for example, the more sexually liberal Taoist versus the more straight-laced Confucian. The classic texts of Indian *ars erotica* also display clear differences that reflect the different mores of different periods.

18. Foucault's emphasis on the essential esoteric nature of these arts is also rather misleading. For many periods of China's long history, according to van Gulik, the handbooks of sex, which were frequently illustrated, "circulated widely" and "were well known and the methods given by them widely practiced" not only by esoteric specialists but "by the people in general." The handbooks began to fall into decline in the Sung period, and still more in the Ming period with its greater Confucian prudishness, but the handbooks' practices and "principles still pervaded sexual life" (*SL*, pp. 79, 94, 121, 192, 228, 268).

19. See *SL*, p. 138: "If a man continually changes the woman with whom he copulates the benefit will be great. If in one night one can copulate with more than ten women it is best. If one always copulates with one and the same woman her vital essence will gradually grow weaker and in the end she will be in no fit condition to give the man benefit. Moreover, the woman herself will become emaciated."

20. It followed from this logic that male masturbation was "forbidden (except for extreme occasions) and nocturnal emissions were viewed with concern." As long as it did not involve ejaculation, homosexuality was not condemned

in classical Chinese culture, but nor did it form part of the ancient sexual handbooks (*SL*, p. 48).

21. In one document from the Later Han period, we read of a Taoist master who "lived to the age of over 150 years by practicing the art of having sexual intercourse with women" and that by such art "one's grey hair will turn black again and new teeth will replace those that have fallen out" (*SL*, p. 71).

22. Another passage from the *Fang-nei-pu-i* that emphasizes multiple partners nonetheless makes clear that this multiplicity does not have pleasure as its highest end. "The method is to copulate on one night with ten different women without emitting semen even a single time. This is the essence of the Art of the Bedchamber. A man must not engage in sexual intercourse merely to satisfy his lust. He must strive to control his sexual desire so as to be able to nurture his vital essence. He must not force his body to sexual extravagance in order to enjoy carnal pleasure, giving free rein to his passion. On the contrary, he must think of how the act will benefit his health and thus keep himself free from disease. This is the subtle secret of the Art of the Bedchamber." The text also discusses the method for controlling ejaculation and making its energy "ascend and benefit the brain" (*SL*, pp. 193–194). A Sui Dynasty sex handbook, *Fang Nei Chi*, offers a health-oriented graduated schedule of ejaculations according to one's age and strength of constitution, ranging from strongly built fifteen-year-olds who can ejaculate twice a day to strong men of seventy who may ejaculate once a month; "weak ones should not ejaculate anymore at that age" (*SL*, p. 146). A different Sui Dynasty handbook, *The Ars Amatoria of Master Tung–Hsuan*, which also offers methods of controlling ejaculation, is less nuanced in prescriptions of frequency: "only emit semen two or three times in ten" (*SL*, p. 132).

23. See Richard Burton and F. F. Arbuthnot, trans., *The Kama Sutra of Vatsyayana*, including a preface by W. G. Archer and an introduction by K. M. Panikkar (Unwin: London, 1988), page references will be to this edition [hereafter *KS*]. Besides this famous (and controversial) translation, I have consulted two other translations: W. Doniger and S. Kakar (Oxford University Press, 2003); S. C. Upadya (Castle Books: New York, 1963). Alex Comfort, ed. and trans., *The Koka Shastra*, with a Preface by W. G. Archer (Stein & Day: New York, 1965) [hereafter *KKS*]. See also F. F. Arbuthnot and Richard Burton, ed. and trans., *Ananga Ranga* (Medical Press: New York, 1964) [hereafter *AR*]. The dating of the *Kama Sutra* is particularly uncertain, ranging from 300 BCE to 400 CE, while that of the *Koka Shastra* (whose formal title is *Ratirahasya* or *Secrets of Rati*) ranges from the eleventh to twelfth century, and *Ananga Ranga*'s from the sixteenth to the seventeenth. Besides these primary texts (and the commentary of the editions cited), my research also draws on J. J. Meyer, *Sexual Life in Ancient China*, 2 vols. (London: Kegan Paul, 2003) and S. C. Banerji, *Crime and Sex in Ancient India* (Naya Prokash: Calcutta, 1980).

24. This is especially so with the *Ananga Ranga*, which, Archer notes, excludes more than 30 kinds of women as partners for sexual intercourse, while the *Kama Sutra* only excludes two (*KS*, pp. 30–31).

25. The *Koka Shastra* (p. 133) recommends the staging of the act in a "brightly-lit room filled with flowers[,] incense … burning," "lively conversation," and with the gentleman "singing … cheerful songs," while *Ananga Ranga* (pp. 96–97) describes the setting "best fitted for sexual intercourse

with women" as follows: "Choose the largest, and finest, and the most airy room in the house, purify it thoroughly with whitewash, and decorate its spacious and beautiful walls with pictures and other objects upon which the eye may dwell with delight. Scattered about this apartment place musical instruments, especially the pipe and the lute; with refreshments, as cocoa-nut, betel leaf, and milk, which is so useful for treating and restoring vigour; bottles of rose water and various essences, fans, and chauris for cooling the air, and books containing amorous songs, and gladdening the glance with illustrations of love-postures. Splendid Diválgiri, or wall lights, should gleam around the hall, reflected by a hundred mirrors, whilst both man and woman should contend against any reserve, or false shame, giving themselves in complete nakedness to unrestrained voluptuousness, upon a high and handsome bedstead, raised on tall legs, furnished [with] many pillows and covered by a rich chatra, or canopy; the sheets being besprinkled with flowers and the coverlet scented by burning luscious incense, such as aloes and other fragrant woods. In such a place, let the man, ascending the throne of love, enjoy the woman in ease and comfort, gratifying his and her every wish and whim."

26. The methods and joys of foreplay and coitus are distinguished (in the *Koka Shastra* and *Ananga Ranga*) as "'outer' and . . . 'inner' forms of lovemaking" (*KS*, p. 125) or "external enjoyments" and "internal enjoyments" (*AR*, pp. 97, 115). The Indian classification recognizes that outer actions and pleasures (kissing, for example) can continue well beyond foreplay.

27. Nor can desire be too weak. Indeed it is the proportionate fit of the organs and its production of sufficient enjoyment and desire that "enables the husband to turn his mind [away from the problems of mechanics of penetration] towards the usual arts which bring women under subjection" to the enthralling pleasures of sexual love (*AR*, p. 22).

28. Some styles of nail scratching and biting are not meant to leave visible marks, but simply to give more tactile pleasure (*see AR*, pp. 105, 107; *KS*, pp. 143, 146).

29. Indian erotic arts also deploy elements of symbolic action that refer suggestively to other elements of the sexual performance, thereby seeking to promote them. The "transferred kiss" is one given not to the lover but to a child or object simultaneously viewed by the lover so as to suggest the desire to kiss the lover (*KS*, p. 141). The "Ghatika" kiss, designed to stimulate the man toward the act of coitus by also symbolizing it, is when the woman "thrusts her tongue into his mouth, moving it to and fro with a motion so pleasant and slow that it at once suggests another and a higher form of enjoyment" (*AR*, p. 102).

30. Vatsyayana also cites some ancient verses on this matter: "The love of a woman who sees the marks of nails on the private parts of her body, even though they are old and

almost worn out, becomes again fresh and new. If there be no marks of nails to remind a person of the passages of love, then love is lessened in the same way as when no union takes place for a long time" (*KS*, p. 144).

31. Alex Comfort, "Introduction," in *KKS*, p. 63.

32. Comfort, "Introduction," pp. 49, 63.

33. See the *Brihadaranyaka Upanishad*: "In the embrace of his beloved, a man forgets the whole world—everything both within and without; in the same way he who embraces the Self knows neither within nor without." Comfort, "Introduction," p. 28.

34. Such ritualized aestheticization can be found in the Japanese tea ceremony, which has its roots in ritual tea drinking in Zen monasteries (in China before Japan) but has long flourished beyond these religious contexts while still maintaining a strong sense of aesthetic ritual with a Zen-like devotion to harmony, gentleness of spirit, reverence, purity, and tranquility. See D. T. Suzuki, *Zen and Japanese Culture* (Princeton University Press, 1989), pp. 272–274.

35. K. M. Pannikar, "Introduction," in *KS*, pp. 74–75.

36. Painters thus came to deploy, as classical representations of love, the various female types and situations delineated by the erotic texts and by the literary works these texts inspired. See Pannikar, "Introduction," p. 75; Comfort, "Introduction," p. 70. Eight of these classical figures are described in *AR* (pp. 113–114).

37. The *Kama Sutra* devotes a chapter (ch. 9) to positions and methods of oral sex but has nothing to say about methods of anal sex, merely noting that it is done (*KS*, p. 153). In the later, more straight-laced *Koka Shastra* very little is said of oral sex and anal sex is not mentioned. Neither oral nor anal sex is discussed in the still more prudish *Ananga Ranga*, though later erotic writers recognize oral sex. See Comfort, *KKS*, p. 124.

38. Comfort, *KKS*, p. 49.

39. The *Kama Sutra* also contains elaborate recommendations for the aesthetic stylization of life in general, not just for specifically erotic matters. See its chapter "On the Arrangements of a House, and Household Furniture; and about the Daily Life of a Citizen, his Companions, Amusements, etc.," which contains suggestions of how to aesthetically organize the living conditions and daily routines of a gentleman or man about town (which I prefer to "citizen" for translating the Sanskrit term *nayaka*) These lifestyle recommendations range from ablutions, cosmetics, clothes, meals, and siestas to amusements such as festivals, drinking parties, discussions of the arts, and aesthetic pastimes (for example, games of verse and decorating oneself with flowers).

40. I am grateful to Pradeep Dhillon for help with Sanskrit and to *Naked Punch,* who first invited me to address this topic at the London School of Economics in February 2006. I also thank the owners of *Der Standhafte Philosoph* for permission to use this image.

JALE NEJDET ERZEN

Islamic Aesthetics: An Alternative
Way to Knowledge

I. INTRODUCTION

One important difference between Islamic and Western aesthetics is that, in the former, there has been little if any critical discourse on art and beauty until very recently. Yet, from the eighth to the thirteenth centuries, a vast literature related to the arts, from architecture to poetry and music, existed in Islamic countries. This literature was initially stimulated by the translations of classical texts, such as those of Plato, Aristotle, and Euclid. These translations were soon followed by Arabic texts that developed ideas of theory and practice, which have become classical references in the Islamic artworld. Gülru Necipoğlu's *The Topkapı Scroll*, an important modern source on the aesthetic basis of arts and crafts in the medieval Islamic world, gives us detailed information on this literature and on the aesthetic implications of the decorative patterns and the mathematical and geometrical principles at the foundations of these arts and crafts.[1] These texts were not formulated as texts about aesthetics, but rather as technical manuals or scientific books.

Insofar as there has been any criticism of the arts in the Islamic world prior to the modern age, it exists in the artwork, in the artistic expression itself. In other words, one thinks or comments about an artwork through another work. There is poetry that responds to other poetry, musical compositions that respond to other music. Indeed, in cultures where tradition is a dominating force, artists compete by producing their own interpretations as a way of commenting on each other's work, rather than by trying to make something totally original or new. The work then constitutes both a critique

and an innovation. In Islam (as in many other non-Western cultures) the only way to move away from a tradition, or to be original, would be through knowing the tradition itself. Such movements may create new approaches in artistic practice, but they can never be radical because they must always stay within traditional norms.

One limitation of this dependence on tradition is that it does not produce an analysis and evaluation—a theory—of its own arts and aesthetic approaches. Even when such attempts are made, the results are often descriptive rather than analytical or conceptual. For example, even as late as the early twentieth century, there was little documentation and writing on Turkish architecture and its history.[2] What analysis and evaluation of Islamic art and aesthetics there was, was done by Orientalists who viewed Islamic art and aesthetics mainly through Western values and concepts. Islamic or oriental forms in general would be explained by their narrative or figurative content or, at best, shown in a positive light through their association with the values of modern Western art, such as the absence of the appearance of three-dimensionality in painting.[3] Even the most sympathetic approaches rarely ventured into the background and sources of the deep cultural meaning of the forms, but concentrated mainly on history, influences, and descriptions of style and technique.[4]

Basic differences between Islamic and Western cultures are manifested not only in how language is—and is not—used to talk about art, but also in profound differences in their approaches to the world in general. It is this dimension that I pursue in this paper. In Islam, for example, there is a conviction that the relationships of humans to the world and human perceptions of it are not fixed, not codifiable, and cannot be captured using language that expresses generalized concepts. Some Sufi teachings deny that definitions of truths about the world and human relationships to it can be captured in language.[5] Literal explanations provided by words are considered only superficial, so discussion is conducted in various kinds of riddles, and points of view are best expressed in symbols or in artistic expression.

Taking these constraints into consideration, I attempt to clarify various Islamic ways of seeing the world and how they establish meanings for artistic forms.[6] I concentrate here mostly on the Sufi tradition, which can be taken as representative of various heterodox Islamic traditions after the fifteenth century, when musicians, miniaturists, calligraphers, and poets were often believers in one of those traditions—whether Alaoui, Sufi, or Bektashi—and in transcendentalism. In the final section of the paper, I discuss some consequences for the possibility of an Islamic aesthetics in contemporary art.

II. TIME AND SPACE

The ways of conceiving and perceiving space and time underlie the most basic symbolic forms of a culture. According to Islam, for example, the world is perceived from a constantly moving and changing vantage point. Cafer Çelebi, in admiration of the work of Mehmet Ağa, the architect of the Blue Mosque (Sultan Ahmet Mosque in Istanbul, c. 1605), describes this well: "When looked at from one angle, one type of form or circle was seen, and when one looked again from another angle, other types of designs and patterns emerged, and other forms appeared. However much the point of view changed, that many times forms were transformed into other shapes."[7] Because the world is accepted as constantly changing, freedom of expression is not an important issue for art or for the artist.[8] Neither does the artist lay claim to some privilege or priority in how his or her work is to be seen, as the work might if it were conceived as created from a fixed point of view.

Similarly, the Islamic view of the world contains no assumption that the world itself is fixed or stable. In Islamic aesthetics, no definitive final state of an artwork or of an utterance (as in criticism)

is pursued as a value. In domestic architecture, no fixed function is given to a space, and the divisions of the spaces themselves are not fixed. Architecture is taken to be constantly changing, according to light and to function; the way one acts in a certain space, the way one lives in it, transforms it. The constant transformability of space is instead pursued as a value.[9] Similar implications hold for the way pictures and visual images are constructed and seen. Several different points of view can be taken when drawing landscapes or cityscapes, as is obvious in miniatures.[10]

Various forms or aesthetic structures for artistic expression in the Islamic world can be traced to certain underlying principles of belief. These beliefs concern the deeper, metaphysical aspects of a worldview, and they impact one's sense of art's meaning and expressiveness in a profound manner. These principles are: (1) the principle of constant change within permanence, (2) the principle of the uncertainty of human cognition, and (3) the principle of love, or understanding with the heart. These principles are mentioned and elaborated on directly by ancient Islamic philosophers such as Ibn-Arabi and Hallac Mansur, as well as by more recent commentators on Islam and Sufism. The understanding of some of these principles, such as "uncertainty of the human condition," can also be derived from allegories and symbolism in the artworks.[11]

1. The Principle of Constant Change Within Permanence

What is typically seen as "merely decorative" or as "arabesque" from the Western point of view is actually an expression of the constant flux of the world and of how all creation is interrelated. Various visual arrays are designed to reflect the constant movement of the world. For example, the basic forms of movement that are reflected in painted, mosaic, or stalactite stars are based on the understanding that the human world, which is symbolized by directionality and the orthogonal (a square or a rectangle), is constantly moving within the permanent universe, the spiritual world, which is symbolized by the circle. In classical Ottoman architecture of the sixteenth century, the two dominant structural forms, the cubic base and the domical cover, express this relationship. Stars and constellations that appear on domes are hardly merely decorative, but have deep significance in their reference to the orientation of humans and of the human world in relation to the universe. They also refer to the breath of the universe, and the expansion and contraction of that breath: the universe and the world and the environment take shape from the breath of God.[12]

In the Sufi tradition, the stimulation of all five senses is crucial to attaining truth. Consider Avicenna, who wrote: "Know that access to that by which our soul becomes knowing begins by way of the senses."[13] Here, the emphasis is on sense perception; however, Avicenna also mentions the importance of the imagination and of emotion.[14] Education, as in early Greek culture, begins with the discipline of the body and hence with music and dance. One is constantly moving and involved in exercising all the senses rather than in conceptualizing about them or about a supposed stable, external object of perception. The involvement of all the senses, moreover, is taken to lead to a profound knowledge of the Absolute, a knowledge that is therefore in the most basic or fundamental way aesthetic. Any kind of artistic involvement may be a path to the knowledge of God, who is manifested in the physical, sensible appearance of the world. For the artist, the goal is to create something worthy of the creation of God.

The sensory or aesthetic means to knowledge is best understood by the fact that, in Sufi, it is through symbols that one is awakened; it is through symbols that one is transformed; and it is through symbols that one is expressive. Symbols are realities contained within the nature of things. The entire journey to God is a journey in symbols, which refer to both the universal aspect of creation and the particular aspect of tradition. In fact, the whole of the visible, sensible world and its many manifestations is the symbol of God. Symbols are the "place of encounter" between the "archetypes or the intelligibles and the sensible, phenomenal world."[15] Thus, the sensible becomes the link between meaning and form, whether the symbols are general—such as basic geometric forms and the patterns resulting from their relations, or spirals, or numbers—or particular, such as those that arise in individual works of visual art and music. Examples of particular symbols are the image of the rose petal in painting, which refers to the skin of the prophet, and the use of certain musical keys or orders (*maqam*) in certain rhythms to refer to love or separation or death.

In Sufi, as in Islam in general, one can never say that an artist creates a symbol. Symbols are given; they are there to be discovered. The artist does not claim originality; it is a gift that the artist can see the value and beauty of the universe. The artist attempts to put forward sensible forms that are worthy of the beauty of creation and that will attract one to the original beauty created by God. Artists may put forward sensible forms almost unconsciously, as if in a trance, or by giving themselves to the act of creativity. In this selflessness, which is a kind of unconsciousness, tradition creates the bond to the spiritual or to God.[16] The process, as a whole, of presenting sensible forms as a work of art, as a beautiful thing, as a symbol, is a path for coming closer to the spiritual. This dynamic quality of the process is not only characteristic of Islamic arts and of Sufism; it belongs also to many other non-Western artistic traditions, including the traditional Japanese approach to the arts, where artistic practices are defined as "ways."[17] Ultimately, it is the *process* of *making* a work that is important.

Artistic expression through symbols is a way of coming closer to the spiritual and to a state of peace. Through this act, this "invocation," as one might translate it, the soul attains peace: "the resistance of the restless is gradually worn down" by artistic expression, such as in dance, music, chanting, or poetry.[18] The Islamic world is known as the world of peace: Dar el Sulh—or Dar el Salam. Islamic arts, including architecture, strive to attain complete harmony through the synthesis of opposites, such as dark and light, inside and outside, square and circle. Though the architecture, for example, is sometimes seen as being overly decorative or as having a quality of "horror vacui," its decorative qualities are a reflection of the beauty and richness of the universe, and with them the tensions of architecture, the tensions of structure, are brought into balance.

One of the most important symbolic, structural, and compositional forms is the spiral. It has introverted and extraverted movement; it is both concentric and eccentric. It represents the inner being and the outer world; it signifies constant change upon permanence. In miniatures, the basic compositional principle is the arrangement of major visual movements in the spiral form.[19] At architectural sites, this principle is also in operation. In the site organization of the Imperial Complex of Suleiman the Magnificent (Istanbul, c. 1557), one circulates among the different buildings of the complex and enters the main portal through spiral movements. The path is never linear.[20]

Decorative qualities of architecture are also the elaboration of structures that are believed to be the basis of all the universe and of all existence, such as the patterns that result from some basic geometries, which are symbolic of relationships between humans and God, or of some basic movements, which are thought to underlie the processes of time and the structures of space. These not only constitute the basis from which elaborate decorative patterns in architecture are produced, but also condition other spatial arts and the forms of music. Both Sufi and Islamic artistic expression in general are to be understood in relation to these basic understandings and interpretations of existence.

2. Principle of the Uncertainty of Human Understanding: Illusion or Reality?

Another basic claim about how humans are related to the world is about human perception, in particular, that what one sees may be illusion or reality. This uncertainty is expressed in many artistic and architectural forms—such as mirrors, reflections, and screens—which abound in Islamic architecture. They create a visual effect where the real and the illusory are confused, where appearances are seen as though through a veil, where the multiple repetitions of the same confuse the boundaries of the real world.

A well-known example is the Alhambra Palace and its gardens. The gardens are designed as sequences of small, connected garden courts. As one looks through the openings between the connected spaces, one sees an unending series of spaces with repeated arches cut into hedges. Water, which has many symbolic meanings, produces illusions and repeated images that create uncertainty about the reality of any of these appearances. Small water ponds adorning these spaces also create a dreamy world of reflections and "veils" created by water sprays.

Another example from Andalusia is the Cordoba Mosque, whose forest of columns and arches creates a sense of indefinable limits. The repetitive character of many elements in Islamic architecture is responsible for the perceiver's doubts about what is real. Repetition also points to the principle

of constant change; what is otherwise perceived as simple and monotonous can be seen in many ways and from a variety of viewing angles. (Something similar happens in the work of the conceptual artist Sol LeWitt.) The spiral form of circulation and the circular form of directionality are also important movements for taking different points of view.

Mirrors and mirror-like reflections, which abound in Islamic architectural works as elements of decoration, are vehicles for displaying the world's many different appearances. Multidimensionality is a way of implying the impossibility of knowing reality as it is. This second principle is reflected in the impossibility of knowledge about the Absolute because the Absolute manifests itself in infinite ways. Except for the ninety-nine names attributed to God, God cannot be known.

Another element that adds to confusion between appearance and reality is the use of lattice screens made of wood or metal. Screens typically have beautiful patterns through which changing effects of lights and shadows create a playful imagery. At the same time, however, the world is shown as if through a veil. Like many patterns used for decoration, screens reflect Islamic beliefs about how one perceives the world—as moving and as through a veil—but Ibn-Arabi says, "yet one is not ordinarily aware of this [movement] because of the extreme thinness and fineness of the veil."[21]

3. The Principle of Love: Understanding with the Heart

This principle is perhaps the one most deeply connected with spirituality. In Islam, existence as a whole is possible because of Love. Because God wanted to make his presence known, he created humankind to admire and love him, and made himself manifest through the world. As a person is part of the world, one is also part of God. As the whole world is the manifestation of God, one finds God within oneself. It is through admiring God's creation that one understands the spiritual world and becomes close to it. As artists view their work with admiration, they lose themselves in its beauty. They become like what they admire; observers become similar to what they look at. Art serves this mimetic purpose since all creation is the reflection of God.

These three principles—of change, of uncertainty, of love—point to a conception of the perceptual world as constructed of opposites that work in conjunction with each other: sacred and profane, humans and God, lover and beloved, male and female. Meaning is created in their conjunction, accessible through love, rendering us similar to what we try to understand. To understand the world, one has to become like artists who, drawing or painting, somehow become similar to what they draw or paint, and who approach the world with love. To approach with love one has to see the beauty. Thus art and understanding become intimately related.[22]

III.   THE PROBLEMATICS OF MODERNIZATION

It is an important question today whether one can still talk about Islamic aesthetics and whether an aesthetic approach that has its grounding in traditions and lifestyles that are no longer sustainable can possibly survive and have a role in contemporary artistic practice. If the answer is negative, we can talk about Islamic aesthetics only as a thing of the past. However, if we look at certain artists' work in Turkey during the era of modernization (roughly the late nineteenth century) and today, we can often see an Islamic approach, even if in the guise of Western painting styles and techniques and in the language of Western contemporary art.

Notwithstanding long years of exposure to Western art, certain ways of seeing have been slow to change. A typical Islamic sensibility that surfaces in the modern art of Islamic countries is the profuse use of patterns and calligraphic effects to produce rich surface qualities in a work. The use of diverse color contrasts and tonal effects in the same painting, for example, produces visual qualities similar to those of architectural decoration on Islamic buildings. It is also common to find fantastic creatures and a mixture of plant and animal forms in modern Islamic arts, not so much to create a surrealistic style, but rather to convey the sense of confusion and uncertainty about what is real and what is imagined.

During the twentieth century, especially as a result of modernization, many artists outside the West tried to create a modern language using elements reminiscent of their historic culture. One typical approach is to use the representation of space in ways that are similar to what is done in miniatures: piling depth planes on top of each other, eliminating three-dimensionality, and rendering size independently of distance. Other traits, as mentioned before, include geometric patterning, texture, and calligraphic movement. Figures may be truncated or placed without regard to where the pictorial surface ends. These features of painting should not be interpreted as the direct copying of traditional motifs and styles, but rather as choices artists make because they consider them to be true to the common visual experience within their culture.

Today, many artists still attempt to create an aesthetic based on a traditional Islamic worldview, such as is described by the three principles above. One approach is to create hybrid expressions, which may be seen as symbolic in the way traditional Islamic principles of understanding involve the integration of opposites. An engaged art involving political, sexual, and social commentary can be constituted using calligraphy, traditional decorative patterns, and images belonging to Islamic cultural traditions. The work of Murat Morova, a Turkish artist whose work is strikingly contemporary, yet still expresses an Islamic aesthetic understanding, provides us with a good example of this approach.[23]

The criticism that many modern visual works of art in Islamic cultures are merely decorative and lack significant content is an important problematic, at least in the eyes of many contemporary critics. Yet, these features need not be viewed as weaknesses. One can assume that the richness and complexity of visual effects that are sought after by many modern artists in the Islamic world are related to visual habits rooted in deep structures of tradition. At a time when such traditions were still alive and images carried the symbolic significance of a worldview, they carried deep meanings and were never merely decorative. Today, with modernization and the penetration of technology into everyday practices, the symbolism has apparently dissolved. Yet visual habits often remain, even when their religious and theoretical groundings do not, influencing artists' technique and style and the resultant surface qualities of their work. In addition, visual habits and preferences remain in the popular taste. The human figure does not have the deep spiritual references that it has in much Western art, especially its religious painting, so that figural painting becomes generally narrative. Abstraction no longer contains the symbolism of traditional worldviews, so the stark, subdued, and subtle, as features of style, are usually seen as alien and unaesthetic. Islamic artists striving for a modernist expressive style find themselves in a serious plight. In this regard, sustaining an Islamic aesthetics in modern and contemporary art depends on its being embedded in an engaged worldview, as in the case of some contemporary artists who create new visual configurations that count as an Islamic aesthetic because of their spiritual affinities.

I have attempted to explain how certain forms and orders of Islamic art reveal and reflect basic values and views about human existence and the relation of the human to the spiritual. Focusing on certain principles of Islamic understanding of the world, I tried to clarify how they are form-generating principles that create an environment, a world that caters to an Islamic way of seeing. Finally, I briefly described a dilemma faced by modern and contemporary artists. Worldviews are profound structures that have direct bearing on artistic practices even when the worldview is no longer shared. Yet, it is in part because patterns of visual experience are slow to change that they can become an important aspect of an artist's own cultural identity, and of his or her work.

JALE NEJDET ERZEN
Faculty of Architecture
Middle East Technical University
Ankara, Turkey 06531

INTERNET: erzen@arch.metu.edu.tr

1. Gülru Necipoğlu explains that the medieval Islamic scholar Al-Farabi classified mathematical sciences "into seven specialized fields (arithmetic, geometry, optics, astronomy, music, weights, mechanics) each of which had both theoretical (al-nazari) and practical (al-'amali) branches." Gülru Necipoğlu, The Topkapi Scroll—Geometry and Ornament in Islamic Architecture (Santa Monica: Getty Center for the History of Art and the Humanities, 1995), p. 132. Al-Farabi, Al-Ghazali, Ibn-Khaldun, Ibn Rushd, Ibn Sina, Al Jazari, and Ibn Al-Haytham can be reasonably taken as the most important medieval Islamic writers whose work reflects aesthetic views and concepts related to architectural and decorative applications. See Necipoğlu, The Topkapı Scroll, pp. 363–380.

2. Albert Gabriel was one of the early scholars who made drawings and elevations of architectural works in Turkey. Albert Gabriel, Les Monuments Turcs d'Anatolie, I, II (Paris: E. de Boccard, 1940).

3. On the influence of Islamic art on Matisse, see Yves Alain Bois, Painting as Model (MIT Press, 1990).

4. Both Oleg Grabar and Richard Ettinghausen were

great scholars of Islamic art; however, one rarely finds aesthetic interpretations in their books. See Richard Ettinghausen and Oleg Grabar, The Art and Architecture of Islam (Yale University Press, 1987); David Talbot Rice, Islamic Art (New York: Thames and Hudson, 1965).

5. See Laleh Bakhtiar, Sufi—Expressions of the Mystic Quest (London: Thames and Hudson, 1976), p. 17. A similar view may be found in Zen Buddhism. See T. Daisetz Suzuki, Zen and Japanese Culture (Princeton University Press, 1959), pp. 5–18.

6. An explanation of what constitutes a worldview and its relation to symbolic forms can be found in Erwin Panofsky, Perspective as Symbolic Form, trans. C. S. Wood (New York: Zone Books, 1991). See also Allister Neher's discussion in "How Perspective Could Be a Symbolic Form," The Journal of Aesthetics and Art Criticism 63 (2005): 359–373.

7. Cafer Efendi, Risale-i Mimariyye: An Early Seventeenth-Century Ottoman Treatise on Architecture, facsimile, trans. and notes by Howard Crane (Leiden: E.J. Brill, 1987), p. 34.

8. Bakhtiar, Sufi, p. 17.

9. Such a position also explains the lack of any musical notation in the Islamic world until the eighteenth century. Cem Behar, Klasik Türk Musikisi Üzerine Denemeler [Essays on Classical Turkish Music] (Istanbul: Bağlam Yayınları, 1987). Behar explains why music had to be memorized and repeatedly practiced, but not notated or written down.

10. Especially notable is the work of Levni, the eighteenth-century Ottoman miniaturist, in which one finds multiple perspectival systems in one view. See Esin Atıl, Levni ve Surname (Istanbul: Koçbank, 1999).

11. References for Islamic thought on these principles include: René Rebetez, La Odisea de la Luz (Bogota: Ediciones M. Roca, 1997); Al-Ghazali Muhamad, The Alchemy of Happiness, trans. Henry A. Homes (Albany: Munsell, 1873); Annemarie Schimmel, Mystical Dimensions of Islam (University of Carolina Press, 1975); Dahdal Masser Musa and Al-Husayn ibn Mansur Al-Hallaji, D.D. Dissertation, (Erlangen: Erlangen University 1983); Idries Shah, The Way of the Sufi (Middlesex: Penguin Books, 1968); Le Mesnevi, Mevlana Jalaludin Rumi, trans. Veled Celebi Izbudak (Istanbul: MEB Sark-Islam Klasikleri, 1966); Henry Corbin, Avicenna and the Visionary Recital (New York: Routledge and Kegan Paul, 1960); Henry Corbin, Creative Imagination in the Sufism of Ibn Arabi (Princeton: Routledge and Kegan Paul, 1969).

12. Bakhtiar, Sufi, p. 16. One important source about this principle being expressed in decorative patterns is the Topkapı Scroll, which has been analyzed by Gulrü Necipoğlu in The Topkapi Scroll.

13. Necipoğlu, The Topkapı Scroll, ch. 5. As articulated by Necipoğlu, there were very developed theories on perception that greatly influenced the arts, as in the writings of Ibn Al-Haytham. See The Optics of Ibn Al-Haytham: Books I–III, On Direct Vision (originally, Kitab al-manazir), trans. and with a commentary by Abdelhamid I. Sabra, 2 vols. (London: Warburg Institute, 1986) (mentioned in Necipoğlu, The Topkapı Scroll); also for the importance of sensory perception, see Bakhtiar, Sufi, pp. 18–19.

14. Avicenna, born in Bukhara in 980, wrote: "[F]or all beauty which is suitable and goodness which one perceives (kul cemal mulayim wakhayr mudrak), that one loves and

desires (*mahbib wa mashug*) the principle of perceiving them (*mabda idrakihi*) relies on the senses (*his*), imagination (*hayal*), the estimative faculty (*wahm*), conjecture (*zan*) and the intellect (*agl*)." (Valerie Gonzales, *Beauty and Islam*, [London: I.B. Tauris Publishers, 2001], pp. 16–18).

15. Bakhtiar, *Sufi*, p. 25.

16. It is a plausible generalization that in most non-Western arts the artist does not claim to be a creator. See Ken-ichi Sasaki, "Issues in Contemporary Culture and Aesthetics," in *Aesthetic Life in the Anti-Urban Culture of Japan*, ed. Heinz Paetzold (Maastricht: Jan van Eyck Akademie, 1996), pp. 59-65.

17. Haruhiko Fujita, "Arts and Ways," in *IAA Yearbook*, ed. Jale Erzen (2003), available at http://www.2.eur.nl/fw/hyper/IAA/index.htm.

18. Bakhtiar, *Sufi*, p. 24.

19. A. Papadopoulo, *L'Islam et l'Art Musulman* (Paris: Mazenod, 1976). For the spiral, see pp. 458–469.

20. See Jale Nejdet Erzen, "Site Organization," in *Sinan Ottoman Architect* (Ankara: METU Faculty of Architecture, 2004), pp. 153-167.

21. Bakhtiar, *Sufi*, p. 17.

22. Beşir Ayvazoğlu, *Aşk Estetiği* [*Aesthetics of Love*] (Istanbul: Ötüken Neşriyat, 1993).

23. Murat Morova's works can be accessed at www.geocities.com/kareninarivista/biennalecountries.htm.

DOMINIC MCIVER LOPES

Shikinen Sengu and the Ontology
of Architecture in Japan

There is nothing to see, and they won't let you see it.
Basil Chamberlain

If we compare the architecture of Western civilization to a museum, Japanese architecture [is like] a theater.
Toyo Ito

Visitors to Ise Jingu in Japan may pick up a free brochure with a caption history of the shrine, photographs of important rites under way, descriptions of the site's principal features, and a plan view drawing. This last catches the eye right away. Paired with each sanctuary compound, or *goshoden*, is an open space, the *kodenchi*, whose dimensions duplicate the *goshoden*'s (Figure 1). Curious philosophers who look into the pairing of *goshoden* to *kodenchi* will find themselves rethinking the ontology of architecture.

I. ONTOLOGY AND CULTURE

It might seem that no topic in aesthetics need less attend to cultural variation than the ontology of art. Ontology is after all a branch of metaphysics and metaphysics abstracts from cultural contingency. However, contemporary work in the ontology of art ties ontology to culture in a way that ought to encourage cross-cultural studies in the ontology of art.

Philosophers have for some time studied theories of art in the context of cultural variation.[1] A theory of art states—perhaps in the form of a definition—the features that make items works of art. Candidate art-making features include having significant form, affording an experience with marked aesthetic character, or occupying a specified role in an institution.[2] Armed with such a theory, we may ask three questions. Do members of any given culture make works of art? Do they

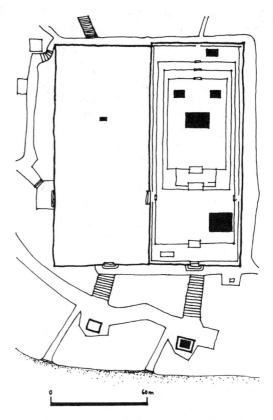

FIGURE 1. Plan view detail of the *naiku* at Ise Jingu. Right: the current sanctuary or *goshoden*. Left: the *kodenchi*, the empty site of the next *goshoden*, to be completed in 2013.

have a concept of art—do they group together as a kind the items that have the art-making features? Do they know the theory of art—do they know that artworks have the art-making features?[3]

An ontology of art is not a theory of art. The world arguably includes material objects, properties, events, and abstracta like sets and types; and an ontology of art places artworks in one or more of these categories. Thus it does not imply a theory of art: the statement that some works of art are material objects does not settle what makes any material object a work of art. Nor does a theory of art imply an ontology of art: the claim that all and only artworks have significant form leaves open whether artworks are material objects, events, or abstracta—any of these may have or lack significant form. Finding that members of a given culture make art, have a concept of art, and know the theory of art leaves open the ontology of art in the culture.

In crafting ontologies of art, philosophers take a cue from the tacit ontological conceptions implicit in appreciative practices.[4] They assume that an adequate ontology of art must be consistent with and help illuminate those practices. Sometimes, an ontology of art leads us to revise our appreciative practices; but if, upon reflection, our appreciative practices are sound, then they furnish materials for a good ontology of art. As David Davies puts the principle, a work of art is an item belonging to the ontological category whose members have the properties that appreciative practice, on reflection, requires us to attribute to the work.

For example, Nelson Goodman observes that appreciations of a work and forgeries of it always differ in content, but whereas some artworks can be forged (such as paintings), others cannot be forged (such as poems).[5] He therefore distinguishes single-instance works, whose duplicates are never instances, from multiple-instance works, which can be copied. Single-instance works are material particulars or token events and multiple-instance works are compliance classes. Although Goodman's ontology of art is not widely accepted, his methodology is entirely orthodox in the sense that it is intended to fit our appreciative practices.[6]

If a phenomenon is a cultural invariant, then nothing can be learned about it by studying it in different cultures (except, of course, that it is a cultural invariant). Perhaps sound art appreciation is a cultural invariant. If it is, then the ontology it implies is also invariant, since anything implied by an invariant is also invariant. The ontology of art in one culture will generalize to all others, and we need not look beyond our own shores for a full ontology of art. It follows that the relevance of cross-cultural studies to the ontology of art depends on whether sound practices of art appreciation vary culturally.

According to pluralist ontologies of art, no ontological category contains all artworks. If some are material objects, then some are not—perhaps they are token events or abstracta. Works are assigned to ontological categories so as to accommodate sound appreciative practices. Since the practices are usually taken to govern groups of works, each group is placed in an ontological category. The question is then how to group works. Initially at least, it makes sense simply to group works into art forms. Thus paintings are material objects, musical works are abstract objects, and so on. What determines ontological category is, roughly, art form.

If art forms are cultural invariants, then pluralist ontologies of art need not attend to cultural variation; but art forms are unlikely to be cultural invariants. Nothing rules out their varying within or across cultures in ways that impact the ontology of art. Peter Kivy and Jerrold Levinson famously hold that musical works are abstracta, but both are careful to qualify their views as applying to European art music in the grand tradition from Bach to Stravinsky.[7] In the same spirit, Stephen Davies develops a pluralist ontology of musical works, including Javanese gamelan.[8] What goes for music may go for other art forms.

According to monist ontologies of art, all works of art belong to the same ontological category. This implies that appreciative practices are invariant enough to embed a uniform ontology of art. For example, David Davies identifies the work of art with a token event, namely, the artist's act of specifying a focus of appreciation. The focus of appreciation comprises a content, a vehicle for expressing the content, and a set of understandings by means of which the vehicle expresses the content.[9] The vehicle may be an object, a performance, or something else, but the work itself is the artist's act of specifying the focus of appreciation—it is not the focus that gets specified. Thus all works of art from all times and places belong to the same ontological category: all are token events.

Even so, Davies's monism about works allows for pluralism about vehicles for expressing content. A painting and a sonata are both, according to Davies, acts of specifying a focus of appreciation, but in each case the focus may have different elements. In the case of the painting, the focus might comprise a material object plus a set of understandings through which material objects bear content. In the case of the sonata, the focus might comprise an abstractum plus a set of understandings through which abstracta bear content. Again, works in different art forms have different vehicles or different content-determining understandings.

Art forms are not likely to be cultural invariants, but Davies's monism also accommodates cultural variation in art forms. The following three propositions are mutually consistent.

Every work of art is an act of specifying a focus of appreciation (monism is true).
The vehicular component of the focus of appreciation varies culturally.
The understandings by means of which the vehicular component bears content vary culturally.

Differences in sound appreciative practices from culture to culture can imply all three propositions together.

In sum, cross-cultural studies are relevant to the ontology of art as long as sound practices of art appreciation vary enough that they imply different ontologies. Pluralist ontologies of art represent this variation as a variation in the ontological categories of works. Monist ontologies of art represent it as a variation in the elements that make up foci of appreciation specified by artworks. However, the question remains whether sound practices of art appreciation do in fact vary in ways that imply different ontologies.

II. SHIKINEN SENGU

Ise Jingu, located on the coast about one-hundred kilometers southeast of Kyoto, is among Japan's most important and most visited Shinto shrines. It is also one of the oldest, though, as we shall see, the *shikinen sengu* makes dating a tricky business.

Each Shinto shrine is consecrated to the worship of one or more *kami*, and Ise Jingu is primarily dedicated to Amaterasu Omikami, the sun goddess, from whom the Japanese emperors claimed descent. Legend tells that it was founded in the first century BCE by Emperor Suinin, though historical evidence indicates a founding in the fifth or sixth centuries CE, around the time when the nearby court at Yamato was establishing itself as the imperial family. As this family's shrine and hence indirectly a national shrine, it has served since then to represent and promote the authority of the emperor and to focus Japanese nationalism.[10] Many Japanese consider that they should visit the shrine at least once in their lifetime and more than 6 million do visit every year.

The shrine occupies two parcels of land six kilometers apart. The smaller *geku* (or outer shrine) comprises a cluster of about two dozen buildings, the most important being a sanctuary for Toyoke Omikami, the goddess of clothing, food, and housing—purveyor to Amaterasu. The *naiku* (or inner shrine) comprises a roughly equal number of structures set in a forest of 5,500 hectares. The structures are modest in scale and are built in a plain style of unfinished Japanese cypress with thatched miscanthus roofing, in obvious resistance to Buddhist and Chinese influence. One of these structures, the *goshoden*, houses Amaterasu herself in the form of a mirror.

Remarkably, the *goshoden* (and all other sanctified structures, including the Uji Bridge) has been rebuilt about every twenty years (with occasional breaks) since the eighth century CE in a cycle called the *shikinen sengu*. Moreover, the rebuilding is not exactly *in situ*. As Figure 1 shows, the *goshoden* sits next to a vacant lot, the *kodenchi*, where the *goshoden* is rebuilt. *Goshoden* and *kodenchi* in this way swap sites with each *sengu* cycle.

The *sengu* is a major material and ritual undertaking.[11] The work takes about eight years, from the initial preparation of the *kodenchi* grounds to the final transfer of the *kami*. Timber from more than 15,000 trees is required, along with 900 meters of silk, 3.75 kilograms of gold, and 260 kilograms of lacquer. Ancient techniques and tools of ancient design are used. News reports put the cost of the 2013 *sengu* at 55 billion yen. In addition, every stage of building is marked by rites, thirty-five in all, some modest, some involving more than one hundred thousand participants, and others elaborate and esoteric.

One might seek out the meaning of the *sengu* in its rationale, but there is no widely accepted explanation of the practice. According to one theological explanation, Shinto requires that *kami* be lodged in fresh and beautiful shrines; according to another, the *sengu* articulates Shinto doctrines of purity and renewal.[12] According to a broader cultural explanation, the *sengu* embodies *mujukan*, an awareness of the transience of life, nature, and artifacts.[13] The close relationship between Ise Jingu and the imperial household suggests a political explanation, that in undertaking the enormous, recurring expense of the *sengu*, the household renewed its unwavering commitment to the shrine and thus its national authority.[14] Architectural explanations have also been proposed: the *sengu* ensures that the skills needed to maintain the shrine are passed down from one generation of artisans to the next, or it maintains the purity of building materials and preserves ancient architectural forms.[15] However plausible or implausible these explanations, the *sengu* is a fact.

Moreover, the *sengu* is no mere curiosity: it arguably distills one strand of architectural practice in Japan. This can be seen in other sacred architecture, in vernacular building, and also in a distinctively Japanese brand of modernism.

More than thirty other shrines are regularly rebuilt. Kasuga Taisha in Nara is rebuilt every thirty years, Kamo Mioya Jinja in Kyoto every fifty years, and Nukisaki Jinja in Gumma Prefecture every thirteen years, for instance. Many more are rebuilt on an irregular schedule—Izumo Taisha in Shimane Prefecture, which rivals Ise Jingu in age and status, has been rebuilt twenty-five times. Buddhist monasteries and temples are also rebuilt as needed—for example, Kofukuji in Nara has now been taken down to its foundations and is slated for completion in 2010.

Traditional Japanese vernacular architecture characteristically features wood, paper, and other relatively ephemeral building materials, which are allowed to weather, and traditional houses are rebuilt every few decades. Thus tourists in Japan are struck by the absence of old town centers—Kyoto's Gion district being a well-known exception. Almost all the historic sites that attract visitors have been rebuilt several times. Kinkakuji, which is perhaps Kyoto's best-known site, was burnt to the ground in 1950, rebuilt in 1955, and regilded in 1987—but nobody regards this as remarkable or as diminishing the site's value.

Modernist architecture is seen in Japan as extending tradition. This conception of Japanese modernism grew out of a campaign to rehabilitate traditional architecture following World War II.[16] The oligarchs had associated traditional architecture, especially Ise Jingu, with extreme nationalism and, after the war, critics and scholars replaced the nationalist associations of traditional architecture with modernist ones. The most articulate statements of this rehabilitation are an essay by Kanzo Tange, the dean of Japanese postwar modernist architecture, in *Ise: Prototype of Japanese Architecture*, and Yasutada Watanabe's *Shinto Art: Ise and Izumo Shrines*.[17] The latter opens with a striking autobiographical passage in which the historian tells how his prewar "fearful reverence for the awesome prestige of Japan's most sacred shrine" gave way after the war to a revelation of the shrine's "delicate balance and harmony of proportion."[18] These writers were so influential that, as one historian remarks, "modern architectural practice in Japan was inexorably bound up with and could not be understood outside the context of premodern architecture, a position that is still pervasive in the literature of Japanese architecture to the present day."[19]

Two elements of tradition were stressed in comparing traditional architecture to modernist architecture. First, traditional post and lintel construction was likened to the modernist use of the grid. At the same time, Japanese modernism was thought to sustain a tendency in Japanese architecture to perpetuate architectural form without much concern for the actual building itself.[20] Typifying this strand of Japanese modernism are the "metabolist" architects of the 1960s and 1970s, who treated architectural structures as kits of elements swapped in and out in cycles of growth, decay, and renewal. Metabolism is the tip of the iceberg.[21] Tange himself replaced his 1957 Tokyo City Hall with a new one in 1991. Well-publicized houses by Kazuo Shinohara and Masaharu Takasaki were replaced within ten years of their construction. The Nomad Restaurant by Toyo Ito, Japan's best-known young architect, was put up for a three-year lifespan. Ito's buildings are often made to look impermanent, as are Shigeru Bam's buildings, which are made of paper.

Botond Bognar suggests several explanations of this architecture of impermanence.[22] High land prices in Tokyo make the ratio of building cost to land value among the lowest in the world, so that 30 percent of central Tokyo's urban fabric is replaced annually. In Japan, craftsmanship is valued more than uniqueness and antiquity in an object. The *sengu* is also a factor: "Japanese architecture and urbanism, in the tradition of 'ritual' building and rebuilding, constitute a culture of making-and-remaking rather than that of making-and-holding." As Bognar sees it, however, cycles of rebuilding reconcile impermanence with continuity: "ephemerality ... can paradoxically yield lasting or enduring achievements."[23]

Maybe the tourist who complained that there is nothing to see at Ise had equipped himself with appreciative tools suited to European architecture that ill fit the strand of Japanese architecture to which Ise Jingu belongs. We need not think all Japanese architectural appreciation takes the very same form—a fascinating twist is the outdoor museum of buildings (including Frank Lloyd Wright's Imperial Hotel) at Meijimura, outside Nagoya. Still, the *shikinen sengu* suggests that some Japanese architecture might require a different appreciative attitude.

III. MUSEUM AND THEATER

Assume that the age attributed to a building is a factor in its appreciation: an appreciation of a building as old would have a different content were it appreciated as young. Here, then, are two propositions:

(O) Ise Jingu is more than one thousand years old.
(Y) Ise Jingu is no more than twenty years old.

(For simplicity, let "Ise Jingu" refer to the *goshoden* at the *naiku*.) These are obviously inconsistent, and a standard ontology of architecture implies that (Y) is true and (O) is false. However, one commentator writes that the *naiku* and *geku* are "ever new yet ever unchanging" and another that "both shrines are very old and very new. They are very old because they are identical with the ones that stood there at least as early as 685 ... They are very new because they are ceremonially rebuilt every twenty years."[24] Taking such statements seriously means that both (O) and (Y) are true. (O) and (Y) are both true only if there is an ambiguity to resolve. An alternative to the standard ontology must resolve the ambiguity.

The standard ontology that forces a choice between (O) and (Y) captures a key feature of architectural appreciation in the West. Copies of a building are not instances of a work. To see a replica of the Seagram Building is not to see the Seagram Building, and to see a reconstruction of the Parthenon as it was in 300 BCE is not to see the Parthenon. We cannot appreciate Europe's great architecture by means of a trip to Las Vegas.

Thus architectural works contrast with multiple-instance works like Beethoven's sonatas: to hear any performance of the Opus 111 Piano Sonata is to hear the sonata.

According to the standard ontology, a building is a material object individuated as common sense individuates objects like tables and chairs. It is made up of parts, each part roughly identical to a bunch of molecules, and it comes into existence when the parts are assembled. Its persistence is a matter of some controversy. It survives the replacement of some parts and it does not survive the simultaneous replacement of all its parts. However, it is unclear whether it survives the gradual replacement of all its parts until no parts remain that were its parts when it was assembled. (It is unclear because surviving in this way generates some well-known puzzles.[25])

If a building is a material object individuated as common sense individuates tables and chairs, then (O) is false.[26] Ise Jingu is made up of parts that were joined together no more than twenty years ago. Although it sits next to the spot where a different building stood, it is not the survivor of that building. The reason is that no building survives the simultaneous replacement of all its parts. Indeed, there was a time when both buildings stood side-by-side, and a material object cannot stand beside itself. (Happily, since the *sengu* does not involve the gradual replacement of each part of the *goshoden* until no original parts remain, there is no need to confront the well-known puzzles.)

An alternative ontology of Ise Jingu that is consistent with both (O) and (Y) must interpret them in such a way that they are also consistent with each other. In addition, it should fit Ise Jingu as an expression of the wider strand of Japanese architectural practice.

Recent architecture provides a precedent for one alternative to the standard ontology.[27] Although they remain uncommon, there are multiple-instance works of architecture. An example is Tom Sandonato and Martin Wehmann's kitHAUS. To appreciate kitHAUS for what it is, one must appreciate it as a work that has instances. Although the instances are material objects, the work itself is an abstractum—assume it to be a type.

Taking kitHAUS as a model, one might propose that Ise Jingu is a multiple-instance work whose instances are material objects built on alternating, adjoining patches of ground about every twenty years. The proposal is consistent with both (O) and (Y). Ise Jingu's current instance is no more than twenty years old and in that sense (Y) is true. Since the type is at least as old as its first token, the type is more than one thousand years old, and in that sense (O) is true. What is old is the type and what is young is its current instance.

However, Ise Jingu is different from works like kitHAUS and the differences suggest that it has a different ontology. The constitutive properties of a type are the properties that its instances have necessarily. The properties that instances of kitHAUS have necessarily are material and spatial features specified in the construction drawings—instances of kitHAUS must fit the drawings. By contrast, the features of Ise Jingu captured in a drawing of it are inessential to it. Although there is evidence that the current incarnation does roughly resemble the earliest ones, a proof that there have been radical design changes over the centuries would not be taken to show that the shrine long ago ceased to exist and was replaced by an impostor. That is, the *sengu* allows for changes in material and spatial specifications from one rebuilding to the next and the evidence is that there have been many changes.[28] So the constitutive properties of kitHAUS and its ilk are not constitutive properties of Ise Jingu.

What then are the constitutive properties of the shrine? One answer profits from the proposition that the shrine belongs to an architectural practice that includes other traditional Japanese architecture and the distinctively Japanese modernism practiced by architects such as Ito and Bam. A constitutive feature of buildings in this strand of architectural practice in Japan is that they change— they weather, decay, and soon perish. Buildings in the West normally resist change (or make minor concessions to it—for example, by gaining patina). Although they do in fact decay, their decay is destructive. By contrast, the decay of Bam's paper building does not destroy it, if the decay is part of the building; and the destruction of the old *goshoden* does not destroy Ise Jingu. Whereas the Seagram Building is a material object conforming to material and spatial design specifications, Ito's Nomad Restaurant is a three-year event conforming to temporal design specifications. Likewise, a constitutive feature of Ise Jingu is that it involves twenty-year cycles of building, weathering, decay, rebuilding, and demolition.

Modeling Ise Jingu on kitHAUS therefore detaches the shrine from a wider strand of architectural practice in Japan. According to the model, Ise Jingu is a repeatable work whose instances are material objects conforming to material and spatial design specifications. If, however, the shrine represents a larger architectural practice, as Japanese historians and critics think it does, then its constitutive features are temporal ones.

Acknowledging this point, one might amend the proposal that Ise Jingu is a multiple-instance work. Its instances are not material objects necessarily conforming to spatial design specifications. Instead, they are events of about twenty years' duration in which a structure is built, weathers, decays, and perishes. This amended proposal reconciles (O) with (Y) and also acknowledges the place of the shrine in a wider architectural practice.

Even so amended, the proposal still detaches Ise Jingu from other works said to belong to the same architectural practice. Ito's Nomad Restaurant and Bam's paper buildings are not multiple-instance works. They are individual events. Thus the amended proposal implies a dual ontology. Rebuilt structures like Ise Jingu are multiple-instance event types; structures that are not rebuilt are token events.

One might accept the dual ontology. If acceptance means that there are two appreciative practices, one for works like the Nomad Restaurant and another for works like Ise Jingu, then the view that the shrine belongs to the larger architectural practice must be qualified. But an alternative is to seek an ontology that reconciles (O) and (Y) and also accommodates the ontological unity of an architectural practice that includes Ise Jingu and the Nomad Restaurant.

Here is an alternative to the multiple-instance ontology. Buildings in one strand of architectural practice in Japan are neither types nor material objects: they are all token events. Sometimes, a building is the history of a material object from its fresh beginnings through weathering and decay until it is taken down. Sometimes, the event includes one or more rounds of reconstruction. If Kinkakuji is a material object, then what tourists visit today is a replica of the Kinkakuji built by Shogun Yoshimitsu in 1394. If it is a token event that includes rebuildings, then what tourists see today is what the shogun built. In the case of Ise Jingu, the event is rule governed and ritualized, and it is made up of a sequence of buildings and rebuildings on alternating, adjoining sites in a twenty-year cycle, the *sengu*.

The advantage of this proposal is that it fits Ise Jingu, traditional Japanese architecture, and distinctively Japanese modernism to a single ontology. Thus Ise Jingu is not an exception; it is a central case of a single architectural practice. This is exactly how it is conceived in the literature on architecture in Japan. At the same time, there are differences between ephemeral works like Nomad Restaurant and works of rebuilding like Ise Jingu. This proposal represents those differences. Nomad Restaurant lasts only three years, whereas, in Ise Jingu, permanence is achieved through rebuilding: the two events differ in duration and only one involves rebuilding. That does not amount, however, to a difference in ontology: both are token events.

Other ontologies might reconcile (O) and (Y) and respect the unity of the strand of architectural practice that takes in Ise Jingu, traditional vernacular architecture, and Japanese modernism. For that reason, it would be premature to take that strand of Japanese architectural appreciation as implying that Ise Jingu is a token event. Nevertheless, Ise Jingu does prompt ontologists of architecture to look at a wider range of ontological options than come into sight when they confine their attention to the Seagram Building and kitHAUS.

IV. CONCLUSION

Faced with the prospect that some architectural works are to be appreciated more like plays than like statues, one might deny that the recommended mode of appreciation is sound. If it is not sound, no ontology it implies carries any weight. Turning the tables, one might ask whether the European mode of architecture appreciation is sound: maybe it is corrected by moving to the Japanese model. A third option is cultural pluralism: there is more than one ontology of architecture because sound architecture appreciation varies across cultures.[29]

DOMINIC MCIVER LOPES
Department of Philosophy
University of British Columbia
Vancouver, BC V6T 121, Canada

INTERNET: dom.lopes@ubc.ca

1. For example, H. Gene Blocker, "Is Primitive Art Art?" *The Journal of Aesthetic Education* 25 (1991): 87–97; Julius Moravcsik, "Why Philosophy of Art in Cross-Cultural Perspective?" *The Journal of Aesthetics and Art Criticism* 51 (1993): 426–435; Stephen Davies, "Non-Western Art and Art's Definition," in *Theories of Art Today*, ed. Noël Carroll (University of Wisconsin Press, 2000).

2. Clive Bell, *Art* (London: Chatto and Windus, 1914); Monroe Beardsley, "An Aesthetic Definition of Art," in *What Is Art?* ed. Hugh Curtler (Yale University Press, 1983); George Dickie, *The Art Circle* (New York: Haven, 1984).

3. The questions are distinct. See Dominic McIver Lopes, "Art Without 'Art,'" *The British Journal of Aesthetics* 47 (2007): 1–15.

4. For defense of the method, see Amie Thomasson, "The Ontology of Art and Knowledge in Aesthetics," *The Journal of Aesthetics and Art Criticism* 63 (2005): 221–229; David Davies, *Art as Performance* (Oxford: Blackwell, 2004), ch. 1.

5. Nelson Goodman, *Languages of Art*, 2nd ed. (Indianapolis: Hackett, 1976).

6. The point withstands complaints about Goodman's ontology of music. Goodman identifies a work of music with sound events that perfectly comply with the score. One wrong note in an attempt to perform a work entails that the work is not actually performed. Goodman replies that this implication does no real injury to our appreciative practices. In making this reply, he recognizes that facts about appreciation cannot be ignored. See Goodman, *Languages of Art*, pp. 186–187.

7. Jerrold Levinson, "What a Musical Work Is," *Journal of Philosophy* 77 (1980): 5–18, the point is made on 6; Peter Kivy, "Platonism in Music: Another Kind of Defense," *American Philosophical Quarterly* 24 (1983): 245–252, the point is made on 245. See also Lydia Goehr, *The Imaginary Museum of Musical Works* (Oxford University Press, 1992).

8. Stephen Davies, *Musical Works and Performances* (Oxford University Press, 2001).

9. Davies, *Art as Performance*, p. 146. See also Gregory Currie, *An Ontology of Art* (London: Macmillan, 1989).

10. William Coaldrake, *Architecture and Authority in Japan* (London: Routledge, 1996); Jonathan Reynolds, "Ise Shrine and a Modernist Construction of Japanese Tradition," *Art Bulletin* 83 (2001): 316–341.

11. For details, see Felicia Bock, "The Rites of Renewal at Ise," *Monumenta Nipponica* 29 (1974): 55–68; Cassandra Adams, "Japan's Ise Shrine and Its Thirteen-Hundred-Year-Old Reconstruction Tradition," *Journal of Architectural Education* 52 (1998) 49–60; Jingu Administration Office, *The Rituals that Are Part of the 61st Shikinen Sengu* (2001), available at http://www.isejingu.or.jp/english/sikinen/sikinen2.htm.

12. Bock, "The Rites of Renewal at Ise," p. 56; Yasutada Watanabe, *Shinto Art: Ise and Izumo Shrines*, trans. Robert Ricketts (New York: Weatherhill and Tokyo: Heibonsha, 1974), pp. 51–52.

13. Günter Nitschke, *From Shinto to Ando: Studies in Architectural Anthropology in Japan* (New York: St. Martin's Press, 1993).

14. Coaldrake, *Architecture and Authority in Japan*.

15. Bock, "The Rites of Renewal at Ise," p. 57; Coaldrake, *Architecture and Authority in Japan*, p. 323; Adams, "Japan's Ise Shrine," p. 49.

16. Reynolds, "Ise Shrine and a Modernist Construction of Japanese Tradition."

17. Kenzo Tange and Noburo Kawazoe, *Ise: Prototype of Japanese Architecture* (MIT Press, [1961] 1965).

18. Watanabe, *Shinto Art*, p. 11.

19. Reynolds, "Ise Shrine and a Modernist Construction of Japanese Tradition," p. 317.

20. Reynolds, "Ise Shrine and a Modernist Construction of Japanese Tradition," p. 331. See also Noburo Kawazoe, "The Ise Shrine and Its Cultural Context," in *Ise: Prototype of Japanese Architecture*, p. 202.

21. Botond Bognar, "What Goes Up Must Come Down: Recent Urban Architecture in Japan," *Harvard Design Magazine* 3 (1997): 1–8.

22. Ibid.

23. Bognar, "What Goes Up Must Come Down," pp. 4, 7.

24. Kawazoe, "The Ise Shrine and Its Cultural Context," p. 206; John Burchard, "Introduction," in *Ise: Prototype of Japanese Architecture*, p. 9.

25. Ship of Theseus and related puzzles. For example, Roderick Chisholm, *Person and Object* (La Salle: Open Court, 1979), ch. 3.

26. Ise Jingu's being a material object is consistent with (O) if we individuate material objects without regard for common sense.

27. One might extend this ontology to all buildings in order to accommodate restoration practices. See Robert Wicks, "Architectural Restoration: Resurrection or Replication?" *The British Journal of Aesthetics* 34 (1994): 163–169.

28. Watanabe, *Shinto Art*, pp. 52–55, 170–172.

29. Thanks to Susan Herrington for Figure 1 and for enlightening discussions of Ise Jingu. Thanks also to the faculty exchange program between the University of British Columbia and Ritsumeikan University in Kyoto for the opportunity to study Japanese aesthetics.

YURIKO SAITO

The Moral Dimension of Japanese Aesthetics

Japanese aesthetics was first introduced to the non-Japanese audience around the turn of the twentieth century through now classic works, such as *Bushidō* (1899), *The Ideals of the East* (1904), and *The Book of Tea* (1907), all written in English and published in the United States.[1] Since then, Japanese aesthetic concepts, such as *wabi*, *sabi*, *yūgen*, *iki*, and *mono no aware*, have become better known, some even popularized today.[2] Some traditional Japanese art media, such as flower arrangement, *Noh* theater, haiku, martial arts, and, perhaps most prominently, tea ceremony, are now widely studied and sometimes practiced outside of Japan. The authors of all these studies generally characterize Japanese aesthetics by focusing on aesthetic concepts and phenomena that are "unique to" Japan and "different from" non-Japanese aesthetic traditions, the Western aesthetic tradition in particular.

Meanwhile, recent scholarship in Japanese studies examines the historical and political context during the rapid process of Westernization (late nineteenth century through early twentieth century) that prompted Japanese intellectuals at the time to rediscover and reaffirm the character, and sometimes superiority, of their own cultural tradition and values, particularly aesthetics. Some argue that, whether consciously or not, this promotion of cultural nationalism paved the way for the political ultra-nationalism that was the ideological underpinning of colonialism.[3]

Despite recent efforts to introduce, popularize, or contextualize Japanese aesthetics, uncharted territories remain. In this paper I explore one such area: the moral dimension of Japanese aesthetics. I characterize the long-held Japanese aesthetic tradition to be morally based by promoting respect, care, and consideration for others, both humans and nonhumans. Although both moral and aesthetic dimensions of Japanese culture have, independently, received considerable attention by scholars of Japanese aesthetics, culture, and society, the relationship between the two has yet to be articulated. One reason may be that there is no specific term in either Japanese or English to capture its content. Furthermore, although this moral dimension of aesthetic life is specifically incorporated in some arts, such as the tea ceremony and haiku, it is deeply entrenched in people's daily, mundane activities and thoroughly integrated with everyday life, rendering it rather invisible. Similarly, contemporary discourse on morality has not given much consideration to this aesthetic manifestation of moral values, despite the emergence of feminist ethics, ethics of care, and virtue ethics. Although they emphasize humility, care, and considerateness, discourses on feminist ethics primarily address actions or persons, not the aesthetic qualities of the works they produce.

Japanese aesthetics suggests several ways for cultivating moral sensibilities. In what follows, I focus on two principles of design: (1) respecting the innate characteristics of objects and (2) honoring and responding to human needs. Exploring them is important not only to illuminate this heretofore neglected aspect of Japanese aesthetics, but also to call attention to the crucial role aesthetics does and can play in promoting a good life and society, whatever the particular historical or cultural tradition and artistic heritage may be.

I

The Japanese aesthetic tradition is noted for its sensitivity to, respect for, and appreciation of the quintessential character of an object. This attitude gives rise to a guiding principle of design that articulates the essence of an object, material, or subject matter, regardless of whether it is considered artistic.[4] In this section, I show how this attitude is embodied in Japanese garden design, flower arrangement, haiku composition, and painting, as well as cooking and packaging.

The earliest expression of such a guiding principle of design can be found in the oldest extant writing on garden design, *Sakuteiki* [*Book on Garden Making*], written by an eleventh-century aristocrat. The author states that the art of garden making consists of creating *the scenic effect* of a landscape by observing one principle of design: "obeying (or following) the request" of an object (*kowan ni shitagau*). Referring specifically to rocks here, this principle suggests that the arrangement of rocks be dictated by their innate characteristics. For example, the gardener "should first install one main stone, and then place other stones, in necessary numbers, in such a way as *to satisfy the request . . . of the main stone*."[5]

In later centuries, the same design strategy extended to the placement and maintenance of plant materials. Instead of allowing unmitigated growth, inevitable death, or destruction by natural processes, Japanese gardeners meticulously shape and maintain trees and shrubs by extensive manipulation.[6] Unlike topiary in European formal gardens, however, where shapes are imposed on the plant materials regardless of their own characteristics, a tree or a shrub in a Japanese garden is shaped according to its individual form. A fifteenth-century manual, for example, instructs the gardener to "observe the natural growth pattern of the tree, and then prune it *to bring out its inherent scenic qualities*." The gardener should express the essential features of a particular material through elimination of inessential and irrelevant parts.[7] The whole art making here requires the artist to work closely *with*, rather than *in spite of* or *irrespective of*, the material's natural endowments.

Similar principles also govern the art of flower arrangement (*ikebana*), which was elevated to an artistic status during the sixteenth century. Although this art form begins, paradoxically, by cutting off a living flower or branch, thereby initiating its death, its primary aim is to "let flower live," the literal translation of *ikebana*, or to "let flower express itself" (*ikasu*).[8] This can be achieved by further cutting of branches, leaves, and blossoms so that only the essential parts defining the particular plant can be clearly delineated. One contemporary

commentator summarizes that "the ultimate aim of floral art is to represent nature in its inmost essence."[9]

The same design principle applies to the art of representation, such as haiku, a 5-7-5 syllable verse form, established in the seventeenth century by Matsuo Bashō (1644–1694). According to Bashō, the *raison d'etre* of poetry is to capture the essence of nature by entering into and identifying oneself with it, summarized in his well-known saying: "Of the pine-tree learn from the pine-tree. Of the bamboo learn from the bamboo."[10] For this, he calls for "the slenderness of mind," as one has to overcome one's personal feelings and concerns in order to grasp and appreciate the qualities of the objects for what they are. Sometimes described as "impersonality," the ideal of haiku making should be object centered, rather than subject governed.[11] When successful, the poet's effort will "'grow into' (*naru*) a verse," rather than "'doing' (*suru*) a verse."[12]

Bashō's contemporary, Tosa Mitsukuni (1617–1691), developed a similar theory regarding the art of painting. For him, mimesis is the main purpose of a painting, but it is "the spirit of the object" that the painter must grasp and present.[13] Toward this end, the painter can and should omit certain elements, making the overall effect "incomplete" and "suggestive," facilitating more readily the presentation of the essential characteristics of the subject matter, such as bird-ness. Exhaustively faithful, realistic renditions, as found in both Chinese painting and his rival Kanō School paintings, according to Mitsukuni, are like prose, which contrasts with the poetry of Tosa School paintings.[14] Probably conscious of the teachings by Bashō and Mitsukuni, another painter, Tsubaki Chinzan (1800–1854), claims that "even when painted with black ink, bamboo is bamboo; with red ink, bamboo is also bamboo. If the spirit of bamboo is embodied in the brush, the *ambience* of bamboo will naturally arise. This is the essence of painting."[15]

This principle for respecting a natural object also applies to producing objects of everyday life. From lacquerware to pottery, paper to textile, woodwork to metalwork, Japanese crafts are transmitted generation after generation, firmly rooted in respect for the materials, methods, tools, and traditions of each craft. Jack Lenor Larsen writes: "Craftmakers working within Japan's ancient traditions respond to the generations of passed-on knowledge. This collective memory includes a deep respect for material and process, and respect too for the intended user."[16]

Packaging and food can be used to illustrate these principles.[17] Traditional Japanese packaging is well known for its aesthetic and functional use of materials. Various packaging materials are designed not only for protecting the content, but also for emphasizing their innate characteristics. The design is suggested by the qualities of the material itself. For example, Japanese paper lends itself to folding, twisting, layering, tearing, and to being made into a cord by tight twisting. A bamboo stalk can be sliced into thin strips that are both flexible and strong, which can then be woven, or it can be cut into sections in order to take advantage of its natural section dividers. Bamboo leaves and bark can be used for wrapping food items because of their thinness, flexibility, and gentle aroma. Similarly, some woods, such as cedar, impart a distinct, pungent aroma to a package's contents. Straw can be tied, woven, or bound. Examples of Japanese packaging that creatively utilize these native characteristics of materials include ceremonial envelopes made with layers of folded paper tied with paper cord, bamboo baskets, cedar boxes for pound cake and preserved seafood, bamboo leaf wrappers for *sushi*, and straw strings woven to hang eggs.[18] These designs are not only practical and economical; they also express an attitude of quiet respect and humility toward the material.

The aesthetics involved in Japanese food, which engages all the senses, is also well known. In addition to various forms of sensory attraction, such as picture-perfect arrangement and choice of container, an important focus of Japanese food is the preparation of ingredients. In general, each type of ingredient is cut, cooked, and seasoned so that the best of its inherent qualities can be brought out. For example, fish may be presented without having been cooked or having been grilled whole with a skewer weaving through the length of the body in order to create a wavy shape suggestive of its movement in the water. Various condiments and ornaments, such as herbs, blossoms, leaves, and seaweed, are arranged so that their individual characteristics are retained and showcased. In *ni-mono*, a Japanese version of vegetable stew, each vegetable is cooked and seasoned separately to retain its respective color, taste, and texture. They are then all arranged carefully in a bowl together, but in a way such that each can be presented in the best light, instead of being dished out as a heaping mound of mixture. The outcome of such labor-intensive fussiness is that each ingredient retains and expresses its own characteristics, while also serving as a complement to the others, and the consumer enjoys the symphony with each instrument playing its own tune, as it were.

Taking the Japanese lunchbox as a microcosmic illustration of this Japanese aesthetic sensibility and worldview, Kenji Ekuan, a noted industrial designer, describes its contents as follows: "Our lunchbox . . . gathers together normal, familiar, everyday things from nature, according to season, and *enhances their inherent appeal*. . . . The aim of preparation and arrangement revealed in the lunchbox is to include everything and *bring each to full life*." In short, the mission of Japanese "culinary artifice" is "to render fish more fishlike and rice more ricelike."[19]

This attitude of respect toward the innate characteristics of objects and materials is not limited to the Japanese aesthetic tradition. Partly influenced by this Japanese aesthetic sensibility, the arts and crafts movement that began during the late nineteenth century in Britain also upholds the notion of "truth to materials." In calling for "honesty" in materials, John Ruskin, the initiator of the arts and crafts movement, claims that "the workman has not done his duty . . . unless he even so far *honours* the materials with which he is working as to set himself to bring out their beauty, and to recommend and exalt, as far as he can, their peculiar qualities."[20] The subsequent arts and crafts movement continued to advocate respecting and working with "*the very essence of things*."[21] Referring to textiles, William Morris, for example, advises: "Never forget the materials you are working with, and try always to use it for doing what it can do best."[22] This attitude, according to one commentator, has been handed down to contemporary craftspeople: "These modern designers uphold *aesthetico-moral* principles such as 'truth to materials,' and try to bring out the unique quality of that material."[23]

Some contemporary artists also embrace this respectful attitude toward their materials. British artist David Nash, who works with wood and trees, is described as engaging in "consistent efforts to tap nature's initiative."[24] Working with materials available on site, Andy Goldsworthy and Michael Singer emphasize the materials' inherent beauty and sense of place, as well as celebrating the ephemerality of their creations, one essential feature of objects located outdoors. Another environmental artist, Alfio Bonamo, describes a particular challenge and lively tension when "working ... directly with natural materials," primarily felled trees, "not knowing exactly where the process will lead you, feeling and listening to what they have to say" and trying to maintain "the essence of its (each component's) identity."[25]

Whether in regards to traditional Japanese arts, crafts, or contemporary art projects, this principle of artistic production has an important moral dimension. If prerequisites for our moral life include understanding, appreciating, and respecting the other's reality, the capacity to experience and appreciate things on their own terms can contribute to applying this principle. As Yi-Fu Tuan puts it, "one kind of definition of a good person, or a moral person, is that that person does not impose his or her fantasy on another"; instead, such a person is "willing to acknowledge the reality of other individuals, or *even of the tree or the rock*" and "to stand and listen."[26] The sensitivity and respect for the objects' essential characteristics, underlying the attitude toward design and creation discussed above, help cultivate this moral capacity for relinquishing the power to impose our own ideas and wishes on the other.

Japanese art and design practitioners, whose vocation determines their way of life in general, have been deeply influenced by Zen Buddhism, transmitted to Japan in late twelfth century to early thirteenth century by priests Eisai (1141–1215) and Dōgen (1200–1253). Zen Buddhism's thoroughgoing admonishment of egocentric and anthropocentric viewpoints is summarized by Dōgen as follows: "acting on and witnessing myriad things *with the burden of oneself* is 'delusion.' Acting on and witnessing oneself *in the advent of myriad things* is enlightenment." Dōgen continues, "studying the Buddha Way is studying oneself. Studying oneself is forgetting oneself. Forgetting oneself is being enlightened by all things."[27] This transcendence of ego is facilitated by our recognizing and overcoming all-too-human schemes of categorizing, classifying, and valuing. Unlike Immanuel Kant, who was skeptical about the possibility of experiencing a thing-in-itself (the noumenal world), Zen is optimistic about our ability to experience directly the thus-ness or being-suchness of the other (*immo*). In this direct, unmediated encounter with the raw reality of each object and phenomenon, our ordinary valuation and

hierarchy disappear, rendering "a horse's mouth," "a donkey's jaw," "the sound of breaking wind," and "the smell of excrement" equally expressive of their respective realities, or Buddha nature, as other more noble or elegant objects and phenomena.[28] We are thus encouraged to recognize and appreciate a diversity of objects, not just those that we ordinarily enjoy and cherish. Thus, the respectful attitude toward the object, material, or subject matter inherent in Japanese artists' and designers' practice, guided by the Buddhistic transcendence of ego, is not only an aesthetic strategy, but also a moral virtue that characterizes enlightenment.

Evidence suggests that the principle of "truth to materials" advocated by the arts and crafts movement and contemporary artists derives its inspiration from this Japanese design philosophy and its spiritual roots in Buddhism. Despite William Morris's disparaging remarks on Japanese art, one commentator on the arts and crafts movement remarks: "Many designers from the 1860s onwards were to see in Japanese work a logic, fitness and control that European design lacked."[29] Among contemporary artists, David Nash's approach to his work is often characterized as "Zenlike."[30] Furthermore, it is reported that, while working in Japan, Nash quickly developed "a remarkable sense of mutual self-recognition" with his Japanese hosts.[31]

This respectful attitude toward materials expressed aesthetically also has pragmatic ramifications, particularly today as we struggle to find an alternative to our problematic attitude toward nature evidenced by our indifference to "unscenic" aspects of nature, such as invertebrates, weeds, and wetlands, leaving them vulnerable to destruction. Since the aesthetic appeal of an object is a powerful incentive for its protection, many environmentalists, beginning with Aldo Leopold, are concerned with cultivating a different aesthetic sensibility toward those seemingly unattractive aspects of nature.[32] The willingness to cast aside our ordinary standards and expectations for aesthetic value and appreciate each object and material for its own sake can thus contribute to nurturing this sorely needed sensibility.

There is a further pragmatic benefit in appreciating each natural object on its own terms. Today's designers, committed to promoting sustainable design, work on the same principle of listening to and working with the materials. For example, Sim Van der Ryn and Stuart Cowan, early advocates of sustainable architecture, encourage "listening to what the land wants to be," rather than imposing a design upon nature irrespective of its own workings and patterns.[33] The same principle underlies an agricultural practice that mimics the working of the native land, such as the prairie, in designing a sewage treatment system that assimilates wetland, and a program of re-meandering de-meandered streams. Commenting on their river restoration project, Marta González del Tánago and Diego Garcia de Jalón stress the importance of engaging in a "dialogue" with the river, and developing a grasp of "what the river wants to do" and "the aesthetic canon of ecological processes."[34]

These "green designers" derive inspirations from the moral outlook shared by Taoism and Buddhism. Van der Ryn and Cowan, for example, emphasize the importance of "humility" in design practice and point to Taoism as providing them with a model.[35] Victor Papanek, another early advocate of green design, also recommends that designers "find sorely needed *humility*," and derives his own inspiration from Buddhism.[36]

The Japanese aesthetic activities described in this section are intended to articulate and enhance the inherent characteristics of materials. This respectful attitude toward the other, in this case the nonhuman, is valuable not simply for sharpening aesthetic sensibility but also for developing a moral perspective, particularly needed today as we struggle to formulate a morally sound relationship with nature.

II

In this section, I discuss another way in which Japanese aesthetics contributes to moral life: cultivation of a respectful, caring, and considerate attitude toward others, in this case other humans. Of course, cultivating such an attitude toward other humans is not limited to the Japanese tradition. In the Japanese tradition, however, it is often practiced through *aesthetic* means. I will illustrate this aesthetic cultivation of moral virtues in tea ceremony, garden design, and, once again, food arrangement and packaging.

The Japanese practice of expressing one's sensitive, caring, and considerate attitude through artifacts and actions has a long tradition, dating back to the court culture of the Heian period (794–1185). Dubbed the "cult of beauty" by Ivan Morris,

Heian aristocrats' lives revolved around communicating their moral status *aesthetically*, as expressed in the composition and writing style of poems, attire, and customs surrounding lovemaking.[37] Exchanging poems was the primary vehicle of courtship in this culture, and a person's moral worth was assessed aesthetically, not only by the content of the poem but also by its style of calligraphy, type of paper, accompanying fragrance, and adornment, such as a branch or a flower. Sei Shōnagon, a court lady writing in the tenth century, for example, describes one such courtship letter that "is attached to a spray of bush-clover, still damp with dew, and the paper gives off a delicious aroma of incense."[38] She also contrasts a lover's elegant leave-taking with a clumsy one, criticizing the latter as "hateful." "Elegant" behavior consists of taking time and lingering as he prepares to leave the lady, with wistful longing. In contrast, a man's behavior is "charmless" and "hateful" if he makes a big commotion as he looks for things when getting dressed and hurriedly gets ready for the day; in short, he is concerned only with what he has to do (get up, get dressed, and leave) and shows no regard for the lady's feelings. Sei Shōnagon thus declares that "one's attachment to a man depends largely on the elegance of his leave-taking."[39]

It is true that aesthetic choices involved in letter writing and lovemaking are motivated by one's desire to win the prospective partner's heart. It may also be the case that the specific content of aesthetic choices, such as the color and fabric combination of a lady's many-layered kimono to indicate her suitability as an object of love, can be dismissed as historical trivia.[40] However, the foundation of such sensibility is the other-regarding nature of aesthetic choices. This requires us to go outside our ego-oriented world and to put ourselves in the other's shoes by *imagining* what it would feel like to receive a letter written in a certain style and infused with a certain incense, or to see the lover leave with a certain manner after lovemaking. Exercising such capacities to imagine what others feel is seen as an indispensable requirement of moral life, not merely a psychological possibility.[41]

The communication of one's caring attitude through aesthetic means also underlies the art of tea ceremony, usually credited with providing the model for civilized behavior and rules of etiquette that are still alive and well in Japan today. The almost excessive fussiness of the host's preparation for the ceremony is guided by the host's desire and obligation to please the guests. This includes not only the obvious, such as preparing tea and snacks and choosing the tea bowl, but also such considerations as (1) when to refill water in the stone basin and sprinkle water on plants in the garden; (2) what implements and decorations to choose for providing a cool feeling in the summer and warmth in winter; (3) whether or not to brush off the snow accumulated on trees, rocks, and basins; and (4) how to leave water droplets on the kettle's surface to allow for appreciation of the way they gradually dry over the hearth.[42]

Decisions regarding these minute details are guided by imagining what would make the guests feel most comfortable and entertained. Interpreting *Nambōroku*, the compilation of teachings by Master Sen no Rikyū (1521–1591) by his disciple, Nambō Soseki, a contemporary commentator, Kumakura Isao, notes Nanbō's frequent use of the term '*hataraki*,' literally meaning function. Kumakura explains that it refers to the way the host's heart and intention are expressed in his or her body movements, manner of tea making, and in various objects' appearance.[43] Another Japanese philosopher, Hisamatsu Shin'ichi, comments on the moral dimension of tea etiquette: "Inherent in the way of tea is the morality that goes beyond everyday life. Thoughtfulness toward the guest is the foundation of tea manners, which realize this attitude in the formal manner. This heartfelt consideration is both profound and elevated in its moral dimension."[44] What is relevant for our purpose here are not the specifics of the host's aesthetic decisions, but rather the fact that the host's concern for the feelings of guests is expressed through aesthetic means.

Heian court sensibility and tea ceremony illustrate the way this care and consideration are embodied in the aesthetic choices regarding discrete items, such as the paper chosen for a letter or a rustic-looking tea bowl used in an autumn tea ceremony. Japanese aesthetic tradition also provides examples of how these other-regarding concerns are expressed by design that responds to the temporal sequence of our sensual experience. Although material objects, whether garden, food, or packaging, are spatial entities, our experience of them necessarily *takes time*. Their spatial arrangements and composition affect, or even dictate, the sequential order in which our experience unfolds. Some sequences, such as those accentuated by anticipation, surprise, or fulfillment of expectation,

are more likely to satisfy us by holding our attention and interest than are other sequences characterized, for example, by repetition and monotony. Designing a spatial arrangement that is experientially satisfying requires not only a sophisticated aesthetic sensitivity and skill but also the ability to imagine how the experience unfolds for its user, recipient, or viewer. In other words, such a design process also engages the moral capacity of care and respect for other people. Let me illustrate this sensitivity to the temporal sequence of our experience by describing aspects of Japanese garden design, food serving, and packaging.

First, in Japanese gardens, the direction of visitors' movements is determined by the placement of stepping stones and bridges. Made with rocks of varying sizes, shapes, textures, and colors, stepping stones are arranged in an irregular manner, making strolling at times awkward and inconvenient. Besides forcing us to slow down and savor each stone's characteristics, which we sense not only through our eyes but also with our soles, the irregular positioning of each stone controls both the direction and speed of our stroll, providing changing vistas and a varied pace. A similar effect is achieved by bridges, often made with two planks or slates placed in a staggered manner, an application of *suji kaete* (changing the axis), another design principle specified in the aforementioned *Sakuteiki*. This arrangement makes us pause in the middle of the bridge and turn slightly before continuing to cross. If we look at these paths and bridges from a purely functional point of view, that is, simply as devices to get us from point A to point B, we would judge that they are not designed well. However, functional efficiency is not the goal. Both devices make our stroll and crossing more engaging, enriching, and stimulating than a straight walk by providing different angles and distances from which to experience different parts of the garden.

Additionally, the strategy of *miegakure*, literally meaning "now you see it, now you don't," sometimes also referred to as "Zen view" by Western designers, intentionally blocks or partially obscures a scenic view or a tea hut by dense planting, giving us only hints and glimpses of what is to come.[45] Anticipating a full view excites us and invites us to proceed, and the final, usually sudden, opening of the full vista is quite dramatic. A series of gates found in tea gardens as well as in temple or shrine compounds also accentuates the sequentially ordered spatial experience. Gates make us conscious of the unfolding layer of spaces along the passageway into *oku*, translated as the innermost, the remote depth, or deep recess, invoking a sense of "unwrapping."[46] The choreography of these devices that enhance the temporal dimensions of our experience in Japanese gardens can produce stunning effects.

Sensitivity to the temporal nature of our experience expressed by spatial arrangement is also a feature of food serving. In addition to accentuating the innate characteristics of each material, as noted earlier, the meticulous arrangement of various ingredients invites us to dismantle it by chopsticks one morsel at a time in our desired sequence. Furthermore, the consumer often has to decide in what order to eat the food. A typical Japanese meal consists of several dishes, including a bowl of rice, a bowl of soup, a pickle plate, and two or three other plates of vegetables, fish, and meat, all served at once. Sometimes, in a resort hotel or an upscale Japanese restaurant, dinner is served on one, sometimes two, individual tray table(s), holding so many dishes that one must stare at them for a moment before deciding with which plate of food to begin the feast. Even when there is one container holding everything, as in a lunch box, the Japanese version of "fast food," so many ingredients are packed in with thoughtful arrangement that it is necessary to take time to survey the entire box in order to decide on the order of eating.

The overall effect of such a spatial arrangement is that it accentuates the temporal sequence of the eating experience. The cook's sensibility is reflected in the spatial arrangement on the plate or in the box, which sets the stage for the diner to compose his or her own gustatory symphony. Such an experience would not be possible if the food were haphazardly mixed or heaped onto one plate, or, paradoxically, if each dish were served in a Western "linear" manner. Graham Parkes explains that "most of the meal is served at one time, rather than course by course as in the West. The advantage of this 'nonlinear' way of eating is a remarkably wide range of tastes, as one gradually works one's way through the various combinations of flavors afforded by a large number of small dishes laid out at the same time."[47]

Japanese gift packaging is another example of design attuned to the temporal sequence of the recipient's experience.[48] In addition to the respectful use of materials discussed above, Japanese packaging provides aesthetic experience by inviting us to engage our bodies and to take care and time in unwrapping it. Sometimes, the maneuver needed for opening consists of one step: untying the cord made of straw, opening a bag of bamboo sheath, peeling off bamboo wrapping, or removing the lid of a wooden box. However, often more than one step is needed. A gift is sometimes wrapped in *furoshiki*, the traditional square-shaped carrying cloth, so the first thing to do is to untie its corners to reveal a gift inside, which itself is also housed in a box. To get at some candies, one may then open a box and untwist the thin paper inside that wraps the individual candies. A piece of pottery is usually first wrapped in a cloth, then placed in a wooden box with the potter's signature in calligraphy on the lid, which is then tied by a cloth cord, requiring at least three steps for opening. Finally, when opening a ceremonial envelope containing money, the ornamental paper cord must be removed first and then, carefully, the envelope, made with a distinctive fold, opened, only to find another piece of paper that needs to be unfolded. Joy Hendry characterizes these "layers of wrapping" as "a way of expressing *care* for the object inside, and therefore care for the recipient of the object."[49]

Of course, other kinds of packages also require time to open, such as the familiar plastic blister packaging that wraps everything today from pens and scissors to toothbrushes and batteries, and at times require skill or sheer strength, engaging our bodies. However, we normally do not derive an aesthetic satisfaction from opening these packages. One difference between this experience and opening Japanese gift packages is that the task required for the former can be rather taxing, as we wonder whether the thick plastic protecting its contents is meant not only to be child-proof but adult-proof as well. Furthermore, opening these packages sometimes requires tools, such as scissors and a staple remover, whereas opening Japanese gift packages requires only gentle movements of our hands, inviting us to *take care* in opening. Finally, because force is often necessary for opening blister packages, its aftermath is messy: packaging materials are ripped and torn apart. In contrast, Japanese gift packages are aesthetically pleasing after opening because nothing is destroyed, prompting us to save and savor them either for their own sake or for some other use. Although it is possible to destroy those Japanese gift packaging materials just as we destroy plastic bubble packaging, we are led to feel that the respectful sensitivity toward the material and the recipient embodied in the beautiful packaging requires reciprocal respect and sensitivity on our part during and after opening.

Care and sensitivity evident in the design of Japanese packaging, aesthetically manifested, carries over to an unlikely dimension of everyday life: disposal of garbage. A Japanese manual for non-Japanese businesspeople, for example, when discussing "aesthetics and perfectionism," notes that "when eating a mandarin orange, many Japanese will remove the peel in one, unbroken piece, and place segment membranes inside the outer peel, so that the leftover materials end up in a neatly wrapped little package."[50] I find the same sensibility underlying this familiar practice in the way my parents stuff their garbage bags for pickup. Because their municipality mandates that garbage bags be transparent, they try to hide unappetizing-looking contents, such as food debris, by using innocuous-looking garbage, such as unrecyclable plastics and papers, as a buffer between the bag and the food debris. (In Japan, unlike in the United States, the garbage bags are placed in a designated community spot.) This seemingly superfluous gesture is motivated by their thoughtfulness in not giving an unpleasant visual experience to the neighbors and passersby, even for a short time.[51]

Of course, this other-regarding attitude toward materials and people is hardly unique to Japanese tradition. Particularly in the field of design today, there is an increasing attention to and call for "care" and "thoughtfulness," paralleling the aforementioned demand for respect for nature and materials. It is noteworthy that such a plea is a reaction against the prevailing design process that the designers themselves admit has not paid enough attention or respect to users' or inhabitants' experiences. They take recent designs to task for exuding the qualities of "arrogance," "narcissism," "impudence," "formal authority," "showiness," and as "ego trips."[52] Juhani Pallasmaa, an architect, criticizes the contemporary architectural profession as encouraging the super-stardom of individual "geniuses" whose creations are for the sake of self-aggrandizement, alienating the users and inhabitants.[53] Similarly, Victor Papanek writes that designers and architects tend to think of themselves as artists whose mission is to make artistic "statements." As a result, he observes that "a good deal of design and architecture seems to be created

for the personal glory of its creator."[54] Van der Ryn and Cowan express a similar sentiment by criticizing the architect in Ayn Rand's *The Fountainhead*, who is depicted as a hero committed to the "'pure' process" that is not "'contaminated' by any real-world constraints or needs: social, environmental, or economic."[55]

These critics offer an alternative model of design process that reflects other-regarding attitudes, such as "courtesy," "responsiveness," "humility," "patience," and "care." These qualities are embodied in an appropriate size for human scale, spatial arrangement sensitive to the bodily-oriented experience as well as its temporal sequence, or design features that are simply delightful to the senses. Resultant design not only provides a positive aesthetic experience, but also leads to a pragmatically serious consequence, such as a healthy environment instead of a "sick" building. The degree of healthfulness is commensurate with the way our sensory experience is affected. For example, consider the recently emerging "green" buildings that utilize the benefits of such sustainable materials as sunlight, fresh air, breeze, rainwater, and vegetation. Such a building "honors" the senses, one critic points out, and it is "comfortable, humanising and supportive," "healthy and healing," "caring for the environment," "nourishing to the human being"; in short, it is where we feel "at home."[56] Humans are sensory, as well as conceptual, creatures, and designing and creating objects and environments that respect the users and inhabitants would necessarily have to respond to their bodily experiences. Papanek quotes the Zen adept's teaching to "think with the whole body" and reminds us that "we need to come to our senses again."[57]

The aesthetic value of designed objects and built environments that respond to our multisensory and temporary sequential experiences is not only in the enhancement of pleasure. It also communicates a moral attitude affirming the importance of others' experiences. "Good design," Donald Norman writes, "takes *care*, planning, thought" and "*concern* for others."[58] Similarly, in discussing the importance of "care" in architecture, Nigel Taylor points out that a building that appears to be put together thoughtlessly and carelessly, without regard to our experience as users or its relationship to the surrounding, "would offend us aesthetically, but, more than that, part of our offense might be ethical. Thus we might reasonably be angered or outraged, not just by the look of the thing, but also by the visible evidence that the person who designed it didn't show sufficient *care* about the aesthetic impact of his building."[59] He cites Roger Scruton's discussion of "appropriateness" as a criterion of architectural criticism, which Scruton calls "an embodiment of moral thought." Commenting on Scruton's praise of a railway wall in London, Taylor points out that "the anonymous designers of this wall *cared* about the wall they designed" and "'caring' is a moral concept." He concludes by stating that "to care like this for how something looks, and thereby for the people who will look at it, is to exhibit not just an aesthetic but also a moral concern. Or rather, it is to exhibit an aesthetic attentiveness which is itself moral."

We should note that this other-regarding attitude expressed aesthetically, whether in traditional Japanese culture or in today's design practice, requires a corresponding sensibility on the part of those who experience the object to recognize and gratefully appreciate the sensitivity and considerate-ness embodied in the object and the act of producing it. As noted above, a beautifully and thoughtfully wrapped gift encourages respect and care in opening it. The aforementioned manual for people doing business in Japan correctly advises that "if the situation makes it desirable for the receiver to unwrap the gift, he or she will do so carefully, keeping the wrapping paper in a hypothetically reusable condition before admiring the gift. This derives from a concern for appearance as well as *an expression of gratitude to the giver.*"[60] Writing in the same vein on the etiquette of eating a Japanese meal, another author first establishes the cardinal principle of etiquette: "the most important rule is to be grateful for the cook's thoughtfulness and consideration . . . and to humbly acknowledge the cook's sincere heart while savoring the food . . . Failure to do so would not only diminish the taste but also ignore the thoughtfulness of the host."[61] Of course, "thanksgiving" for food is hardly unique to Japanese culture, but in Japan this "thanks-giving" is not simply directed toward the nourishment provided by the prepared food, but also toward its sensuous dimension.

From the Japanese aesthetic point of view, a person who rips apart a beautifully wrapped gift or gobbles up a Japanese lunchbox meal without savoring each ingredient is considered not only deficient in aesthetic sense and manner but also lacking in moral sensibility. In this sense, thoughtful design, such as in the Japanese gift package and food presentation, functions as a vehicle of communication. Communication here, however, is not that of a certain emotion, idea, ideology, or religious feeling, as in the communication or expression theories of art espoused by Leo Tolstoy and R. G. Collingwood. It is instead moral virtues, such as thoughtfulness and consideration, which are conveyed and acknowledged through specific design features. For this communication to occur, the experiencing agent must possess both a keen aesthetic sensibility and a moral capacity to gratefully acknowledge, and reciprocate, the consideration and respect conveyed aesthetically.

In all these examples, the distinction between the aesthetic and the moral is blurred. A person's aesthetic sensibility, whether in providing or receiving an aesthetic experience, can be an important measure of his or her moral capacity. The aesthetic considerations in our lives are thus neither mere dispensable luxuries nor, to borrow Yrjö Sepänmaa's phrase, "high cultural icing."[62] Nor are they confined to works of fine arts that tend to encourage or facilitate our disengagement from everyday life. Rather, promotion of and support for sensitively designed objects and environments is an indispensable ingredient of what Sepänmaa calls "aesthetic welfare."[63] He points out that a true welfare state should guarantee not only "health care, education, and housing," but also "an experiential aspect of welfare. An aesthetic welfare state should offer a beautiful living environment and a rich cultural and art life" because they provide "the basic conditions of life." Such environments and artifacts provide an experientially verifiable indication that people's needs and experiences are taken seriously and responded to with care. They exemplify moral qualities such as respect, care, sensitivity, and considerateness through their color, texture, size, arrangement of parts, smell, and acoustics. To the extent that these moral qualities are expressed by sensuous means, it is an aesthetic matter, and cultivating those moral virtues aesthetically, I believe, is as important as practicing them through our actions.[64]

What would happen if we succeeded in cultivating some moral virtues but failed to develop an accompanying aesthetic sensibility? We would become a person Marcia Eaton describes as leading "a moral/unaesthetic life," who "may litter streets or deface buildings" and "destroy beautiful buildings only after taking care that there are no people in them."[65] Such a person, Eaton continues, "fails to see that a world with fewer beautiful buildings is less worth inhabiting." I think most of us believe that something is lacking in such a person's character or life. Or, put differently, we may have a difficult time imagining such a person, as we may consider littering and defacing a building to be incompatible with moral goodness *even if* (hypothetically) those acts do not harm other people. However, the problem is not simply a deficiency of one's character or impoverishment of one's aesthetic life. The cumulative effect of neglecting this dimension of our aesthetic life is that it undermines the core of what a good life and an ideal society should be. It is important to have laws protecting our rights, freedom, equality, and welfare. However, in a good society we should also be able to *experience* moral values in our everyday environment. Care, respect, sensitivity, and consideration toward the other, whether human or nonhuman, should be the moral foundations of a good society, as well as of a good life. Being able to enjoy the ease, comfort, and aesthetic pleasure provided by artifacts induces a sense of belonging. It confirms that our needs, interests, and experiences are important and worthy of attention. In turn, it encourages us to adopt the same attitude toward others, not only in our direct dealing with them, but also in creating an environment that is reflective of care, thoughtfulness, and mindfulness.

People surrounded by poorly designed artifacts will despair that nobody pays attention to or cares about their experiences. They will be demoralized and feel that it does not make any difference if they remain indifferent and insensitive to other's experiences. "Why bother? Nobody else seems to care," they will say.[66] This attitude is not conducive to developing moral sensitivity and civility. Or, alternatively, they might be spurred to become activists for cleaning up the surroundings and promoting a more humane environment and better artifacts. If they react in this second way, it is because they feel that the creation of aesthetically sound artifacts and environment is an important social agenda.

Concern for the aesthetic in our everyday life is neither frivolous nor trivial. It has a close connection to the moral dimension of our lives. Eaton points out that, ultimately, there is a "connection between being a person who has aesthetic experi-

ence and being a person who has *sympathies and insights of a kind required for successful social interaction.*"[67] Arnold Berleant characterizes a "humane" urban environment as one that "assimilates human perceptual characteristics, needs, and values to a functional network of human dimensions, that engages our imaginative responses, that symbolizes our cultural ideals and evokes our unspoken understanding, ... that, in short, enlarges the range, depth, and vividness of our immediate experience."[68] He then observes that "such an urban environment acts at the same time as an aesthetic one" and points out that in this instance "the moral and the aesthetic join together." Japanese aesthetics provides a rich tradition and diverse examples of this morally sensitive dimension of our aesthetic lives.[69]

YURIKO SAITO
Department of History, Philosophy, and Social Sciences
Rhode Island School of Design
Providence, RI 02903, USA

INTERNET: Ysaitorisd@aol.com

1. The first was written by Nitobe Inazō and the other two by Okakura Tenshin. In this paper, I observe the Japanese custom by putting a Japanese author's family name first and the given name last, except when quoting from a contemporary Japanese author's work that is written in English or from an English translation.

2. *Wabi* refers to simplicity, imperfection, and forlornness celebrated in the art of tea ceremony. *Sabi*, literally meaning both loneliness and rusticity, is the aesthetic ideal of haiku. *Yūgen* is the sublime loftiness of *Noh* performance, while *iki*, sometimes translated as "chic" or "stylishness," was identified as a unique Japanese aesthetic sensibility by Kuki Shūzō in his seminal work, *Iki no Kōzō* [*The Structure of Iki*] (1929). *Mono no aware* refers to the sympathetic sensibility toward things, nature in particular, also identified as a "pure" Japanese aesthetic sensibility uncontaminated by foreign (specifically Chinese) influence, by a nativist philologist, Motoori Norinaga (1730–1801). In recent years, *wabi* and *sabi* have become popularized outside Japan, mostly through manuals for interior decoration that celebrates minimalism, imperfection, and aging surface.

3. Here is a list of recent works on this research area available in English (given name first here). Kōjin Karatani, "Japan as Museum: Okakura Tenshin and Ernest Fenollosa," in *Japanese Art After 1945: Scream Against the Sky*, ed. Alexandra Munroe (New York: Harry N. Abrams, Inc., 1994), and "Uses of Aesthetics: After Orientalism," in *Edward Said and the Work of the Critic: Speaking Truth to Power*, ed. Paul A. Bove (Duke University Press, 2000); Leslie Pincus, *Authenticating Culture in Imperial Japan: Kuki Shūzō and the Rise of National Aesthetics* (University of California Press, 1996); Michael F. Marra, ed.,

Japanese Hermeneutics: Current Debates on Aesthetics and Interpretation (University of Hawai'i Press, 2002); Yumiko Iida, *Rethinking Identity in Modern Japan: Nationalism as Aesthetics* (London: Routledge, 2002); Emiko Ohnuki-Tierney, *Kamikaze, Cherry Blossoms, and Nationalisms: The Militarization of Aesthetics in Japanese History* (The University of Chicago Press, 2002).

4. I explore this aspect of Japanese aesthetics further in "Representing the Essence of Objects: Art in the Japanese Aesthetic Tradition," in *Art and Essence*, ed. Stephen Davies and Ananta Ch. Sukla (Westport: Praeger, 2003).

5. Tachibana-no-Toshitsuna, *Sakuteiki: The Book of Garden-Making, Being a Full Translation of the Japanese Eleventh Century Manuscript: Memoranda on Garden Making Attributed to the Writing of Tachibana-no-Toshitsuna*, trans. S. Shimoyama (Tokyo: Town & City Planners, 1985), p. 20, emphasis added. The other places with reference to the notion of "obeying the request" are pp. 7, 10, and 13. I explore this principle of Japanese garden design in "Japanese Gardens: The Art of Improving Nature," *Chanoyu Quarterly* 83 (1996): 40–61.

6. The methods of manipulation include: pruning, clipping, shearing, pinching, plucking, the use of various gears such as wires, ropes, poles, and weights, and even the application of retardant to stunt the growth of some parts.

7. Zōen, "Illustrations for Designing Mountains, Water, and Hillside Field Landscape," trans. D. A. Slawson, in D. A. Slawson, *Secret Teachings in the Art of Japanese Gardens: Design Principles, Aesthetic Values* (Tokyo: Kodansha International, 1991), §56, emphasis added. Allen Carlson uses the expression, "a look of inevitability," to refer to this design principle for the Japanese garden, in his "On the Aesthetic Appreciation of Japanese Gardens," *The British Journal of Aesthetics* 37 (1997): 47-56. It is interesting to note that William Morris refers to the same term in his instructions on how to design a pattern after a plant: "above all, pattern, in whatever medium, should have the inevitability of nature." William Morris, "Textiles," in *Arts and Crafts Essays* (Bristol: Thoemmes Press, [1893] 1996), p. 36.

8. For the paradox involved in the art of *ikebana*, see Ryosuke Ohashi's entry on "Kire and Iki" in *Encyclopedia of Aesthetics*, ed. Michael Kelly (Oxford University Press, 1998), vol. 2, p. 553.

9. Makoto Ueda, *Literary and Art Theories in Japan* (The Press of Case Western Reserve University, 1967), p. 86.

10. Recorded by Bashō's disciple, Hattori Dohō, in "The Red Booklet," first published in the eighteenth century, in *The Theory of Beauty in the Classical Aesthetics of Japan*, ed. and trans. Toshihiko and Toyo Izutsu (The Hague: Martinus Nijhoff Publishers, 1981), pp. 162–163.

11. Makoto Ueda explains this notion of impersonality as follows: "The poet's task is not to express his emotions, but to detach himself from them and to enter into the object of nature. A pine tree has its own life, so a poet composing a verse on it should first learn what sort of life it is by entering into the pine tree: this is the only way by which he can learn about the inner life of the pine." Ueda, *Literary and Art Theories in Japan*, p. 158.

12. Dohō, "The Red Booklet," p. 134.

13. Ueda, *Literary and Art Theories in Japan*, p. 137.

14. Ueda, *Literary and Art Theories in Japan*, pp. 138–139. Ueda explains Mitsukuni's view by stating

that "the painter can give spirit to his painting only by *growing into the object of the painting himself*—that is to say, by *identifying his spirit with the spirit of the object* in his painting" (p. 138, emphasis added).

15. Tsubaki Chinzan, "Chinzan Shokan" ["Correspondence of Chinzan"], from the nineteenth century, my translation, in *Nihon no Geijutsuron* [*Theories of Art in Japan*], ed. Yasuda Ayao (Tokyo: Sōgensha, 1990), p. 251, emphasis added.

16. Jack Lenor Larsen, "The Inspiration of Japanese Design," in *Traditional Japanese Design: Five Tastes* (New York: Japan Society, 2001), p. 12.

17. I explore the aesthetics of Japanese packaging further in "Japanese Aesthetics of Packaging," *The Journal of Aesthetics and Art Criticism* 57 (1999): 257–265.

18. The discussion here is best accompanied by the visual images from Hideyuki Oka's *How to Wrap Five Eggs: Japanese Design in Traditional Packaging* (New York: Harper and Row, 1967) and *How to Wrap Five More Eggs: Traditional Japanese Packaging* (New York: Weatherhill, 1975), as well as images from Shigeru Uchida, ed., *Package Design in Japan* (Köln: Benedikt Taschen Verlag, 1989).

19. Kenji Ekuan, *The Aesthetics of the Japanese Lunchbox*, trans. Don Kenny (MIT Press, 2000), pp. 6 (the long passage), 77 ("fishlike . . . ricelike"), emphases added. Short of actually experiencing Japanese lunchbox, Ekuan's book has abundant photographic images of Japanese lunchboxes, as does Junichi Kamekura et al., *Ekiben: The Art of the Japanese Box Lunch* (San Francisco: Chronicle Books, 1989). Kamekura shows not only the food arrangement but also various forms of packaging for box lunches sold on train stations. This Japanese design principle of respecting and taking advantage of the materials' native characteristics is not limited to more traditional, natural materials. Contemporary designers apply it to new materials. For example, Tadao Andō's architecture often emphasizes the concrete-ness of concrete, while Issey Miyake, in his apparel design, explores synthetic materials and rubber.

20. John Ruskin, *The Stones of Venice*, Vol. II (1853), cited by Nigel Whiteley, "Utility, Design Principles and the Ethical Tradition," in *Utility Reassessed: The Role of Ethics in the Practice of Design*, ed. Judy Attfield (Manchester University Press, 1999), p. 192.

21. Cited by Gillian Naylor, *The Arts and Crafts Movement: A Study of its Sources, Ideals and Influence on Design Theory* (MIT Press, 1971), p. 106, emphasis added. Although Morris generally favors handicraft over mechanized production, he does advocate the same principle for the latter as well, summarized in his recommendation: "let your design show clearly what it is. Make it mechanical with a vengeance . . . Don't try, for instance, to make a printed plate look like a hand-painted one" (Naylor, *The Arts and Crafts Movement*, pp. 106–107).

22. Morris, "Textiles." pp. 37–38.

23. Nigel Whiteley, *Design for Society* (London: Reaktion Books, 1993), p. 92, emphasis added.

24. Ann Wilson Lloyd, "David Nash," *Sculpture* (1992): 22–23. In light of this commitment, Nash himself is critical of his own project, *Ash Dome*, a planting and training of twenty-two ash trees to form a dome-like structure. "Knowing what I know now, I wouldn't have done it. It's actually manipulating the trees more than I feel comfortable with" (cited by Lloyd, p. 22).

25. Alfio Bonanno et al., "Materials," in *Ecological Aesthetics: Art in Environmental Design: Theory and Practice*, ed. Heike Strelow (Basel: Birkhäuser, 2004), pp. 96, 98.

26. Yi-Fu Tuan, "Yi-Fu Tuan's Good Life," *On Wisconsin* 9 (1987), emphasis added. I develop the aesthetico-moral implication of this view as it applies to nature appreciation in "Appreciating Nature on Its Own Terms," *Environmental Ethics* 20 (1998): 135–149.

27. Dōgen, *Shōbōgenzō: Zen Essays by Dōgen*, trans. Thomas Cleary (University of Hawaii Press, 1988), p. 32.

28. The specific examples of a donkey's jaw and a horse's mouth come from the chapter on Busshō [Buddha Nature], the sound of breaking wind and the smell of excrement from the chapter on Gyōbutsu Iigi [The Dignified Activities of Practicing Buddha] from Dōgen Zenji, *Shōbōgenzō: The Eye and Treasury of the True Law*, trans. Kōsen Nishiyama (Tokyo: Nakayama Shobō, 1986).

29. After praising Japanese draftsmanship for its skillful naturalism, Morris claims that "with all their brilliant qualities as handicraftsmen, ... the Japanese have no architectural, and therefore no decorative, instinct. Their works of art are isolated and blankly individualistic, and in consequence, unless where they rise, as they sometimes do, to the dignity of a suggestion for a picture (always devoid of human interest), they remain mere wonderful toys, things quite outside the pale of the evolution of art, which ... cannot be carried on without the architectural sense that connects it with the history of mankind" ("Textiles," pp. 34–35). The passage in the text is from Naylor, *The Arts and Crafts Movement*, p. 117.

30. Lloyd, "David Nash," p. 22.

31. John Beardsley, *Earthworks and Beyond: Contemporary Art in the Landscape* (New York: Cross River Press, 1989), p. 50.

32. I explore this challenge to environmental aesthetics in "The Aesthetics of Unscenic Nature," *The Journal of Aesthetics and Art Criticism* 56 (1998): 101–111.

33. Sim Van der Ryn and Stuart Cowan, *Ecological Design* (Washington, DC: Island Press, 1996), p. 35.

34. Marta González del Tánago and Diego Garcia de Jalón, "Ecological Aesthetics of River Ecosystem Restoration," in *Ecological Aesthetics*, p. 192, emphasis added.

35. Van der Ryn and Cowan, *Ecological Design*, pp. 7, 136. Zen Buddhism incorporates many aspects of Taoism.

36. Victor Papanek, *The Green Imperative: Natural Design for the Real World* (New York: Thames and Hudson, 1995), p. 12, emphasis added. This attitude underlying ecological design raises an important question, which I will simply mention without trying to answer. How can one decipher "what the river wants to do" and "what the land wants to be"? These metaphorical expressions need to be supported by riparian hydrology and prairie ecosystem, so that specific design strategies can be formulated. Whether such knowledge comes from formal scientific investigation or local wisdom accumulated over many generations, it is based on some kind of human organizational scheme.

37. Ivan Morris, *The World of the Shining Prince: Court Life in Ancient Japan* (New York: Kodansha International, 1994), ch. VII. See also Donald Keene, "Feminine Sensibility in the Heian Era," in *Japanese Aesthetics and Culture: A Reader*, ed. Nancy Hume (SUNY Press, 1995), pp. 109–123.

38. Sei Shōnagon, *The Pillow Book of Sei Shōnagon*, trans. Ivan Morris (Hammondsworth: Penguin Books, 1981),

p.62. The next two passages are both from page 49. Readers learn the extent to which these aesthetic concerns permeated the aristocrats' daily life by the description of a fictional princess who rebelled against them. This "lady who admired vermin" in *Tsutsumi Chūnagon Monogatari* [*The Riverside Counselor's Stories*], written between the end of the Heian period and the beginning of the Kamakura period that marks the age of warriors, is depicted as breaking all the codes of proper behavior in aesthetics. She uses "very stiff and coarse" paper on which she writes poems full of imagery of "vermin and caterpillar fur" with *katakana* script that is more angular and reserved for male courtiers and monks rather than "the beautifully flowing *hiragana*." Her attire and appearance are also the opposite of what were considered to constitute feminine beauty at this time. See Michele Marra, *The Aesthetics of Discontent: Politics and Reclusion in Medieval Japanese Literature* (University of Hawaii Press, 1991), pp. 63–64.

39. During the Heian period, female aristocrats were supposed to remain hidden inside their residence or inside a carriage, allowing only a glimpse to the male suitors. This required the male suitor to gain entry into the lady's residence, as well as her heart, by showing his aesthetic sensibility in poems. Even after the relationship began, couples never lived together and the man had to commute to her place for the night of lovemaking. This makes the time of morning leave-taking another test of his moral-aesthetic sensibility. In a way, when it came to love affairs and setting the aesthetic standard, women at this time had an upper hand.

40. For this point, see Liza Crihfield Dalby, *Kimono: Fashioning Culture* (Yale University Press, 1993), p. 222; Morris, *The World of the Shining Prince*, pp. 194–195.

41. I thank the editor and anonymous referees for pointing out that what is important is the exercising, rather than the mere possession, of such capacities.

42. These items were culled from remarks scattered throughout *Nanbōroku* in *Nanbōroku wo Yomu* [*Reading Nanbōroku*], ed. Kumakura Isao (Kyoto: Tankōsha, 1989).

43. *Nanbōroku wo Yomu*, p. 242.

44. Hisamatsu Shin'ichi, *Sadō no Tetsugaku* [*The Philosophy of the Way of Tea*] (Tokyo: Kōdansha, 1991), pp. 53–54, my translation, emphasis added. He means by "formal" sensuous, rather than the contrary of "informal" or "casual." Eiko Ikegami makes a sociological interpretation of the social and political role served by the aesthetic expression of hospitality, sociability, and civility in the tea ceremony and other traditional Japanese arts, in *Bonds of Civility: Aesthetic Networks and the Political Origins of Japanese Culture* (Cambridge University Press, 2005).

45. Donald A. Norman, *Emotional Design: Why We Love (or Hate) Everyday Things* (New York: Basic Books, 2004), pp. 109–110. He derives his discussion of "Zen view" from Christopher Alexander et al., *A Pattern Language: Towns, Buildings, Construction* (Oxford University Press, 1977), pp. 642–643.

46. See Fumihiko Maki, "Japanese City Spaces and the Concept of *Oku*," *The Japan Architect* (1979): 51–62, on the discussion of the concept of *oku*. A good, general discussion and various examples of *oku* can be found in Joy Hendry, *Wrapping Culture: Politeness, Presentation and Power in Japan and Other Societies* (Oxford: Clarendon Press, 1993).

47. Graham Parkes, "Ways of Japanese Thinking," in *Japanese Aesthetics and Culture*, p. 80.

48. The examples discussed here are primarily gift packaging, not packaging for everyday items that we buy for ourselves, such as pens, toothpaste, noodles, coffees, and the like. However, Japan is a gift-giving culture. In addition to two annual gift-giving seasons, Japanese give gifts for every conceivable occasions; hence, gift packaging does not occupy a special place in people's lives. Its frequency and prevalence make it a common occurrence.

49. Hendry, *Wrapping Culture*, p. 63, emphasis added.

50. Yasutaka Sai, *The Eight Core Values of the Japanese Businessman: Toward an Understanding of Japanese Management* (New York: International Business Press, 1995), p. 56.

51. This other-regarding sensitivity expressed in design is not free from criticism. In comparing Japanese and Western automobile designs, designer Hara Kenya admits that the former invites a criticism that it lacks strong self-expression and manufacturer passion. The reason is because the auto design is made to accommodate Japanese consumers' desires, rendering it warm, kind, and obedient. However, ultimately, he is more critical of European and American design for being "egotistical" and "selfish." See Hara Kenya, *Dezain no Dezain* [*Design of Design*] (Tokyo: Iwanami Shoten, 2003), pp. 133–134.

52. These terms are culled from Juhani Pallasmaa, "Toward an Architecture of Humility," *Harvard Design Magazine* (1999), Van der Ryn and Cowan, and Papanek.

53. Pallasmaa, "Toward an Architecture of Humility."

54. Papanek, *The Green Imperative*, p. 203.

55. Van der Ryn and Cowan, *Ecological Design*, p. 147.

56. David Pearson, "Making Sense of Architecture," *Architectural Review* 1136 (1991): 68–70, see p. 70.

57. Papanek, *The Green Imperative*, pp. 76, 104.

58. Donald A. Norman, *The Design of Everyday Things* (New York: Doubleday, 1990), pp. 25, 27, emphasis added.

59. Nigel Taylor, "Ethical Arguments about the Aesthetics of Architecture," in *Ethics and the Built Environment*, ed. Warwick Fox (London: Routledge, 2000), pp. 201–202. Citations in the next three sentences are from pp. 203, 205.

60. Sai, *Eight Core Values of the Japanese Businessman*, p. 57, emphasis added.

61. Shiotsuki Yaeko, *Washoku no Itadaki kata: Oishiku, Tanoshiku, Utsukushiku* [*How to Eat Japanese Meals: Deliciously, Enjoyably, and Beautifully*] (Tokyo: Shinchōsha, 1989), p. 12. The awkward, but literal, translation of the title is mine.

62. Yrjö Sepänmaa, "Aesthetics in Practice: Prolegomenon," in *Practical Aesthetics in Practice and in Theory*, ed. Martti Honkanen (University of Helsinki, 1995), p. 15.

63. Sepänmaa, "Aesthetics in Practice: Prolegomenon," p. 15.

64. Tangible examples of "aesthetic welfare" can be seen in a number of projects by Auburn University's Rural Studio. Building or restoring structures in one of the most impoverished communities in the United States, the students have to make do with a low or nonexistent budget, forcing them to come up with creative solutions by reusing available materials. However, instead of cheap- and crude-looking structures that are common among impoverished communities, their efforts often result in stunning results that also respond sensitively and humanely to the residents' and communities' needs and lifestyles. Those structures embody respect and celebration, rather than a patronizing attitude, toward the economically disadvantaged residents' humanity and dignity. Descriptions and photos of their projects are compiled by Andrea Oppenheimer Dean and Timothy Hursley, *Rural Studio: Samuel Mockbee and an Architecture of Decency* (New York: Princeton Architectural Press, 2002) and *Proceed and Be Bold: Rural Studio After Samuel Mockbee* (New York: Princeton Architectural Press, 2005).

65. Marcia Muelder Eaton, *Aesthetics and the Good Life* (Fairleigh Dickinson University Press, 1989), p. 179. The next passage is also from p. 179.

66. This may happen in a run-down neighborhood where there is no attempt at cleanup or beautification either by the residents themselves or the municipality.

67. Eaton, *Aesthetics and the Good Life*, p. 165.

68. Arnold Berleant, *The Aesthetics of Environment* (Temple University Press, 1992), p. 80.

69. I thank the editor and anonymous referees for their helpful comments on the first draft. I also thank Steve Rabson for editing the final version of the manuscript as well as for his insightful suggestions.

ERIC C. MULLIS

The Ethics of Confucian Artistry

禮云禮云，

玉帛云乎哉

樂云樂云，

鍾鼓云乎哉

In referring time and again to observing ritual propriety,

how could I just be talking about gifts of jade and silk?

In referring time and again to making music,

how could I just be talking about bells and drums?

Analects 17:11

In the West, Confucian thought was originally presumed irrelevant to serious philosophical study. For example, in his *Lectures on the History of Philosophy*, G. W. F. Hegel remarked that the morality presented in the *Analects* was "good and honest, and nothing more." And further, with regard to deep philosophical inquiry, "there is nothing to be obtained from his [Confucius's] teachings."[1] There has been a resurgent interest in Confucianism, however, as it has become clear that the early translations of the Chinese classics are fraught with difficulties. More nuanced translations have provided grist for novel discussions regarding virtue ethics, environmental ethics, and the performance of language, as well as aesthetics.

In this paper I investigate a point of intersection between art and ethics from a Confucian perspective. Confucian philosophy addresses the issue by first stressing the development that artists must undergo in acquiring their arts, emphasizing the development of artistic ability and ultimately the process of person-making. Practicing an art is necessarily a moral affair as it entails transforming the self, finding a place within a tradition, and otherwise entering into significant relationships with others. Second, Confucianism also says something on the matter of the relationship between aesthetic and ethical value. It denies the moral autonomy of works of art and argues that art objects should serve the interests of the communities and states that they inhabit. I show that this stance rests on an implicit belief about the ontology of works of visual art. Using the art of Chinese calligraphy as an illustration, I begin with a discussion of the relation between art and ritual, which encompasses both the religious and the moral, broadly conceived. I then describe the contributions that this approach has for contemporary debates over the ethical criticism of works of art.

I. RELIGIOUS RITUAL AND ITS SECULARIZATION

A. C. Graham notes that Confucius (551–479 BCE) saw himself as the preserver and restorer of a declining culture.[2] For him, the early Zhou Dynasty (1045 - 771 BCE) demonstrated how political harmony could be achieved and culture could flourish. The institutions central to Zhou culture and cherished by Confucius were its rituals and arts—its *li* (禮). For this reason, in the Confucian *Analects*, a great deal of importance is placed both on ritual propriety and the practice and appreciation of arts such as music, poetry, and archery.[3]

The association of ritual and art began in the Shang Dynasty (1766 - 1122 BCE), when ritual vessels were decorated with images of animals and inscribed with pictographs, the ancient precursors of written language. During the Zhou Dynasty a transition was made from the use of pictographs to graphs characterized by smooth and flowing strokes and, in general, increasing attention was directed toward overall composition and style.[4] The movement away from religious toward purely artistic usage culminated much later in China's history; however, Confucius—living after the fall of the Zhou Dynasty—was instrumental in continuing the trend of ritual and art toward the secular. The rituals and arts that previously had been used to serve the gods were seen as instrumental in serving humankind. Rituals such as funeral rites, wedding ceremonies, and the celebrations that punctuated the lunar calendar were still practiced, but "ritual" took on the more secular notion of proper etiquette or good manners. Ultimately, Confucius incorporated the rites into secular relationships in order to make the ideal of social harmony—exemplified by the Zhou Dynasty—a more realistic one. Hence, the *Analects* state that "[a]chieving harmony (*he*,和) is the most valuable function of observing ritual propriety (*li*,禮). In the ways of the Former Kings, the achievement of harmony made them elegant, and was a guiding standard in all things large and small."[5]

The consequences that this transition had for Chinese art and aesthetics were nothing short of momentous. The Zhou Dynasty was revered because its *li* provided the foundation for a stable and culturally refined state. For Confucius, since ritual was essential in bringing about social harmony and since the arts were seen as an important component of ritual, the arts, too, were seen as instrumental in actualizing two interrelated social ends: self-cultivation and social harmony. Rituals are essential for social harmony as they delineate various roles and provide normative guidelines for action. In turn, they provide the social framework necessary for self-mastery. Confucius held that "[o]ne stands to be improved by the enjoyment found in attuning oneself to the rhythms of ritual propriety and music."[6] Hence, the early Confucians viewed moral and aesthetic goodness as intertwined, for practicing the arts and rituals allowed one to cultivate the self and to ultimately become a good person, a process that, on this view, is essential for the establishment and maintenance of a good state.

The association of moral and aesthetic goodness was also expressed in the criticism of works of art. For example, Confucius detested the overly complex and unorthodox music of Zheng as it threatened the traditional music of the court.[7] Xunzi

(298–238 BCE) later reiterates the point by arguing that "the songs of *Zheng* and *Wei* cause the hearts of men to be dissipated ... the *Succession* dance and the *Martial* music [however] cause the hearts of men to be filled with dignity."[8] These remarks illustrate the early Confucian belief that the arts are capable of affecting their audiences positively *or* negatively, and that the arts ultimately reflect the moral status of the states in which they are practiced. Hence, criticism addresses whether specific works pay homage to traditional forms and whether they are compatible with or function like *li*. Capturing the effects of good music on both individual and state, Xunzi writes: "When [good] music is performed, the inner mind becomes pure; and when ritual is cultivated, conduct is perfected. The ears become acute and the eyes clear-sighted; the blood humour (*qi*,氣) becomes harmonious and is balanced, manners are altered and customs changed. The entire world is made tranquil, and enjoys together beauty and goodness. Therefore it is said: 'music is joy.'"[9]

With these general points made, I continue by exploring what implications this approach had for artists working within this tradition. I take Chinese calligraphy as my example, in part because its history—like that of music, theater, and painting—is deeply interwoven with Confucian thought.

II. APPROPRIATENESS AND APPROPRIATION

'Appropriateness' has two senses, as an adjective and as a verb, which jointly capture the essence of authentic ritual action. The first sense is the more literal one, the "morally appropriate," which entails acting in accord with the norms outlined by the *li*. Confucius said: "Having a sense of appropriate conduct (*yi*,義) as one's basic disposition, developing it by observing ritual propriety (*li*,禮), expressing it with modesty ... this then is an exemplary person."[10] *Yi* is homophonous with another *yi* (宜), which denotes "right," "fitting," or "suitable." Hence, *yi* simultaneously describes how one's cultural environment contributes to the process of person-making and how one finds a place within it.

David Hall and Roger Ames describe the second sense of 'appropriate' as signifying the "disposition of making the ritual action one's own and displaying oneself in that conduct."[11] Conservative readings of Confucius often miss this sense of appropriating meaning from a system of customs and expressing it in novel circumstances. One cannot follow the *li* blindly, but one must learn how to skillfully apply them; this, in turn, produces a sense of authorship that is an essential component of the self-cultivation process. For this reason, Confucius criticizes those who simply go through the motions of ritual action.[12] On the contrary, to appropriate the *li* is to make them one's own, to personalize them by developing a characteristic style of enacting them. A. C. Graham supports this point by noting that Confucius never laid down fixed rules regarding the details of ritual action. For example, merely aping Confucius's style would be a grave error since "his good manners plainly have nothing to do with prescribed forms."[13] And further, with regard to Confucius's project as a whole, "in spite of his fidelity to the Chou [Zhou] he sees the rebuilding of contemporary culture as a process of selecting and evaluating past and present models."[14]

Hence, for the Confucian, a virtue essential to any practice—artistic or otherwise—is the authentic appropriation of its *li*. Without this kind of appropriation, the goods internal to the practice cannot be actualized since "going through the motions" is not to fully participate in the practice. For artists, the *li* pertain both to the relationships between practitioners (teachers, students, colleagues, and so forth) and to the skills that they all acquire and develop of necessity in the company of others. This point of convergence is emphasized in the linguistic association between appropriate ritual actions and the appropriation of actions by individuals in performances of their own.

The character '*li*' (禮) comprises two elements: *shi* (示), which means to manifest or display, and the phonetic element, 豊, which stands for the ritual vase. The character as a whole refers to the rites performed by the ancient kings, which involved the presentation of a ritual vase and other sacrificial offerings. One also finds the ritual vase in the character that denotes the human body (*t'i*, 體), whose other component is *gu* (骨), the skeleton or, more generally, "organic form." This cluster of concepts leads Hall and Ames to conclude that the "notion of formal *li* action overlaps with *t'i*, body, in that *li* actions are *embodiments* or formalizations of meaning and value that accumulate to constitute a cultural tradition."[15] Ritualized action is an affair of habit, whether habitual modes of behavior that occur between members of a practice (etiquette, manners, and so forth) or the development and maintenance of skill matrices necessary for the execution of the art in question. On this account, the human body is at the intersection of the moral and the aesthetic, as the ability to intelligently form habits enables one to become both a good person and a good artist.

Thus, 'appropriateness,' or *yi*, has both moral and aesthetic connotations. It is grounded in ritual, which, as we have seen, includes both moral and artistic practices. A Confucian holds that in developing technique artists gain an embodied knowledge of aesthetic appropriateness. Good calligraphers master brushwork, understand the spatial logic of individual characters, understand the principles of composition, and are aware of stylistic variations; all of them are a part of appropriate execution. This explains why, in this tradition, a sense of appropriateness is generated through the diligent reproduction of famous works. A text that especially lent itself to this process was the "Thousand Character Essay" (*Qian-zi wen*, 千字文), a work that is composed of 1,000 different characters selected by artists from the collective work of the eminent master Wang Xizhi (303 - 361 CE). This text was studied and reproduced by students and famous calligraphers in every known script including seal, clerical, standard, draft-cursive, and modern cursive.[16]

The way to absorb calligraphic *li* is to repetitiously copy the work of past masters, to break down difficult characters into their constituent parts and to put them together again in fluid, controlled movements. This process establishes a somatic relationship between artist and tradition. Wen C. Fong calls these "presentational" characteristics of Chinese characters, which are not exhausted by the way a character appears. Fong writes, "calligraphy embodies an artist's identity, and its gestures form a projection of the artist's body language."[17] Through copying, a student gains growing insight into the master's corporeality, that is, the manner in which the master's movements inform each character's rhythm and form. Students' awareness of the tradition they work within is not limited to reflection; through embodiment and ritualized action, students appropriate the tradition in an intimate way. Their actions acquire significance since they are informed by and build on a tradition of embodied technique.

As noted earlier, copying must move beyond imitation if the art is to be authentically appropriated. Robert E. Harris, Jr. observes that "copying" is a "clumsy English term for processes that are subtly different in Chinese terminology: *mo* (摹), to trace, *lin* (臨), to copy freehand, and *fang* (倣), to imitate in a freer manner."[18] Indeed, the process of tracing great works, copying them freehand, and imitating them in a freer manner by experimenting with script, size, and overall composition paves the way for the personal appropriation of the art. As Confucius stresses, enacting the rites of a tradition is not a mindless process, but the rites must be personalized by various individuals in various situations. Hence, in reproducing the "Thousand Character Essay," the student must avoid blind repetition and find a way to make it his or her own. The great Yuan Dynasty (1260 - 1368 CE) calligrapher Chao Mengfu, for example, produced transcriptions of the "Thousand Character Essay" in several scripts. Further, repetitions by individual artists and their cohorts changed the way the "Essay" is perceived. As Harris notes, it "was transcribed so often as a writing exercise that the text itself may be thought to have disappeared into the calligraphy: that is, the text was so well known that it is doubtful that anybody paid much attention to what it said, accepting it simply as a format for the display of calligraphic skill."[19]

For Confucians, then, one of the most important aspects of taking up an art is participating in a tradition, and artists must strike an appropriate balance between part and whole by simultaneously drawing on the richness of the tradition and finding a way to appropriate it authentically. One must both preserve and contribute to one's cultural tradition, and the first component of actualizing the goods internal to a practice involves participating in this rich sense. More specifically, if one leans toward an extreme, whether extreme individualism or extreme conformity, then the goods of artistic expression, person-making, and increase of skill will be negatively affected. On the one hand, just as aping Confucius's style misses the point of embodying the *li*, merely imitating another artist also keeps one from living the tradition and actualizing the goods that it offers. One will not discover the joys and frustrations of aesthetic expression, and there will be no genuine sense of authorship, if the skill involved is limited to that of mimicry. On the other hand, extreme individualism ignores the relationships that are integral to the continuation of the tradition. Fraternity (*xiao di*,孝弟) is essential for artistic practice, not only because it guarantees the transmission of knowledge from one generation to the next, but also because it sets the stage for fruitful exchanges between peers. As with excessive conformity, excessive individualism limits one's access to a practice's internal goods.

Hence, artistic ability and personal refinement are maximized by avoiding these extremes. The classical Confucian text *The Doctrine of the Mean* states, "equilibrium is the great foundation of the world, and harmony its universal path. When equilibrium and harmony are realized ... heaven and earth will attain their proper order and all things will flourish."[20] The claim is that striking a balance between individual and tradition is essential for flourishing artists and further reminds us that the arts—on the Confucian account—serve primarily humanitarian ends. It is all too easy to stress the individual's relationship with the practice without giving due consideration to what place the practice holds within the culture as a whole. Any practice has moral implications since it entails entering into relationships with others, but in a more general sense, there is also the possibility of extending one's awareness and influence beyond the bounds of the practice itself. To see how, we will need to say something more about the ontological status of works of calligraphy.

III. "ORGANIC FORM" IN CALLIGRAPHY

On the most fundamental level, the belief that the written character is an embodied image that suggests something of the artist's comportment is supported by observing the way the medium captures quality of movement. Since brush and ink are readily influenced by variations in force, speed, and breath, the strokes themselves reveal much about the physical act of writing. This is evident in the conceptual and experiential frameworks used for criticizing calligraphy. Physiological metaphors are used in order to draw attention to the kinesthetic elements of the characters: flesh (*rou*,肉), sinew (*jin*,筋), bone (*gu*,骨), blood (*xue*,血), vein (*mai*,脉), and breath (*qi*,氣).[21] Madame Wei's (272 - 349 CE) famous treatise, "A Diagram of the Battle Array of the Brush," states: "Calligraphy by those good in brush strength has much bone; that by those not good in brush strength has much flesh. Calligraphy that has much bone but slight in flesh is called sinew-writing; that with much flesh but slight bone is called ink-pig ... Every writer proceeds in accordance with the manifestation of their digestion and respiration of energy."[22]

"Flesh," "sinew," and "bone" refer to the formal or structural elements of the characters, while "blood," "vein," and "breath" refer to their energetic qualities. The centrality of these concepts to criticism for Daoists and Confucians alike intimates that works of art are best understood in terms of a "process ontology." On this point François Jullien notes that "artistic activity was seen as a process of *actualization*, which produced a particular configuration of the dynamism inherent in reality."[23] This is especially clear in calligraphy, for in the dynamic process of writing a character, "a particular gesture is converted into a form, just as a particular form is equally converted into gesture."[24] The reciprocal process of absorbing the characters (through repetitious practice) and expressing them is contingent upon and reflects the work of a body that is continually being affected by and is continually affecting its social and physical environment. Each character is something of a signature. A text from the Han Dynasty (206 BCE - 220 CE) makes this clear: "All men differ in their energy (*qi*) and blood (*xue*), and vary in their sinew and bones; the heart-mind (*xin*,心) may be dispersed or dense; the hand may be skilled or clumsy. The beauty or ugliness of calligraphy is in the heart-mind and hand."[25] This culminated in the popular saying, "writing is like the person" (*zi ru qi ren*,字如其人) and was largely influenced by the Confucian belief that artistic practice is an intensely personal affair. Further, the quote's mention of the "heart-mind" brings us to the ethical implications of this view.[26]

It has been shown that the artist's corporeality determines the form of the characters he or she writes. Moreover, since the "heart-mind" is an essential part of the body, it, too, influences the quality of the characters. For example, mental agitation or ill health influence brushwork by producing feeble emaciated lines, lines that exhibit a loss of control. The logical conclusion of this approach is an aesthetic moralism, that is, the identification of calligraphic and moral value. "Stability" and "uprightness" describe both well-written ideograms and well-refined moral characters, as do "decisiveness" and "felicitous placement."[27] Good (*shan*,善) characters can only be written by

good people; harmonious (*he*,和), well-balanced (*ping*,平) characters reflect individuals who have actualized a state of moral equilibrium. Again, this is contingent on the connection between ritual and art, for they are both seen as instrumental in refining the self.

IV. CONTRIBUTIONS TO MORAL CRITICISM

The first section of this paper described Confucianism's advocacy of practicing the arts, for such practice is seen as essential for the self-cultivation process and more generally for cultivating an awareness of one's place within a tradition and culture. Emphasis is placed on the artist's character as well as the effects that his or her work has on its audiences. Furthermore, this is not a reflective awareness, for the effect is contingent on gestural communication; the viewer sees something of the artist's very corporality in the work and—qua embodiment—becomes tacitly aware of a high level of somatic refinement. Hence, in viewing good calligraphy, the observer will see something of the artist's character or state of refinement and will be affected positively.

An essential element of this approach is its understanding of form. As mentioned, *gu* (骨) denotes "bone" or "organic form," a notion that centers not on abstract relationships among lines, shapes, and colors, but on energetic quality. Calligraphy may seem to lend itself to a "purely" formalist mode of appreciation, especially its more modern forms such as the cursive, or *cao* (草), script. However, something important would be lost in an analysis that ignored the way the form of the script presents the artist's bodily activity. No doubt, an aesthetic autonomist who stresses the importance of objective form would argue that this is precisely where Confucian aesthetics goes wrong. Still, I would argue that an analysis of calligraphy in solely formalistic terms would bracket an essential element of the art, that is, the quality of line that is contingent on the quality of physical movement of making that line. The rhythm and intensity of the character originates in the movements of the hand, arm, and torso, and are also influenced by the calligrapher's breath and psychological state. One wonders whether a work's rhythms and tensions spoken of abstracted from such phenomena would be an analysis of the art of calligraphy at all.

Like many who discuss the intersection of art and ethics, Noël Carroll focuses primarily on works that take a narrative form, and he argues that *Uncle Tom's Cabin* has ethical import since it provides "richly particularized episodes of cruelty and inhumanity" and this "engages the reader's imagination and emotions, thereby giving the reader a 'feel' for what it was like to live in slave times."[28] He continues by claiming that most fiction "engages audiences in a constant process of ethical judgment encouraging readers, viewers, and listeners to form moral evaluations of characters and situations."[29] Confucians, however, hold that the organic form of calligraphy can both *acquaint* viewers with moral situations and *cultivate* their moral sensibilities, including fine perceptual discrimination, imagination, and moral reflection, in ways that do not depend on narrative.

The essential component of this process is gestural communication, for calligraphy provides insight into a refined mode of embodiment. Its form provides knowledge about the feel of writing elegant characters, that is, the sense of controlled movement in which the body, brush, ink, and paper become elements of an organic whole. The sensitive viewer becomes aware of the possibility of somatic refinement, not only because the work presents something of the artist's comportment but also because the viewer, too, is an embodied being who communicates with others by writing and gesturing. In his *Manual on Calligraphy* Sun Guoting (c. 648 - 703 CE) notes that Wang Xizhi's late work demonstrates that "his thoughts were well considered and his intent (zhi,志) and breath (qi,氣) in perfect harmony and balance. Never agitated, never sharp, [his] style and demeanor naturally resonate far (zi-$yuan$,自遠)."[30] The work of the experienced calligrapher gives the reader insight into the manner in which the gestural abilities of the human body can—through the use of a sensitive medium—become aesthetic.

In calligraphy, the artist's character is presented by means of embodied form, and the task consequently becomes that of discriminating quality of character or level of refinement by evaluating the quality of the work. Sun's comment illustrates that value is placed on control of the medium and the self-control necessary for this to be achieved. To understand the work's organic form the viewer must make fine perceptual discriminations regarding the work's structure and its movement of energy. Further, the work reveals the state of the artist's heart-mind (xin), how one's emotions influence the creative act, and how clear one's intent (zhi) is. For this reason, the experienced viewer is called to reflect on the possibilities of the self-cultivation process and the effect that it has on the emotions and on the general clarity of the mind.

In sum, on this account, the art of judging calligraphy is akin to that of judging character. In judging another, one observes their etiquette or manners, the way they express their emotions, and their overall style of acting in order to assess whether they are good, trustworthy, and have other moral virtues. Likewise, in judging a work of calligraphy, a critic will observe what the work's form reveals about the artist's moral standing. In judging either character or organic form, consistency is essential not only because each element mutually affects and is affected by the others, but also because inconsistency indicates a loss of control, which, on this view, is both an aesthetic and a moral defect. The level of artists' state of moral refinement is believed to be clear in all their actions—artistic or otherwise—and a keen eye will be able to read artists' level of refinement either by observing their work or everyday actions.

I earlier described the Confucian view that instances of organic form are products of artistic acts that are indicative of a characteristically artistic mode of embodiment. The notion of organic form turns our attention away from art objects toward the performances that bring them into being. These performances, of course, are not isolated affairs, but actions that take place within the broader context of a life. Along these lines, it has been pointed out that it is a strange fact that Western cultures hold rational individuals accountable for their actions in every context except the aesthetic.[31] Westerners generally judge the moral outcomes of others' actions regardless of the arena in which they unfold, whether political, religious, public, or private. Further, these judgments often pertain to the things that people make: craftspeople are judged on the quality of their craft, surgeons on the quality of the procedures they perform, scientists on their inventions, parents on the character of the children they raise, and so on. Works of art and the artists who create them, however, are often construed as immune to such criticism. But if actions that take place outside of the artist's studio are often, if not always, susceptible to moral criticism, then why should those that take place within the studio remain immune to it? An approach that bases itself on moral character views all action as open to ethical criticism, and consequently calls aesthetic immunity into question. The Confucian morality that unites aesthetic value with moral value may seem extreme, but why should it be considered any less plausible than the opposite extreme— aesthetic autonomy—especially when we take into consideration the inconsistent application of the notion of moral responsibility mentioned above?[32]

The notion of moral responsibility has another dimension. Mencius (371 - 289 BCE) cites the case of the famously skillful archer, Yi, who was murdered by a student who had mastered everything Yi had taught him.[33] It could be argued that the student's shot was a "good" one even though it killed his teacher, for it required a great deal of dexterity and skill. Mencius's purpose in citing the story is to show just the opposite, that the shot was indeed a bad one because it assaulted the *li* on several fronts. By killing his teacher—presumably for fame, as the student would have then been the best archer in the land—the student simultaneously ignored the importance of the student-teacher relationship and the norms that maintain it, threatened the integrity of the tradition, and reduced the *art* to a mere means that allowed him to attain an external good. Now, it can be argued that there is a difference between performing an action in a particular circumstance (as in the case of the archer Yi), and using the product of an action, at some later point in time, to bring about other results, such as fame and fortune. An artist may have not only skill and creative vision, but also develop the ability to spot opportunities for material success. He or she may even be quite ruthless in actualizing these external goods, deftly undermining other artists, strategically playing the market, and so on. Further, the work of such artists may have good organic form and otherwise display a high level of artistic skill. Using art as a means to acquiring ends external to the practice—good or bad—may or may not be morally praiseworthy or objectionable, but doing so does not entail anything about the artistic ability of the artist. However, the Confucian stance holds that the notion of artistic mastery is profaned when it is seen as simply denoting the mastery of a skill, independently of how it is used. As noted above, one's work unfolds in the context of one's life, and it is consequently disingenuous to divorce one skill from the next in order to justify the pursuit of external goods. On this ac-

count, the title "master" should be reserved for those who both master an art and the art of living, and perhaps, even though it is a lofty goal, it is one that is well worth pursuing and honoring.

This raises a related question concerning the relationship between moral and aesthetic goodness, namely: Can morally flawed individuals create good art? Answering this entails saying something about the manner in which a Confucian judges the actions and character of others. This topic demands extended treatment; however, it can be said here that emphasis is generally placed on carefully observing action and on the correspondence between what is said and what is done. With regard to the first point, Confucius advised: "Watch their actions, observe their motives, examine wherein they dwell content; won't you know what kind of person they are?"[34] And, with regard to the second, he states that "I am not sure that anyone who does not make good on their word (*xin*,信) is viable as a person. If a large carriage does not have a pin for its yoke, how can you drive [it] anywhere?"[35] Like the carriage pin, making good on one's word is the link between saying and doing, and judging others consequently entails considering the consistency of their actions as well as the correspondence between their words and deeds. In either case, inconsistency demonstrates that the individual lacks self-control or self-awareness.

This does not bode well for artists since, as we have seen, the artistic media that they utilize give the observer clear insight into the totality of an artist's character. If they are correct, a good work of art cannot be executed by an immoral person. Further, artists were saddled with a great moral burden since it was widely held that works of art could readily influence their audiences. Not unlike Plato, Confucius was quite concerned about the effects of works of art with questionable moral content and of the work of morally corrupt artists. Consequently, criticism was polarized in the sense that it tended to view both artists and works of art as *either* good or bad.

There are two ways to respond to this difficulty. The first is to argue that the Confucian conception of the self is flawed in the sense that it does not take into account the fact that individuals have moral strengths as well as weaknesses; the second is to argue that one's moral strengths and weaknesses are not necessarily displayed in every action. With regard to the second point, the Confucian view is that the medium will disclose the entirety of the artist's moral being and that the discriminating eye will perceive it. In turn, with regard to the first point, Confucius is quite clear that the moral ideals that he espouses are difficult to attain. In *Analects* 7:26, he laments that he will never get to meet a sage and goes on to add that he would be content to meet someone who is "constant," that is, someone whose actions are consistent and whose words correspond with their deeds, as described above. However, he is also skeptical about whether he will ever actually meet such a person. Further, in 7:33 he adds: "In the niceties of culture (*wen*,文), I am perhaps like other people, but as far as personally succeeding in living the life of the exemplary person, I have accomplished little." Here, Confucius characteristically effaces himself and his doubt indicates that he realizes that the way of life that he envisions is notoriously difficult to live. If this is the case, then there is room to argue that a Confucian could hold that individuals may have both good and bad moral qualities, and in varying degrees, and hence that Confucian criticism of works of art could reflect these variations instead of judging them simply as good or bad. The moral and aesthetic ideals espoused by Confucianism shaped the ancient conception of aesthetic goodness; however, if it is kept in mind that these ideals are lofty, a more pragmatic conception could also be employed to leave room for the acceptability of works by artists who fall short of them. An artist may not be a sage but may still be capable of creating works of art that have a high degree of aesthetic value.

It has been shown that the Confucian stance on the practice of art and the relationship between aesthetic and moral value makes an important contribution to discussions that center on such issues. This approach holds that the practice of art is necessarily a moral affair since the arts allow the student to cultivate the self, to find a place within a historical tradition, and to benefit from relationships with others who likewise pursue the goods of artistic self-expression. The analysis of calligraphy demonstrates that the form of the work itself is also important in this context, for the form is an expression of the artist's corporeality. The strokes that compose the ideograms are not components of "pure form" but are a product of the artist's gestural communication. The work of art is a manifestation of an artistic mode of embodiment and this contributes to the notion that the artist's work should be seen as an expression of character and as unfolding within the broader context of a life.[36]

ERIC C. MULLIS
Department of Philosophy
Queens University of Charlotte
Charlotte, NC 28274, USA

INTERNET: mullise@queens.edu

1. G. W. F. Hegel, *Lectures on the History of Philosophy* (3 vols.), trans. E. S. Haldane and Frances H. Simson (London: Kegan Paul, Trench, Trubner and Company, 1892–1896), vol. 1, pp. 120–121.
2. A. C. Graham, *Disputers of the Tao: Philosophical Argument in Ancient China* (La Salle: Open Court, 1989), p. 10. This is supported by *Analects* 7:1.
3. *Analects* 7:32, 8:8, 14:39. All references to the *Analects* are taken from *The Analects of Confucius: A Philosophical Translation*, trans. Roger T. Ames and Henry Rosemont Jr. (New York: Ballantine Books, 1998).
4. Li Zehou, *The Path of Beauty: A Study of Chinese Aesthetics*, trans. Gong Lizeng (Oxford University Press, 1994), pp. 35–38.
5. *Analects* 1:12.
6. *Analects* 16:5.
7. *Analects* 17:18. The music of the state of Zheng was seen as unorthodox not only because of its intricacy but also because it added one or two tones to the traditional pentatonic scale. For more, see Kenneth J. Dewoskin, *A Song For One or Two: Music and the Concept of Art in Early China* (Ann Arbor: Center for Chinese Studies at the University of Michigan, 1982), pp. 45, 92–96.
8. Xunzi, *Xunzi*, trans. John Knoblock (Library of Chinese Classics, Hunan Publishing House, 1999), vol. II, 20:7, pp. 658–659.
9. Xunzi, *Xunzi*, vol. II, 20:9, pp. 660–661.
10. *Analects* 15:18.
11. David L. Hall and Roger T. Ames, *Thinking Through Confucius* (SUNY Press, 1987), p. 96.
12. For but one example, see *Analects* 3:12.
13. Graham, *Disputers of the Tao*, p. 12.
14. Ibid.
15. Hall and Ames, *Thinking Through Confucius*, p. 88.
16. See Robert E. Harris Jr., "Reading Chinese Calligraphy," in *The Embodied Image: Chinese Calligraphy from the John B. Elliot Collection*, ed. Robert E. Harris Jr. and Wen C. Fong (The Art Museum, Princeton University, 1999), pp. 15–17.
17. Wen C. Fong, "Chinese Calligraphy: Theory and History" in *The Embodied Image*, p. 29.
18. Harris, "Reading Chinese Calligraphy," p. 19.
19. Harris, "Reading Chinese Calligraphy," p. 16.
20. Wing-Tsit Chan, *A Source Book in Chinese Philosophy* (Princeton University Press, 1963), p. 98.
21. For more, see John Hay, "The Human Body as Microcosmic Source of Macrocosmic Values in Calligraphy," in *Theories of the Arts in China*, ed. Susan Bush and Christian F. Murk (Princeton University Press, 1983), pp. 74–102.
22. Quoted in Hay, "The Human Body," p. 82. For more on this text, see Richard Barnhart, "Wei Fu-jen's Pi-chen T'u and Early Texts on Calligraphy," *Archives of the Chinese Art Society of America* 18 (1964): 13–25.
23. François Jullien, *The Propensity of Things: Toward a History of Efficacy in China*, trans. Janet Lloyd (New York: Zone Books, 1995), p. 75.

24. Jullien, *The Propensity of Things*, p. 76.

25. Quoted in Hay, "The Human Body," p. 83.

26. The character '*xin*' (心) is a pictograph of the physical heart. It is used to refer to the mind as well as the emotions. For an excellent discussion of the connection and the difficulty in translating the character, see Harold H. Oshima, "A Metaphorical Analysis of the Concept of Mind in the *Chuang-Tzu*," in *Experimental Essays on Chuang-Tzu*, ed. Victor H. Mair (University of Hawaii Press, 1983), pp. 63–84.

27. Fong, "Chinese Calligraphy," p. 34.

28. Noël Carroll, "Art and Ethical Criticism: An Overview of Recent Directions of Research," *Ethics* 110 (2000): 350–387, quote from 362.

29. Carroll, "Art and Ethical Criticism," p. 366.

30. Chang Ch'ung-ho and Hans H. Frankel, *Two Chinese Treatises on Calligraphy* (Yale University Press, 1995).

31. For instance, see Mary Devereaux, "How Bad Can Good Art Be?" in *Aesthetics and Ethics: Essays at the Intersection*, ed. Jerrold Levinson (Cambridge University Press, 1998), p. 217.

32. Of course, the autonomist will reply that there is good reason to believe that the artist and the work of art should remain immune from moral criticism, and such a reply is based on a definition of art and a conception of the role of the artist that are both deeply at odds with those advocated by the ancient Confucians. To fully address and critically examine both accounts would require a separate discussion. For a discussion of autonomism and responses to it, see Carroll, "Art and Ethical Criticism," pp. 351–353, 357–360; Wayne Booth, *The Company We Keep: An Ethics of Fiction* (University of California Press, 1988), pp. 3–22.

33. Mencius, *The Works of Mencius*, trans. James Legge (New York: Dover, 1970), 4:24, pp. 328–329.

34. *Analects* 7:26.

35. *Analects* 7:33.

36. An abbreviated version of this paper was presented at the 2006 joint meeting of the North and South Carolina Societies for Philosophy. The author thanks the participants for a lively discussion and also thanks the editor and anonymous referees of this journal for their comments and suggestions.

MARY BITTNER WISEMAN

Subversive Strategies in Chinese Avant-Garde Art

The following review of an underground exhibition held alongside the Shanghai Biennale 2000 appeared in the July 2001 issue of *Art in America*.

Socialist realism, which was still acknowledged in the modern portion of the Guggenheim Museum's "China, 5,000 Years" exhibition in 1998, has vanished without a trace ... [China] essentially skipped the stage of modernist formalism, moving in two Great Leaps, so to speak, from traditional ink painting to Socialist Realism to postmodern eclecticism ...

The urge for practitioners to "catch up" with the West and to stand out from the overwhelming competition leads many to a strategy of shock. If one "Fuck Off" artist uses a dead baby (Sun Yuan in *Honey*, 1999, or Zhu Yu in *Eating People*, 2000), the next, it seems, must use two (Peng Yu [and Sun Yuan] in *Link of the Body*).

After decades of censorship, China's young talents now seem obsessed with testing the limits of tolerance: How much provocation will the government permit? When will viewers begin to react with physical disgust or moral outrage? ... These "progressives" are remarkably like avant-garde artists everywhere ... Nothing is more uniform, it seems, than art-world nonconformity.[1]

It is true that nonconformity is a mark of the avant-garde, but it can be argued, *pace* this review, that to read the work of Chinese nonconforming artists at the turn of the twenty-first century as doing nothing but testing the limits of tolerance is to do the art an injustice and to deprive oneself of a lesson on the possible functions of and, hence, the nature of art. The evidence for this can be found by looking at the art of the Chinese avant-garde as a series of subversions of the claims of certain

beliefs to be true. The first subversion is of the presumption that a communist government with a capitalist economy can carve out a social space in which people can be themselves; the second, that the discourses in place in China are interpretable; and the third, that Western conceptions of art, supposing as they do a chasm between art and nature raw, can be adequate to China at the turn of the new century.

This way of looking raises the question of whether there are concepts specific to a non-Western aesthetics that have been omitted or marginalized in the West and would, were they to enter its critical discourse, enrich specific concepts in Western aesthetics and philosophies of art. More precisely, the question is whether there are traits or concepts present in the one art and absent from the other that are so deeply entrenched as not to be able to leave their context in order to enter the critical discourse of the West. An answer to this requires the separation out of the distinctly non-Western and the transposition of what is separated out to Western criticism.

In the fast-moving history of post-Cultural Revolution art in China there was a further forward leap from traditional ink painting to postmodern eclecticism not mentioned in the review in *Art in America*: from Socialist Realism to Political Pop, whose style, though not its content, was indebted to the art of the 1960s in the West. Political Pop performed the first of the three subversions through which the course of recent Chinese art can be charted. One reason to see the art as subversion is to discover what in it is global and what local. "Global" is here taken to apply to those activities or genres that can shake free of their native soil and be transported to almost anywhere, practices such as the manufacture of clothes for

American companies and the analysis of radiological scans from American hospitals that have moved to China and to India, respectively, and genres such as the installations and performance art that have journeyed from New York to Beijing. A difference between the economic and aesthetic cases leads to a distinction between the global and the local: something is global when it is unmarked by its travels and local when it bears the imprint of the place to which it has traveled. For example, the "Made in China" tag is the only evidence that many articles of clothing designed and sold by American companies are not of American manufacture. The clothing could have been made anywhere, and aside from the tag there is no sign of its having come from China. The installations and performance art made by artists of the Chinese avant-garde, however, are marked by the Chinese present and past, and their origin in the West pales in the face of their Chinese-ness. The imported genres themselves can become so familiar as to lose their "outsider-ness" and come to be thought of as local or homegrown.

China did skip the modernist formalism that reigned in the West throughout the period bracketed by the founding of the People's Republic of China in 1949 and the onset of the Cultural Revolution in 1966. An art conceived as significant form, an art whose content was excoriated for distracting the viewer from the plastic values whose creation is art's purpose, is a luxury Chinese artists cannot afford. The formalist creates forms free of content, message, or meaning of any sort, forms the mere perception of which pleases. Chinese avant-garde artists, on the other hand, perform ritualistic erasures of systems of intelligibility like language and art. In this activity lies the second subversion. It is performed for at least two different sorts of reasons. One is skepticism or cynicism or despair about, finally, the intelligibility of extant languages and arts. The other is the performance of an intellectual exercise: to find out how much content or meaning one can take away and still have anything that does more than merely please. The exercise includes an experiment in imagination: should the erasures succeed and the world be reduced to nothing but empty forms, would the artist's presence, his or her body and its gestures, be enough to remake the world? The answer from China today is yes.

Part of what is distinctive about the work of the Chinese avant-garde is its subject matter and, most important, the attitude the artist takes toward it. The subject matter of the most recent art is precisely the means through which the avant-garde performs its third subversion. The distinctiveness, the "otherness," led the U.K.'s International Trade Commission to find a television program to contain material that constituted an offense against good taste and decency, an offense to public feeling.[2] Forty-two viewers had objected to two pieces of performance art shown on a Channel 4 broadcast of *Beijing Swings* on January 2, 2003 at 11:05 p.m. One was Zhu Yu's *Eating People*, which contained a photograph of the artist eating the body of a dead baby, and the other was Peng Yu and Sun Yuan's *Link of the Body*, in which "the dead bodies of a pair of Siamese twins were smeared with the artists' blood."[3]

The fact that *Link of the Body* was found to offend good taste and decency in Britain and yet won for its artists the 2002 young artist prize in the Contemporary Chinese Art Awards highlights one difference between the global and the local, the regional, the native, what cannot be exported or "shaken off."[4] *Link of the Body* is weakly global in its genre because performance art originated in the West, but the attitudes, ideas, and impulses it expresses are local. Although a British commission found the broadcast of pictures of the work to offend public decency, the Chinese government apparently did not: it did not interfere with the underground exhibition alternate to the Shanghai Biennale 2000 that included *Link of the Body*. This leads to the thought that the avant-garde in the twenty-first century is speaking to something distinctively Chinese and that global audiences welcome this art for its difference, its Chinese-ness, but only so long as the expressed attitudes toward the subject matter do not offend their own local codes of what is acceptable. What the Chinese-ness consists in must, of course, be adumbrated.

The mainland Chinese are living through the reinscription within their culture of the opposing sides of the Cold War that dominated the second half of the twentieth century. Furthermore, the Chinese counterparts of the series of upheavals that caused the breakup of the Soviet Union and its satellites failed to bring about a similar effect, the fall of communism, when they culminated in the demonstrations in Tiananmen Square in 1989. The government forcefully suppressed them, and the coexistence of the communist government and its capitalist economy still defines the "new China."

The people have to come to terms not only with the prima facie contradiction between the virtual obliteration of the idea of the individual under communism and the self-promotion of the individual under capitalism, but also with the change from Mao's prohibition of any commerce with the bourgeoisie to his successor Deng Xiaoping's invitation to foreign investors. This all takes place against the backdrop of the "old China" that persists despite efforts Mao made to cast it into shadow.

Imagine an art that is refashioning itself in a world that has in its last decades seen the end of communism in the Soviet Union and central Europe, the electronic revolution and the subsequent information explosion, and globalization. Imagine an art whose identity is in flux and whose exposure to the arts and ideas of the West was slight between the inception of communism in China in 1949 and the country's opening itself to the West in the late 1970s. Such is the art of China. Its story shows it to be in the service of what is no longer its primary function in the West: the reconstruction of the identity of a people and the reinvention of the idea of art itself. One specific Chinese difference, then, is the role its current art plays in the articulation of what can in China be thought and felt and said. This is the classic role of an avant-garde. The aesthetic avant-garde has been the pride of the West, but its avatars have moved East. The move gives rise to the question of whether and how much this avant-garde is inflected by "China," by its ancient and its recent history. The question is whether and how what might fall out as distinctly Chinese can assert itself in the presence of the global reach of Western practices.

Installation and performance art abound in the work of these Chinese artists, but they are far from simply copying the West. Evidence for this is the presence of two themes with no obvious counterpart in the West, identified by Norman Bryson in *Inside Out: New Chinese Art.*[5] One is the relation of the individual to the social spaces created by the mix of materialism and socialism, spaces identified by Henri Lefebvre as having been produced by social forces as their preconditions and their products.[6] Distinctive of the organization of social space in the People's Republic of China through the mid-1980s was its homogeneity, which the Cultural Revolution sought to further by trying to erase the differences between town and county. On its surface, the space is homogeneous

no longer. The other theme specific to the new art is the individual's relation to the languages that articulate and convey meaning.

Social spaces and their languages comprise Bryson's list. I have another. On mine are items more nearly primitive, resistant though not immune to the incursion of "the languages of criticism and the sciences of man."[7] They are items from a brute and dumb nonsignifying nature, not from a nature domesticated in gardens, national parks, wildlife preserves, and landscape paintings. The list includes worms, gunpowder, dust, dead bodies, and blood. Both of us, however, recognize something in the current art that operates at a level below that of ideology, below where communism and capitalism collide. And below what the one U.K. watchdog considered the boundaries of good taste or decency and respect for human dignity.[8]

I.   FIRST SUBVERSION—OF THE PRESUMPTION THAT A COMMUNIST GOVERNMENT WITH A CAPITALIST ECONOMY CAN CARVE OUT A SOCIAL SPACE IN WHICH PEOPLE CAN BE THEMSELVES

Look first at one distinguishing theme to be found in *Inside Out: New Chinese Art*: responses to the social spaces created by Chinese communism's embrace of capitalism. It is the material for the first subversion that began soon after the end of the Cultural Revolution and appeared as a local version of Pop Art. Artists in Hangzhou, for example, made a series of installations called *Red Humor* in 1986–1987. Wu Shan Zhuan made one in which the walls, ceiling, and floor of a small room were papered with communist slogans, lines from Buddhist texts, advertisements, jokes, the title of Leonardo's *Last Supper*, in a word, the contents of the mind of a mainland Chinese person living in the 1980s. Most of the papers were white with black characters, some few were red, and the whole was splashed with red paint. On the painted red floor were four large white characters spelling out "No one can interpret it," no one, not Deng or the CEO of MacDonald's. The room is a metaphor for a mind, and the subtext of the installation is that no sense can be made of the contents of a mind full of communist dicta and capitalist slogans. When the room is seen as a metaphor for the culture, the subtext is that its disparate languages and the sayings they license cannot carry meaning because there are no shared meanings through which they can be read together.

Wu Shan Zhuan chose the sayings used in *Red Humor* randomly, believing the artist not to be the main factor in the production of art and declaring: "Wu is an example of material. Nothing can escape from being material."[9] And nothing, it seems, can escape being turned into a commodity, a thing that can be traded for money. Indeed, in its January 2006 issue, *Artforum* reported that "it was only two months ago that an individual work by a Chinese contemporary artist surpassed the $1 million mark," and on October 20, 2005, *The New York Times* reported that sales in China's leading auction houses "have risen from less than $100 million in 2000 to about $1 billion in 2003." The growth of the Chinese art market requires its artists to become increasingly subversive if they are to function as a bona fide avant-garde. This is exactly what they have done.

Historical materialism records the history of the conversion of the goods of the earth into materials that will sustain human life. Capitalism is the system through which the goods of the earth are converted into capital, where capital is not what

sustains life but what makes more of itself. Uneasy bedfellows, the two materialisms sleep together nonetheless. In the words of the curator of *Inside Out: New Chinese Art*: "The mass media's overwhelming of the population with propagandist images (such as Mao's art) or advertisement and entertainment symbols (such as Coca-Cola and Marilyn Monroe) apparently levels the differences between Mao's mass culture and Hollywood."[10]

Political themes from the Cultural Revolution joined Pop Art in a series of oil paintings by Wang Guangyi, one of which, *Great Castigation: Coca-Cola* (1993) (Figure 1), combines the image of three workers lined up side by side with the soft drink logo. Only the heads and raised left arms of the second and third workers can be seen. The first clutches a red book and all three hold one large fountain pen whose nib lies just above the second *C* in the white letters 'Coca-Cola' and whose length appears to be the pole of a red flag. If the first *C* is communism, then the second, the one threatened by the pen's nib, is "capitalism." Book and pen replace hammer and sickle. The

FIGURE 1. Wang Guangyi, *Great Castigation: Coca-Cola* (1993). Oil on canvas. Photograph courtesy of the Asia Society, New York.

flag and the back wall, deep yellow on top and red on the bottom, are peppered with ten-digit numbers, perhaps identification numbers of some kind, some white, some black. The conjunction of the two reduces the revolutionary workers and the logo of China's most popular company to kitsch, trivializing the ideologies of Maoism and Western economies. To reduce Maoism to kitsch is to subvert its authority over the people's beliefs and values.

Great Castigation: Coca-Cola is nothing more than an exemplification of materialism, historical and consumer, where "nothing can escape being material."[11] Material cannot generate meaning, people do, but not deliberately. Wang Guangyi, like Wu Shan Zhuan, belongs to an anti-author movement that holds artists not to be major factors in the production of art, and it is consistent with this movement to hold individuals not to be major factors in the production of language, that is to say, their intentions do not issue in meanings. How, then, does language have the authority it has? What is at issue is the source of meaning, and *Great Castigation: Coca-Cola* says that the discourses of neither communism nor capitalism can authorize a set of shared meanings in a culture that contains both. Bryson suggests that gesture and its repetition, not ideology, is what legitimates discourses. The subversion of Mao's authority leads straightaway to a crisis of language and to the second subversion performed by conceptual art.

II. SECOND SUBVERSION—OF THE PRESUMPTION THAT THE DISCOURSES IN PLACE IN CHINA ARE INTERPRETABLE

The second theme found to be specific to Chinese art, then, the relation of the individual to language, follows from the first, the relation of the individual to the social spaces that house the former antagonists in the Cold War. *Red Humor* says that the two languages under one roof cannot be interpreted, and *Great Castigation: Coca-Cola* implies that this is because the signifiers of the only possible sources of meaning, the revolution and the market, are empty. Nor can Chinese tradition enter the breach. It and its art are reduced to nothing when made to share space with the modern art of Europe and America. This is the message of *"A History of Chinese Painting" and "A Concise History of Modern Painting" Washed in a Washing Machine for Two Minutes* (1987) by Huang Yong

Ping. The work is the pile of paper pulp left over from having washed the two books in a machine for two minutes. Because the two had been torn from their respective Chinese and Western contexts and made to share each other's space, the meaning of each was washed away. In the pulp that remains the material identity of each, as well as its meaning, is lost.

Artists are making works that consist, in Bryson's words, "in emptying out the semantic dimension of language," enacting through their art precisely the effects of the contradictions supported by the too-rapid reconfigurations of their social spaces.[12] The unsettling of the language user's identity—revolutionary or bourgeois?—unsettles his or her relation to language, and the language user cannot find himself or herself in it. The response of conceptual artists has been to perform and document actions that not only dramatize the crisis of meaning by eviscerating language's semantic content, but also exemplify what is left over and above syntax: gesture, the body's performance of language. To talk, to write, is to do some physical thing. To listen, to read, is to use ears and eyes. And because there can be no private language, silently to think with words requires also being able to use them to talk and to listen, to write and to read.

Two works of performance art in *Inside Out* can be read to say that since power in China seems no longer to reside at the level of the great ideologies, perhaps it lies in a level below them where individuals can act, where they can "intervene and innovate at their own scale and on their own terms."[13] One work is *Writing the "Orchid Pavilion Preface" One Thousand Times* (1986/1997) by Qui Zhijie, in which the artist does what any student of calligraphy must do and copies again and again a famous fourth-century text. The singular difference of Qui's exercise is that he copies the words onto one piece of paper, which eventually becomes an unreadable black sheet. To do this, then, is to do no more than to encode the characters in the writer's hand, arm, and brain.[14] In the sheer repetitiveness of the activity, Qui did the same kind of thing that is done by every language user with every use of a given word in a language. He embedded the words in the memory of his hand and mind, as each use of a word further embeds it in the language.

Writing the "Orchid Pavilion Preface" One Thousand Times makes of the artist's activity a metaphor for one dimension and one effect of language. The dimension is its use. Natural language is language in use, and for anyone competent in a language, its use is more or less automatic, as writing the "Orchid Pavilion Preface" becomes at a certain point in the exercise. The artist's repeated and systematic performance of language completely covers with signs the sheet that had been blank. The metaphoric effect of the artist's activity is to show language to be opaque because one cannot read *through* it and dense because one cannot read *between* its signs. It says, finally, that language blankets the world and all that is in it, and one cannot read the world through the opacity of the signs that constitute it. The world, it would seem, is lost.

The second work is *Printing on Water* (1996), a performance by Song Dong in the Lhasa River, Tibet. Against the backdrop of mountains the artist stands in a sacred river and, holding above his head a seal carved with the character for "water," again and again brings it down onto the water's surface. There is no coition of word and thing, however. No character, no matter what it signifies, can unite with or imprint itself on water. The calligraphy in *Writing "The Orchid Pavilion Preface" One Thousand Times* cannot be read and the character for "water" in *Printing on Water* cannot be written.[15] The artist is authorizing the seal by using it. But what is he using it for? Not to say anything. The repeated gestures of imprinting or writing are intransitive. In them writing is at its zero degree.

The absence of the world, of the other side of language, of everything that language is about, does not, however, mean that the individual is alone. Indeed, the world is absent precisely because everything is shot through with the language by which the individual is surrounded. Or so it seems. At the height of the New Wave in Chinese art, which succeeded the socialist realism of Maoist art, Xu Bing mounted his *Book from the Sky* (1988) (Figure 2) in the National Museum in Beijing. As did *Red Humor*, it surrounds its viewers with writing. On the walls are plastered scrolls reminiscent of the newspapers pasted on walls for everyone to read. Draped from the ceiling are yards and yards of scrolls in the format of ancient religious texts, and on the floor are books bound in the traditional Chinese way. Xu hand-carved 4,000 blocks from which the scrolls were printed in the style of the eleventh-century Sung Dynasty and "every detail of the piece was exquisite and perfect: the carved characters, the printing, the

FIGURE 2.   Xu Bing, *Book from the Sky* (1987–1991). Hand-printed books, ceiling, and wall scrolls from false letter blocks, installation view at the National Gallery of Canada, Ottawa, 1998. Photograph courtesy of the Xu Bing Studio.

binding, and the meticulous design."[16] Yet all but ten of the characters were Xu's invention. They mean nothing. The viewer is cocooned in writing that cannot be read, in hundreds of illegible scrolls.

The repetitions in both *Writing "The Orchid Pavilion Preface" One Thousand Times* and *Printing on Water* are not in *Book from the Sky*. Xu Bing is not encoding Chinese characters in his muscles and mind by writing them repeatedly, nor is he authorizing the character for "water" by his repeated efforts to print it. Xu's artwork, the work of it, lies in the sheer doing of the project, almost three years of carving 4,000 characters in wood blocks. It is a prayer, a meditation. "He suffered. It was like a morning prayer, the process was more important than the result," said Cao Minglu, curator of *Inside Out: New Chinese Art*. The "process," the exercise, the ritual is like a dance, where a dancer's body knows what to do, and so in exercise and the performance of a ritual does the performer's body. Nothing, said Wu Shan Zhuan, "can escape from being material."[17] Seen in this light, *Book from the Sky* bears witness to words' and books' being things, things to be carved, printed, and bound. This book does not come from Confucianism, to which Xu's art refers, or from the artist's intentions to mean; it comes, the title tells us, from the sky.

The idea of writing at its zero degree leads to the thought of art making at its zero degree, to the third subversion, and to adding my list to Bryson's list of social spaces and their languages. Earthworms and silkworms, gunpowder, dust, blood, and violence, in a word, nature brute, blind, and dumb is what is left, avant-garde Chinese artists suggest, when the world appears to be lost. It is the primitive that is left, whatever has penetrated, punctured, pierced the myriad social and semantic spaces that have failed to fulfill their promises of hospitality and legibility, their claims undermined by the art of the avant-garde.

III.   THIRD SUBVERSION — OF THE PRESUMPTION THAT WESTERN CONCEPTIONS OF ART, SUPPOSING AS THEY DO A CHASM BETWEEN ART AND NATURE RAW, ARE ADEQUATE TO CHINA TODAY

A decade after *Book from the Sky*, Xu Bing installed *The Silkworm Series* in a gallery for the 1998 exhibition *Where Heaven and Earth Meet*. In the gallery is a coffee table with books and magazines, framed pictures on the wall, a TV monitor

screening the lifecycle of the silk worm, and its accompanying VCR, whose cover is open. Silkworm moths lay eggs that hatch into worms that spin their threads over everything they come near, which, in the gallery, is everything, including the mechanical insides of the VCR. The enveloping of things makes them unrecognizable, their words and images unreadable.

The Chinese have raised silkworms for more than 2,000 years, and silk is an emblem of China. Traditional China is present in the silkworm and so is the modern West, in the form of installation art. Nature also is present. Compare this piece with, say, Damien Hirst's exhibition of the carcass of a once life-threatening shark in a tank of formaldehyde or, moving from an exhibition of death to that of dying, with an installation in which flies emerge from maggots, eat, and die when struck by an insect-o-cutor. These works use, they do not represent, the animals that are their subjects. In two of them, creatures are born, and in one, they die soon after birth. Every living thing is born and dies, but in the meantime they interact with other creatures, including human beings and their works. This meantime is the space occupied by Xu Bing's *Silkworm Series*, in which the worms do what naturally they do, spin threads of silk that end up covering all of the paraphernalia of culture in the gallery.

Silkworms cover over; earthworms burrow under. In *New York Earthworm Room*, made for the same exhibition, Cai Guo-Qiang, who like Xu Bing left China after 1989 and now lives in New York, appropriated Walter De Maria's *The New York Earth Room* that has been maintained by the Dia Center for the Arts since 1977. De Maria transported yards of earth to a New York art gallery. De-contextualized, it is no longer part of nature. Cai also transported yards of earth to an art gallery, but he reintroduced nature by putting worms and, therefore, life into it. Grass began to grow as the worms aerated the soil and nourished it with organic material. The earth was in one gallery in the exhibition in which a camcorder was focused on the grass, and in an adjoining gallery were video screens, connected by cable to the camcorder, onto which the earthworms' movements were projected.

The salient difference between the two installations of worms, on the one hand, and the works of Hirst and De Maria, on the other, is that the worms were alive and active while the objects in the works by Hirst and De Maria were not. The worms were de-contextualized: they were active in an art gallery instead of nature. But they continued to make their characteristic contributions: one made silk, the other aerated and nourished soil.

Gunpowder was invented in China long years ago and is as much an emblem of China as is silk. Cai Guo-Qiang has used it widely in his work, from *Traces of Ancient Explosions* (1985), made of gunpowder and oil paint on canvas, to the *Project to Extend the Great Wall of China by 10,000 Meters* (1993), in which 600 kilograms of gunpowder were connected to a 10,000-meter long fuse on the ground at the western terminus of the Great Wall. On February 27, 1993, the fuse was ignited to cause a series of successive explosions. Of the project the artist wrote that "the 10,000 meter wall of light will form a line of *Qi* energy that will wake the Great Wall, which has been sleeping for thousands of years."[18] And it did so by extending the Great Wall westward.

Gunpowder is one instrument of violent destruction, and ground zero dust is the result of another, namely, of the two airplanes that crashed into New York's Twin Towers on September 11, 2001. On the day of the attack Xu Bing collected a bag of dust from the site and with it he later made an installation in a gallery-sized enclosure in the National Museum and Gallery of Cardiff, Wales entitled *Where Does the Dust Itself Collect?* (2002). He sprayed the dust over stencils of letters spelling out two lines of a seminal seventh-century Zen poem. When the dust settled, the stencils were removed and the lines appeared in the dust: "As there is nothing from the first, where does the dust itself collect?" The work won the first Artes Mundi prize, an international arts prize awarded in 2004 for work in the exhibition in the National Museum of Cardiff.

Any worms and any gunpowder whatsoever could have been used without changing the identity of the works of which they were a part, but neither the site of the 10,000-meter wall of light nor the actual dust used to spell out the Zen poem could have been different without destroying the work's identity. And so are these artworks grounded in the world to which they relate not by imitating, representing, or idealizing, but by incorporating it into themselves.

The position on the world's stage of the social and the verbal has been called into question by two of the subversions performed in the artworld

since the end of the Cultural Revolution. What shares the stage with them is the natural, the material, the physical. The artworks introduced so far as examples of the third subversion have used living or once-living nonhuman things, on the one hand, and powders that caused and resulted from explosions, on the other: matter enlivened in the one case and matter plain and simple in the other.

The subject of the final two artworks to be discussed is the human body. The body is not simply matter enlivened; it is matter made human, made conscious of itself, conscious of death, of its inevitable death, and, for the classical Chinese scholar and many an artist of the avant-garde, matter made conscious of its harmony with nature. On the Judeo-Christian-Muslim view, human beings are essentially different from the rest of creation because they alone are enlivened by the breath of God, himself beyond nature's pale. Human beings, matter-made-human, seek to control rather than to harmonize with nature. This difference from the West is manifest in these last two works.

Link of the Body is a performance in which the dead bodies of conjoined infant twins are linked to two artists by tubes through which blood flows into the mouths of the infants; the body of one twin is covered with blood. Linkages abound in *Link of the Body*. The most obvious is the link between the conjoined twins, the result of misdirection in their fetal development. Then there is the indirect connection between the artists by virtue of their each being connected to the twins by a tube of blood, a bloodline, as individuals are connected with their forebears by bloodlines.[19] The artists "feeding" the conjoined twins are a male and a female, as they would have to be were they the twins' parents. The most moving link in the performance is the one between living and dead bodies. It constitutes, I want to say, an acknowledgment of death, not the desecration of a corpse. Perhaps "wonder at" is better than "acknowledgment of" in light of an answer Peng Yu gave in an interview published in 2002. Asked whether her influence had, as her partner just said his had, come from a photographer, Peng said, no, it came from her experience of the death of a childhood playmate.

[F]acing the death of a person is like an electric shock. I had a friend once . . . a little girl . . . [who] died of uremia . . . When I saw her I suddenly had, I'm not sure what kind of feeling, but it was like *life could just fly from a person's body in an instant.* Sometimes I think that the second a person is born, or when a person dies, this is really fascinating, so I search for that kind of thing in my work. Sometimes *it amounts to something you or I don't dare to face*. It's also something very pressing and forces me to keep going. Sometimes I use these materials, do this kind of work, in this process I can get the kind of feeling I was talking about.[20]

She is talking about something that beggars understanding, namely, what happens in the instant a person is born or dies. The link of body to body: at birth the link between the bodies of mother and infant is sundered and the infant becomes a single thing. At death the body becomes matter no longer enlivened, but matter that will decay as every generated thing does, gradually ceasing to be a body as it does. But until it does, it is a human body. The pathos of *Link of the Body* lies in the artists' act of infusing the dead bodies with their own (so it seems) life's blood as though to bring the bodies back or to dare us to face the futility of infusing them, dare us to face the differ-

ence between being alive and being dead, to face what we cannot understand and so can only acknowledge. If this reading of *Link of the Body* has merit, then neither government censure nor physical disgust nor moral outrage is an appropriate response.[21]

Look at a final example of a work whose theme is also blood and the human body, where the body is female and the blood, menstrual. It is a series of twelve photographs by Chen Lingyang, *Twelve Flower Months* (1999), made from November 1999 to November 2000. In each photograph is the flower of the month specific to it together with a mirror that reflects the artist's menstruating body. The shapes of the mirrors, each different as are the shapes of the photographs themselves, are those of windows and doors in traditional gardens, but instead of the mirrors showing the face of a beautiful woman they show the artist's menstrual bleeding from various angles, variously framed, lit, and colored. *Twelve Flower Month for the First Month Narcissus* (1999) (Figure 3) is a square, relentless in

Figure 3.   Chen Ling Yang, *Twelve Flower Month for the First Month Narcissus* (1999). Photograph. Reproduced by permission of the Modern Chinese Art Foundation.

its blackness, hung on the diagonal. An oval mirror suspended on a stand occupies about two-thirds of the left side of the plane and three narcissus flowers and leaves, the right. Reflected are the bottom of the buttocks of the artist and her legs down to the back of the knees. Blood trickles down most of her thigh. The blood, the flowers, and highlights on the wooden stand are a soft rosy red, the leaves are green, the mirror is light-suffused. The whole is quiet, elegant, and beautiful.

The metaphoric connection of women with flowers is undermined when Chen pictures a real connection between female reproductive organs and flowering. The juxtaposition of menstrual periods and blooming flowers highlights the connection of each to the cycle of nature and, hence, to each other. And although, as Chen pointed out in an interview connected with her winning one of the Contemporary Chinese Art Awards in 2002, "[i]n traditional Chinese culture there is the notion of man in harmony with nature," the work still takes its audience by surprise.[22]

About this Chen said that "[w]hen people see this work in a public space, it provokes various reactions. But the work itself also offers the possibility of dispelling such reactions. The possibility of dispelling may come from the traditional elements . . . Provoking and dispelling . . . are inextricably bound together. Only through the process of provoking and dispelling can new possibilities emerge."[23] In *Twelve Flower Months* Chen dresses her bleeding vagina in the clothes of classical China: flowers and mirrors beautifully shaped like the windows in garden pavilions. The artist is treating the flow of her monthly blood as a subject as worthy of art as flowers and mirrors are. Classical in their serenity and their symbolism, the photographs observe their subject in the way traditional Chinese thought observes the world.

Chen Lingyang and Peng Su are young women, one born in 1975, the other in 1974, who have made art that springs from a near preoccupation with and reflection on the nature-imposed limits of birth and death and the female body's reproductive cycle. Matter-made-human is matter made conscious of the mysteries of birth and of death and, for these two artists, made conscious of matter's embeddedness in nature. What does this come to? The idea that they are not, that no human being is, different in kind from the rest of nature. One effect of this is that death is not regarded as something that has gone terribly wrong,

and menstrual blood is not regarded as unclean or the menstruating woman untouchable. They are seen as an integral part of the ceaseless cycles of reproduction, birth, and death. Another effect is that the artists treat with respect the materials they use for the third subversive strategy. They treat them as one treats things that have worth and not just value.

Chen's experience of the rhythm of her body's periods is an experience of the rhythms of nature, of its repetitiveness and its duration. She said of the subject of menstruation that "I found myself harassed by the subject and could not put it out of my mind, it was both strong and apt enough for me to express what I wanted to express . . . Thus, I used this subject for my artwork."[24] Limits, not repetitiveness and duration, are what move Peng Yu. The effort to capture in her work the feeling that "life could just fly from a person's body in an instant" is "something very pressing and forces me to keep going."[25]

Earthworms and silkworms, gunpowder and dust, dead babies and menstrual blood: here is a grand materialism, one deaf to the cacophony caused by the competing voices of communism and capitalism and immune to the divorce of signifier and signified caused by the competing discourses. When signs are emptied of meaning, all that is left for language users to do is to "go through the motions," to speak, to write, to listen, to read the signs that carry with them, at least, the memory of meaning. Intransitive, these activities are language at its zero degree. Writing is at zero when the movements of the calligrapher's hand and brush are performed for their own sake, as the movements of a dance are, and speaking is at zero when one recites a poem in a language whose script one can read but not understand. The evisceration of meaning from the signs of an individual's world leaves him or her with the material of the world, which includes the body and its movements.

Bryson's insight that since power in China seems no longer to reside at the level of the great ideologies, perhaps it lies at a level below them where individuals can act, where they can "intervene and innovate at their own scale and on their own terms" is apt.[26] "Individuals acting" parses out as "bodies gesturing," where the gesturing body of the avant-garde artist is what is reconstructing the identity of a people and reinventing the idea of art itself. The material used in the artists' third subversive strategy constitutes a tutorial on the differences between nonliving, living, and conscious material things. The attitudes toward the various materials taken by artists of the avant-garde teach viewers willing to send themselves to school these distinctions. Lacking a coherent discourse in their dizzyingly fast changing world, the artists work at a level below that of discourse, at the level of matter, matter that the body with its gestures and repetitions transmutes into such material as to start a dialogue with its viewers about who they are as Chinese men and women and what their artworks are.[27]

MARY BITTNER WISEMAN
The Graduate Center of the City
    University of New York
Department of Philosophy
New York, NY 10016, USA

INTERNET: marigold21@comcast.net

1. Richard Vine, "The Report from Shanghai: After Exoticism," *Art in America* 89 (2001): 30–39, quote is from p. 39.

2. The International Trade Commission (ITC) is an "independent" quasi-judicial British agency that advises the legislative and executive branches of government. It found Channel 4 in breach of §1.1 of its Programme Code, available at http://www.ofcom.org.uk/static/archive/itc/itc_publications/complaints_reports/programme_complaints/show_complaint.asp-prog_complaint_id=596.html.

3. From the report of the above ITC ruling.

4. Contemporary Chinese Art Awards (CCAA) is an award-granting foundation established in 1998 by the Swiss collector and ambassador to China, Uli Siggs. The CCAA are the only such awards in China.

5. Norman Bryson, "The Post-Ideological Avant-Garde," in *Inside Out: New Chinese Art*, catalogue for a 1998–1999 exhibition at the San Francisco Museum of Modern Art and Asia Society Galleries in New York (University of California Press, 1998), p. 53.

6. Henri Lefebvre, *The Production of Space*, trans. Donald Nicholson-Smith (Oxford: Blackwell, 1991).

7. The title is that of a conference at the Johns Hopkins University in 1966 at which contemporary French criticism and theory were introduced to the U.S. academic world.

8. The claims being made here are not about the whole of the contemporary Chinese art scene, but about art shown in several exhibitions in the United States. Bryson's judgments are based for the most part on the exhibition *Inside Out: New Chinese Art*. Mine are based for the most part on it and two other publications. One is Zhang Zhaohui, ed., *Where Heaven and Earth Meet: Xu Bing & Cai Guo-Qiang*, catalogue for an 1998 exhibition at the Art Museum of the Center for Curatorial Studies at Bard College (Hong Kong: Timezone 8 Limited, 2005). The other is Ai Weiwei, ed., *Chinese Artists, Texts and Interviews: Chinese Contemporary Art*

Awards (CCAA) 1998–2002 (Hong Kong: Timezone 8 Limited, 2002).

9. Wu Shan Zhuan and Inga Svala, "Tourist Information: Alphabetical Aphorisms," a selection of writings distributed by Wu and Red Humor International, 1992–1993. Cited in *Inside Out: New Chinese Art*, p. 159.

10. Cao Minglu, "From Elite to Small Man: The Many Faces of a Transitional Avant-Garde in Mainland China," in *Inside Outside: New Chinese Art*, p. 152.

11. Wu Shan Zhuan and Inga Svala, "Tourist Information: Alphabetical Aphorisms."

12. Bryson, *Inside Out: New Chinese Art*, p. 56.

13. Bryson, *Inside Out: New Chinese Art*, p. 57.

14. Bryson describes the effect: the power of the text lies not in its content but "in the sheer force of the cultural repetition, especially through the internalization of social authority that is performed within the calligrapher's own body as he attempts to incorporate the text inside his own musculature and gestural reflexes"(*Inside Out: New Chinese Art*, p. 57).

15. All that remains of Song Dong's activity is "the central gesture of the subject's interpellation within the graphic or social field, where power is located entirely within the individual subject's repeated action of creating and re-creating the authority of the seal with his own psychophysical being, again and again." Bryson, *Inside Out: New Chinese Art*, p. 57.

16. Zhang Zhaohui, *Where Heaven and Earth Meet*, p. 9.

17. Wu Shan Zhuan, *Inside Out: New Chinese Art*, p. 159.

18. Zhang Zhaohui, *Where Heaven and Earth Meet*, p. 14.

19. In fact, the connection with ancestors is genetic, but the prescientific and popular view is that blood is what connects present with contemporary and long-gone members of a family.

20. "Sun Yuan and Peng Yu Interview with Ai Waiwai," in *Chinese Artists, Texts and Interviews*, p. 20, emphases added.

21. This reading is made in light of Peng Yu's feelings about death. To read the work through its social context instead is to ask what the unnaturally linked twins stand for: The East and the West? Old China and New China? Communism and Capitalism? Why is one splashed with blood and the other not? What does the bloodied one stand for?

22. "An Interview with Chen Lingyang by Chen Lingyang No. 2 2001/4/28," in *Chinese Artists, Texts and Interviews*, p. 30.

23. Chen Lingyang, *Chinese Artists, Texts and Interviews*, p. 30.

24. Chen Lingyang, *Chinese Artists, Texts and Interviews*, p. 29.

25. Peng Yu, *Chinese Artists, Texts and Interviews*, p. 20.

26. Bryson, *Inside Out: New Chinese Art*, p. 57.

27. The 2006 Milan International Art Fair was devoted to "a unique artistic phenomenon—Chinese contemporary art—that is developing at an amazingly accelerated pace. [There were panels on] the specificities, processes and evolution of contemporary Chinese art from the perspective of a connection with the international art system, and through many layers of perception existing in China and the West, across boundaries that are far more than merely geographical" ("MIArt 2006 Cina Intra/Extra Ovest," info@e-flux.com, February 15, 2006).

ARTHUR C. DANTO

Embodied Meanings, Isotypes, and Aesthetical Ideas

The translator into Hungarian of several of my writings on art theory recently sent me a catalog of the work of a young artist from her country, Ágnes Eperjesi.[1] The translator—Eszter Babarczy—is a gifted critic in her own right, and I cannot do better than quote from her letter, which explains why she felt I would be especially interested in Eperjesi's art.

She thought your ideas about transfiguration and the commonplace applied to her work, and she took inspiration from your essays. Hers is a remarkable and long journey from experimental photography to an absolutely unique venture of collecting wrappings of household products, and taking the humble sign language of ordinary household chores, and recreating them as objects of beauty and irony.

The products, like dishwashers and vacuum cleaners—or underwear—were in all likelihood intended for export to countries anywhere in the world, which implies that they will fit into forms of life that must be much the same the world over. So the images must themselves belong to the sign language of globalism, necessarily universal in that they have to be legible to consumers who cannot be counted on to have a common language. The signs show what the consumers need to know about the products they have purchased—which side of a pair of underpants is front and which side is back, for example. In many, though not, all cases, they are pictograms or even *isotypes*—an acronym for "International System of Typographic Picture Education"—signs of a kind initially invented in 1936 by the Logical Positivist, Otto Neurath, who may have been influenced by Wittgenstein's so-called picture theory of language. Neurath anticipated globalism in saying: "The visual method

becomes the basis for a common cultural life and a common cultural relationship."[2] Just consider their international use in giving traffic directions to drivers who may or may not be able to read the language of the country in which they are traveling, or in guiding us through foreign airports. Isotypes are among the rare practical and positive contributions made by modern philosophy to the common life of humankind. When these pictograms are recycled—or transfigured—into works of art, their implied universality is elevated to a portrait of the society in which the products are to be used.

I would not altogether follow Babarszy in calling Eperjesi's works beautiful and, in truth, I am somewhat at a loss to describe them aesthetically. But I can appreciate that in transfiguring the isotype into an artwork, an interesting reversal of Walter Benjamin's famous distinction has taken place: the art of mechanical reproduction has acquired, through transfiguration, an aura, and in virtue of that the images may acquire an aesthetic interest they heretofore lacked. At least, as art, we look at them as critics, and notice their aesthetic qualities, such as they are. Just knowing that an object is intended as a piece of fine art may trigger the sense that it must be beautiful. Or better, we use this standard term of aesthetic commendation in connection with *them* that we would hardly use in characterizing the pictograms on which they are based. The term 'beautiful' may simply be a compliment paid to art as art, without really being descriptive of the art at all.

The goal of trans-cultural communication may mean that features that imply ethnic differences will be erased—the persons are depicted neither as white nor black nor red nor yellow—leaving figures that are abstractly human, which in a way look quite "modern." But is "looks modern" an

My new boyfriend gets along fine with my daughter.
I hope it's not just a show for now.

FIGURE 1.   Ágenes Eperjesi.

aesthetic characterization or a stylistic one? Modernist design strove for a kind of simplification through its distaste for ornament, and this led to stylization in modernist pictography. This does not explain why the isotypical pictograms are stylized as they are, which comes, rather, from globalist imperatives—so "looks modern" is *façon de parler*. But in any case, the pictogram has undergone some sort of aesthetic transformation in the course of its artistic transfiguration, however we finally describe it. Eperjesi's aesthetic enhancement of workaday images is as distinctive as Andy Warhol's transformations of Polaroids into portraits.

As to Eszter Bararcszy's description of the work as "ironic," that is true—but it is due more to Eperjesi's titles—or perhaps they are captions—than to the images themselves: the covers of *The New Yorker Magazine* have titles, the cartoons have captions. Either way, the titles/captions express thoughts that the images alone do not. Eperjesi has often selected her images with the intention of using them to convey how women in contemporary Hungary regard themselves, and how they think about the housework for which the product designated by the image is intended to be used—usually by women as a matter of course. One of her images shows a man, a woman, and a child on bicycles. It is difficult to determine what

product it stands for, though I would guess that it belongs to what we might think of as the secret life of women. The image could show a woman living a full active life, thanks to the product in question. Whatever its rhetorical aim, Eperjesi captions it this way: "My new boyfriend gets along fine with my daughter. I hope it's not just a show for now" (Figure 1). This is interesting because the woman is evidently a single mother, looking for a new relationship. The irony derives from the implication that while women in contemporary society have been greatly liberated, they remain in a disadvantageous position in relationship to men, as much so in Hungary as in America or western Europe. They are the ones left to do the housework, and to hope that men are not just out to exploit them sexually.

The irony goes well beyond the power of isotypes. The three figures could, after all, just represent a family. Interestingly, most of the women are in Western clothing, which has become fairly isotypical: I imagine that the isotype on the door of women's' toilets, shown with a short flaring skirt, would be recognized in airports everywhere in the world, even by women who wear burkhas. In any case, the titles/captions have to be translated, as the artist has done, from Hungarian into the language of the country in which they are to be shown—English, for example, in the catalog I saw.

English itself is not, for all it ubiquity, isotypical. Even if it were universally used, as Latin once was, there would be a distinction between pictures and words, which means that while isotypes may validate the picture theory of language, they do so in ways having nothing to do with natural languages as spoken or written. The semantics of sentences in a natural language differ from the semantic of a sentence used pictorially, as in a quotation. But even quotations have to be translated.

Tempting as it is to dwell on the artistic semantics of Eperjesi's pictures, my immediate purpose in using her work has to do with its extreme contemporaneity, and to the way it illustrates the pluralistic structure that has increasingly come to define the production of contemporary art, especially since the 1960s when artists first began to explore the possibility of using vernacular imagery. I have already touched on the question of their indeterminate aesthetic qualities, but I want ultimately to discuss this with reference to the problems that artistic pluralism has raised for aesthetic theory, and especially for Kantian aesthetic theory, which more or less dominated discussion until the decade when pluralism became a driving force in art. I understand "Kantian" to mean the view that artistic excellence is one with aesthetic excellence, which is understood to be a matter of pleasure and value distinct from the pleasure of sensual gratification, and internally connected with an ideal of disinterested contemplation. It concerns what the classical aestheticians designated "taste," and the main features of the theory are laid out in the section of the *Critique of Aesthetic Judgment* titled "The Analytic of Taste," which served as the great empowering text for aesthetic theory in modern times, especially, at least in America, in the critical thought and practice of Clement Greenberg.

Immanuel Kant's initial interest was in natural beauty, which it was easy enough to relate to the visual arts, understood—the decorative arts apart, which were appraised in terms of "free beauty"—either as accurate representations of natural beauty, or else as beautified representations of natural objects that in reality fell short of beauty. For what would be the point of making pictures of aesthetically repellent or deficient motifs? Greenberg had no such interest, as far as I can tell, and his chief focus was on abstract painting, which could be treated in terms of "free" beauty. This had the advantage for him that he could treat even representationalist art as if abstract, and hence

subject to formalist analysis. That is to say, he appreciated painting in terms of what we might call the aesthetics of medium, since painterly excellence is determined by what pertains to properties essential to that medium, namely, in Greenberg's view, relationships between flat forms, irrespective of what the forms may signify. Aesthetic value is what these forms convey to visual perception, in which all concepts are put out of play. Kant himself spoke of the pleasure taken in an object *independently of any concept*. For Greenberg, the critic's eye alone mattered, with whatever historical knowledge he or she may possess put for the time in brackets. The task of the artist was to eliminate from painting whatever did not address the critic's eye. The aim was the production of pure beauty for contemplative delectation.

The impact of Greenberg's modernist aesthetics on so-called art professionals in the United States was inestimable. What is astonishing is how pluralism should have emerged at all when the Greenberg-inspired professionals had all the power and authority in the artworld, at least so far as contemporary visual art was concerned. But for reasons that demand an historical explanation I am unable to furnish, the Kant-Greenberg aesthetic began to give way in the late 1950s, and became untenable just when Greenberg published his most considered statement in his 1960 essay, "Modernist Painting." The underground imperative, implied by Robert Rauschenberg in 1961, in the catalog for the exhibition "Sixteen Americans" at the Museum of Modern Art, was to erase the boundary between art and life. (Kant would have spoken instead of erasing the boundary between art and reality so far as both were beautiful.) In Rauschenberg's artistic practice, that meant disregarding the imperatives of medium altogether, giving himself license to make art out of anything—socks, bedclothes, Coke bottles, automobile tires, stuffed animals—"whatever." Purity of medium had become obsolete almost the moment it was declared.

Aesthetics was not rendered irrelevant when Modernism ended in the 1960s, but the kind of aesthetic quality presupposed by the Kant-Greenberg conception almost certainly disappeared, making room for what one may think of as a pluralism of aesthetic modalities. There is, for instance, a Rauschenbergian aesthetic that is almost the opposite of the kind of aesthetic excellence Kant and Greenberg took for granted. It is the aesthetics of grunge and mess, as exemplified in Rauschen-berg's *Bed*, where he slathered paint over the bedclothes and quilt in which the work materi-ally consists. He applied paint, as it was used by Abstract Expressionist painters, to an object of domestic use in connection with which cleanli-ness and neatness are ordinarily mandated—as in hospitals, army barracks, or bedrooms as main-tained by what Matisse once described as "coun-try aunts." Grunge is the aesthetic of disorder, flaunted by rebellious adolescents, and there is lit-tle question that a taste for it can be developed, and even exploited, by marketing torn blue-jeans, tacky tee-shirts, and athletic jerseys to young peo-ple concerned with identifying themselves through a style of affected slovenliness.

Kant's main ambition was to combat what one might call a pluralism of taste, by which I mean the common and somewhat cynical view that beauty is in the mind of the beholder and that differences in taste are relative to differences in beholders' minds. Kant rightly undertook to show that beauty is and ought to be univocal, the same for all. This was a kind of aesthetic colonialism—the view that so-called primitive societies were simply aestheti-cally retrograde in their taste—which was the the-oretical underpinning for the supremacist views of Western taste in what came to be Victorian anthropology. Greenberg was convinced that his critical practice was validated by Kant's *Critique of Aesthetic Judgment*, which he often proclaimed the greatest book ever written on art. In truth, the direction of validation might equally have gone in the opposite direction: the remarkable success of Greenberg's critical judgments could be taken to have conferred a measure of validity on Kant's otherwise exceedingly abstract formu-lations, which derived a surprising confirmation from a body of painting hardly thinkable in his own century.

Two of Kant's claims give particular support to Greenberg's practice, which came to typify aes-thetic attitudes that prevailed in the New York School. First, there was Kant's argument that judg-ments of beauty are nonconceptual, and second, that they are universally valid, that is, they are in no sense merely personal. Greenberg rarely spoke of beauty. His interest was in what he termed "quality" in art, which meant that his views could not easily be extended to the aesthetics of na-ture, which would of course have been of central interest to Kant. In 1961, Greenberg wrote that

"quality in art can be neither ascertained nor proved by logic or discourse. Experience alone rules in this area—and the experience, so to speak, of experience."[3] Greenberg's view here is essen-tially Hume's: that quality is what qualified critics agree is good.

Greenberg cherished Kant for explaining how it was possible to be right or wrong in questions of aesthetic merit. He did not think one had to know anything of the kind that art history concerns it-self with in order to be right or wrong about art. Indeed, he believed that modernism had opened up the possibility of appreciating "all sorts of ex-otic art that we didn't 100 years ago, whether an-cient Egyptian, Persian, Far Eastern, barbaric or primitive."[4] What makes art good has nothing to do with historical circumstance. He once boasted that though he knew little about African art, he would almost unfailingly be able to pick out the two or three best pieces in a group. They need not be best by the criteria by which Africans them-selves judged such matters, but probably that was because they were driven by beliefs that had little to do with aesthetic qualities as he himself under-stood them. There was little to say, in front of a piece of good art, beyond an admiring "Wow!" But that in no sense meant that one was merely venting feelings, as Greenberg's positivist contemporaries in philosophy would have said, having come to the view that aesthetic discourse is noncognitive. That it was, on the other hand, nonconceptual is under-written by Greenberg's way of closing his eyes and opening them only when the work to be judged was in front of him. What immediately flooded the eyes, as if a blinding flash, before the mind had time to bring anything to bear by way of ex-ternal associations, was what aesthetic experience rested upon.

Greenberg's "home-made aesthetics" was val-idated through his actual success in identifying artistic merit, particularly in championing Jackson Pollock, at a time when there was still resistance on the part of many critics to abstract art as such. This would have included conservative art critics on the major New York newspapers—John Cana-day at the *New York Times* and Emily Genauer at the *New York Herald-Tribune*. "They lack the right to pronounce on abstract art, because they have not taken the trouble to amass sufficient ex-perience of it. Without experience enough to be able to tell the good from the bad in abstract art, no one has the right to be heard on this subject."[5] However, European critics were also resistant, including David Sylvester, who came round to agreeing with Greenberg on Pollock's preeminence ("What could I have been using for eyes?"). Greenberg was the "high-brow New York intellectual" referred to in the 1949 *Life* magazine article that made Pollock famous. The massive endorsement of his assessment of Pollock had about it the quality of a scientific proof. It gave him immense authority as well as great power in the artworld.

Where Greenberg and, more excusably, Kant went wrong was in their failure to recognize that there is a nearly boundless set of aesthetic qualities, something that came to be recognized when philosophers of language touched on the vocabulary of aesthetics at about the same time that Greenberg dominated critical discourse in America. I have in mind particularly an *obiter dictum* of J. L. Austin's: "How much it is to be wished [that] we could forget for a while about the beautiful and get down instead to the dainty and the dumpy."[6] Austin stated this in describing his philosophical practice, in his important 1956 paper, "A Plea for Excuses," as *linguistic phenomenology*. Essentially this meant working out the rules that govern linguistic practice—"what we say when," to use the slogan of ordinary language philosophy—and some interesting discoveries were made by analysts such as Frank Sibley, who attempted to prove that aesthetic predicates were not "rule-governed." It would have been interesting to find out if this was the criterion for aesthetic predicates as a class—for "beautiful," "dainty," "dumpy," "grungy" for starters—and if not, what criteria, if any, there are.

Linguistic phenomenology did not survive Austin's death in 1960—the year Greenberg's "Modernist Painting" was published. But aesthetics took a backseat in the ensuing decade to the philosophy of art, beginning, I am obliged to say, with my 1964 paper, "The Art World," which was inspired by Pop and to a lesser degree by minimalism. With the work of Richard Wollheim, and especially of George Dickie, the central issue became the definition of art, and that has more or less been the project for the analytical philosophy of art ever since. What was interesting was how minor a role aesthetics played in that collective investigation—almost as minor as the role aesthetic qualities played in advanced artistic production and criticism in the increasingly

globalized art world, in the United States and England, but also in Germany, Italy, France, Spain, Japan, and finally everywhere that art was made, down to the present moment. The artists that mattered philosophically were preeminently Duchamp and Warhol, Eva Hesse, the minimalists, and the conceptualists, in whose work aesthetics was of negligible significance. And since the definition of art had to deal with the ready-mades and the Brillo Boxes, in which aesthetic qualities were marginal at best, there was a question of whether aesthetics had anything really to do with art at all. This was a revolutionary shift, given that from the outset it had seemed self-evident that aesthetic pleasure was what art was all about.

I was fairly bearish about the importance of aesthetics for art. In my main work in the philosophy of art, *The Transfiguration of the Commonplace*, I emerged with what I thought of as two necessary conditions for a philosophical definition of art—that art is about something and hence possesses meaning; and that an artwork embodies its meaning, which is what art criticism addresses. I condensed this by calling works of art *embodied meanings*. In my latest book, *The Abuse of Beauty*, I more or less acknowledged Austin's discovery that aesthetics is wider than had been traditionally recognized, and asked if there were not a *third* necessary condition, namely, that to be a work of art, something has to have *some* aesthetic quality—if not beauty, then, say, grunge. If not grunge, then something else. I ended the book skeptical that art need have any aesthetic quality at all. I did, however, make a distinction worth emphasizing between *internal* and *external* beauty, and, by generalization, between *internal* and *external* α, when α stands for any aesthetic predicate that may apply.

Here is what I meant by internal beauty. The beauty of an artwork is internal when it contributes to the work's meaning. I offered several examples of this from contemporary art, including Robert Motherwell's *Elegy for the Spanish Republic* and Maya Lin's *Vietnam Veterans Memorial* in Washington, DC. In a subsequent essay I thought a very successful example was the use that Jacques Louis David made of beauty in painting the body of Marat as beautiful in *Marat Assassiné*, which looks like a descent from the cross. The beauty of Marat was like the beauty of Jesus, and the meaning of the painting was that Jesus/Marat died for the viewer, who must acknowledge the meaning of this sacrifice by following their imperatives. If the beauty is not internal in a work of art it is, strictly speaking, meaningless, which means that it is, in Kant's terms, "free beauty" and mere decoration. In brief, my effort was to break away from the Kant-Greenberg aesthetic of form, and instead develop an aesthetics of meaning. It is at this point that one might recognize that the internal/external distinction applies throughout the vast domain of aesthetic qualities to which Austin and the ordinary language aestheticians drew attention in the early 1950s. Let us consider grunge once more. In certain artists—Dieter Roth is a good example—grunge had just the meaning that the work was deliberately anti-aesthetic, meaning anti-beautiful. When Roth first saw the 1962 exhibition of Jean Tinguely in Basel, it was a conversion experience for him. "Everything was so rusty and broken and made so much noise," he said afterward. "I was impressed half to death. It was simply a completely different world from my Constructivism, it was something like a paradise that I'd lost."[7] In a sense, Roth's quest from that moment on was the recreation of a lost infantile paradise, made up of detritus, noises, and noxious smells. He moved from a Kantian to an anti-Kantian aesthetic, as did Duchamp when he applied as his criterion for the ready-mades that they have the zero degree of aesthetic interest—meaning that they caused neither pleasure nor pain to the eye. They were nonaesthetic from the narrow perspective of "the analytic of taste"—but they were entirely aesthetic from the widened perspective that was to open up in the 1960s, when aesthetic blandness became an aesthetic quality, internal to the meaning of the ready-mades, and itself a matter of taste, the way grunge had been for Dieter Roth.

There is, one might say, an aesthetic of ready-made images, of the kind out of which Ágnes Eperjesi makes her art. It is not easy to describe this aesthetic, but it is easy enough to recognize, and it is probably due to the contingencies of design, itself due to the requirement of making the images easy to read and to understand everywhere in the world. There is, to take a kindred form, an easily recognized aesthetic in the coarsely drawn images of the simple advertisements that Andy Warhol used in his first exhibition in April 1961, in the store windows of Bonwit Teller's women's store on 57th Street. They were the kind of advertisements that were printed on pulp paper in cheap publications, advertising cures for acne, baldness,

shyness, and like vexations of the loveless. It is the aesthetics of "cheap black-and-white ads," explained by the need to make salient the blemishes that would cause viewers to buy the product advertised. But that aesthetic gets to be internal to the works Warhol made of them, as the aesthetics of package images gets to be internal to the work Ágnes Eperjesi based on them. Both bodies of work show their origins and draw meaning from them—though this is not the whole meaning of either artist's work.

The upshot of this excursion is that the answer to the question of whether aesthetics survives into the era of pluralism is yes and no. It is "no" if we are thinking of the Kant-Greenberg aesthetic of taste and disinterested contemplation. It is "yes" if we are thinking of the way in which different aesthetic qualities, many of them antithetical to taste as construed by Kant and Greenberg, are internal to the meaning of works of art construed as embodied meanings. In brief, the age of pluralism has opened our eyes to the plurality of aesthetic qualities far far wider than traditional aesthetics was able to countenance. I would say, moreover, that each of these aesthetic qualities is as objective as Kant supposed beauty was. Aesthetics is in the mind of the beholder, but only in the way in which sense qualities are in the mind of the beholder, just as Hume argued they are. "Beauty in things exists in the mind," he wrote, but this in no sense distinguishes it from anything else, inasmuch as "tastes and colours, and all other sensible qualities, lie not in bodies but in the senses."

The case is the same with beauty and deformity, virtue and vice. This doctrine, however takes off no more from the reality of the latter qualities than from that of the former ... Though colours were allowed to lie only in the eye, would dyers or painters ever be less regarded or esteemed? There is a sufficient uniformity in the senses and feelings of mankind to make all these qualities the objects of art and reasoning, and to have the greatest influence on life and manners.[8]

Having taken the matter to this point, however, I must make some amends to Kant, whose view on works of art takes a very different direction in a later section of the *Third Critique*—the brilliant Section 49, "Of the Faculties of the Mind that Constitute Genius," where he introduces his concept of *aesthetical ideas*. The Kant of Section 49 is not the Kant of Kantian aesthetics, which is based almost entirely on the "Analytic of Taste." I owe it to Kant—and to myself—to show how close my views are to his in this section of his book, the mere existence of which shows how Kant was registering the deep changes in Enlightenment culture that the age of Romanticism was developing from within. He certainly realized that taste alone was not the entire story when it comes to art: "We say of certain products of which we expect that they should at least in part appear as beautiful art, they are without *spirit*, although we find nothing to blame in them on the score of taste."[9] By spirit, he means "the animating principle of the mind"; and this principle, he goes on to say, "is no other than the faculty of presenting *aesthetical ideas*."[10] It is characteristic of Kant that he will seek a kind of faculty in order to account for a difference, when the difference, one might say, is really ontological. An "aesthetical idea" is really, as it turns out, an idea that has been given sensory embodiment—he uses "aesthetic" in the way it was used by Alexander Baumgarten, where it generally refers to what is given to sense. What is stunning is that he has stumbled onto something that is both given to sense *and* intellectual—where we grasp a *meaning* through the senses, rather than merely a color or a taste or a sound.

Kant gives as an example one of Frederick the Great's French poems, which we are likely to pass over, thinking that Kant is writing here as a sort of courtier, flattering the monarch, when in fact the poem, whatever its actual merits, does something that poetry often does—mean one thing by saying another. The king speaks in the poem of "finishing ones life and dying without regret" through the image of a beautiful summer day ending peacefully.[11] This is a quite commonplace use of poetry, and has nothing to do with genius, as Kant seems to feel it has. "The aesthetical idea" is merely one meaning given through another, as in irony or in metaphor. We realize that the poet, in this case Kant's sovereign, is talking about the course of a day as a way of talking about the course of a life. It is a beautiful thought, which need have nothing to do with the beauty of the words. The poetic example comes just after two examples from the visual arts: Jupiter is represented as an eagle grasping lightning in its claws, and Juno as a peacock (actually, as a male peacock, with glorious tail feathers). The power of Jupiter is made vivid through the fact that lightning is not something than can ordinarily be grasped—that a being capable of holding lightning must have *extraordinary power*. The image tells us more than "Jupiter is all powerful" alone tells. Presenting the idea of power aesthetically, that is, via an image, "gives occasion to the imagination to spread itself over a number of kindred representations that arouse more thought than can be expressed in a concept determined by words."

It is in regard to the expression of "aesthetical ideas" that Kant speaks of "spirit" and of "the imagination as free from the guidance of rules and yet as purposive in reference to the presentment of the given concept." This was much in the air in the 1790s, when he published his *Third Critique*. In 1792, for example, Francisco Goya composed a set of proposals for reforming the Royal Academy of San Fernando, of which he was at the time assistant director. His fundamental principle must have seemed entirely contrary to the concept of an academy, namely, that there are no rules in painting: *No hay reglas en la pintura*. It follows in particular from this that we cannot base the practice of painting on the canon of Greek sculpture, or on any set of paradigms. His text ended with a plea to allow the "genius" of the students to "develop in full freedom, without suppressing it, and to use means for turning them away from the tendency that shows them the way to this or that style of painting."[12] Historically, Goya's text marks a shift from the neoclassicism that defined his early work to the romanticism of his mature work, but it also expresses a deep truth about art. Strictly speaking, art involves a deep originality and is not something that can be taught.

Aesthetical ideas have nothing much to do with the aesthetics of taste, and they are what is missing entirely from Greenberg's agenda, who seldom spoke of meaning in his discussions of quality in art. In a sense, aesthetics, which has application to natural and physical beauty, has little to do with art, which in Goya's time was imitated in the academies in copying plaster casts of what were felt to be paradigms of classical beauty. There is very little of that in his masterpiece, *Los Caprichos*. However one characterizes them, these are hardly celebrations of ideal beauty. "Caprice" embodies the idea of spirit, but I draw attention to Goya's advertisement for this work, published in the *Diario de Madrid*, where he claimed for "la pintura" a right to criticize human error and vice, "although [such] criticism is usually taken to be exclusively the province of literature."[13] If "no hay reglas en la pintura," there is no rule against using painting for purposes of "holding a mirror up" to "the innumerable foibles and follies to be found in any civilized society." Greenberg would have rejected this as having nothing essential to do with plastic art at all. "Literary" was a term of critical dismissal in Greenberg's vocabulary, and in formalist vocabulary generally.

My own view is that the relationship of aesthetics to art was always external and contingent. The advent of pluralism has changed nothing in this respect. But the theory of art as embodied meanings—or the "aesthetical presentation of ideas"—makes it clear how aesthetic qualities can contribute to the meaning of the work that possesses them. This I am certain is what Hegel intuited when he declared, at the beginning of his lectures on aesthetics, why artistic beauty is "superior" to natural beauty. It is because natural beauty is meaningless—not, incidentally, something Kant could have accepted since for him natural beauty is a symbol of morality, and gives us the sense that the world is not indifferent to our hopes. Beauty, for him, has a kind of theodical meaning, as the philosopher Fred Rush has recently claimed in his writings. Painting natural beauty, as in the immense canvases of the Hudson River School, was an effort to capture this kind of meaning.

But its presence in those works is internal to their beauty as art. One can accept that without for a moment believing that nature itself is God's message in the medium of mountains and mighty waterfalls.

The 1961 works of Andy Warhol I spoke of convey aesthetical ideas—though they have only as aesthetic qualities what belongs to cheap advertisements through their cheapness. They convey the small vexations of the flesh, and the promise that for a mere few dollars our complexion will be clear, our hair grow luxuriant, and that love and happiness will finally come our way. What Ágnes Eperjesi discovered in the throw-away packaging in which consumer products are wrapped are portraits of the society in which those products are used. They are ready-made portraits or better, assisted ready-mades, as her melancholy wit makes clear. Beneath a picture of what looks like a bride in her veil—which may in fact be the negative of a photograph of a woman with a handkerchief—she writes: "Once in a while something gets into my eyes. Then I can let go of my feelings" (Figure 2). An innocent, even bland image of a woman with a hanky is turned into a psychological representation of stifled feelings and a comment on repression for the sake of appearance.

Once in a while something gets into my eyes.
Then I can let go of my feelings.

FIGURE 2.   Ágenes Eperjesi.

ARTHUR C. DANTO
Columbia University
New York, NY 10027, USA

INTERNET: acd1@columbia.edu

1. This essay was written at the invitation of Bernard Lafargue, of the Universite de Pau; and it appeared under the title, "Les Significations incarnées comme Idées esthétiques," in *Figures del'art* 10 (2006). I am grateful to Diarmuid Costello for having drawn my attention to Kant's concept of aesthetical ideas as conveying a philosophy of art quite different from the rather shallow one implied by the "aesthetics of taste." He felt that Kant's concept has something of the same logic as my own view of artworks as embodied meanings. Kant was annoyed when critics claimed that some of his ideas had been anticipated by earlier writers when, as he said, no one had the wit to see them before they appeared in his writings. I certainly did not have the wit to see Kant as having anticipated ideas of my mine, but no one can begrudge having Kant as a predecessor. My own feeling is that aesthetical ideas dropped out of aesthetic theory until they emerged in the guise of embodied meanings in a very different artworld than Kant could have imagined. If I am right, aesthetics really wandered in the wilderness until the anti-aesthetic bias of contemporary art set it on course once again. Robert J. Yanal's "Duchamp and Kant: Together Again," *Angelaki* 7 (2002): 161–166, was very much on the right track, had I been able to follow his thought, and the same may be true of Thierry de Duve's *Kant After Duchamp*, which makes a heroic effort to transform Kant's aesthetic into the kind of philosophy of art one can live with today. For obvious reasons, his is not a path I can follow.

2. Otto Neurath, "Visual Education: a New Language." *Survey Graphic* 26. (1937): 25; this essay can be found at: http://newdeal.feri.org/survey/37025.htm.

3. Clement Greenberg, *The Collected Essays and Criticism, Volume 4: Modernism with a Vengeance (1957-1969)*, ed. John O'Brian (University of Chicago Press, 1993), p. 118.

4. Greenberg, *The Collected essays and Criticis,* p. 309.

5. Greenberg, *The Collected essays and Criticis,* p. 119.

6. J. L. Austin, *Philosophical Papers,* ed. J. O. Urmson and G. J. Warnock (Oxford: Clarendon Press, 1961), p. 131.

7. Dirk Dobke and BernadetteWalther, *Roth Time: A Retrospective of Dieter Roth* (New York: Museum of Modern Art, 2003), p. 64.

8. David Hume, "The Skeptic," *Essays Moral and Political*, n. 2.

9. Immanuel Kant, *Critique of Judgment*, trans. J. H. Bernard (New York: Hafner Publishing Co., 1951), p. 156.

10. Kant, *Critique of Judgment*, p. 157.

11. This and the following two quotations are from Kant, *Critique of Judgment*, § 49.

12. Francisco Goya, "Address to the Royal Academy of San Fernando Regarding the Method of Teaching the Visual Arts," in Janis A. Tomlinson, *Goya in the Twilight of the Enlightenment* (Yale University Press, 1992).

13. Francisco Goya, *Diario de Madrid*.

NOËL CARROLL

Art and Globalization: Then and Now

I. ARE WE GLOBAL NOW/YET?

Though there can be little doubt that the world is becoming a much "smaller place" in terms of the amount of time it takes to move information, people (including business executives, tourists, workers, academics, and, unfortunately, slaves), as well as goods, jobs, investment capital, fashions, corporations, services, and so forth around it, there is a legitimate controversy about whether this condition deserves to be regarded as a new historical epoch in its own right, namely, the epoch of globalization. For, on the one hand, the interconnectedness, signaled by barbarisms like "globality," is, as critics point out, exaggerated by enthusiasts, since many parts of the world have not been integrated into the pertinent global networks. For example, much of sub-Saharan Africa has not been. Thus, the present epoch is not truly *global*, if that is supposed to imply that every part of the world is in lively commerce and contact on a relatively equal footing with every other part of the world. Rather, the current state of affairs is very uneven.

Furthermore, on the other hand, the historically minded observe that capitalism, perhaps the driving engine behind the globalizing tendencies of the present, has always had worldwide ambitions with respect to markets and resources. So, on this view, globalization is merely an advanced stage of capitalism—an admittedly both more extensive and intensive version of capitalism than what came before, but not something utterly new under the sun. Globalization, that is, is not a unique historical moment, though we in the West may be vain enough to regard our lifetimes as the dawning of a new age. After all, we have already done this at least twice before in recent memory—first with the Age of Aquarius and then with postmodernism.

Indeed, even before the emergence of capitalism, there was exchange between Europe and Asia, often through Istanbul, as well as between Rome and India, and, of course, among the Hellenistic empires that arose in the aftermath of Alexander the Great. The trade along the Silk Route was longstanding. Hence, globalization is not especially recent; it is, arguably, a process with a probably immemorial lineage. The Mongol and Muslim conquests put large parts of the world in contact. And, the age of Western colonial imperialism was, needless to say, a form of globalization, albeit lamentable in a great many respects. In the nineteenth and twentieth centuries, the introduction of new technologies of transportation—like the railroad, the automobile, and the airplane—and new technologies of communication—such as the telegraph, the photograph, the telephone, the movies, radio, TV, video, facsimile copying and transmission, and satellite delivery systems—must be regarded as ingredients in a *continuing* process that today has been further accelerated with the advent and dissemination of digital processing and the Internet. But, again, this looks more like a difference in degree from the past rather than a difference in kind.

In short, the phenomenon of globalization, understood as a new phase of world history, is dubious because it is incomplete—regions of the world lie outside the global village—and, in any event, the process has been ongoing for centuries.[1] Although skeptics would agree that today we are witnessing much *more* of the same, they would stress dramatically that what needs to be underscored theoretically is that it—however we label it—is essentially "the same."

In this article, which focuses on art in the global context, I want to suggest that something new is evolving—an integrated, interconnected, transnational artworld—while, at the same time, advancing that hypothesis in a way that avoids skeptical misgivings about globalization.

One area where the temptation to herald the coming of the age of globalization is especially enticing is that of art and culture. People are eating McDonald's cheeseburgers and drinking Coke everywhere. In Singapore there are more than forty Starbucks.[2] But the traffic is not simply one way. Even Americans are being exposed to an unprecedented range of cuisines. The difference between what was available in the supermarket when I was a youth in the 1950s and the variety of items on the shelves today from different ethnic food cultures around the world is stunning. Even small American cities are likely to have at least one Asian market, which is not only there for the émigré population, but is visited by the native-born as well.

Nor is the exchange merely between American mass culture and the rest. We have before us hybrid phenomena as diverse as "Thai boxing by Moroccan girls in Amsterdam, Asian rap in London, Irish bagels, Chinese tacos and Mardi Gras Indians in the United States, and Mexican school girls dressed in Greek togas dancing in the style of Isidore Duncan."[3]

Of course, the factor that probably accounts for the virtually irresistible impression that many of us have of a new epoch of globalization is, in a word, *media*. Communication across great distances has never been faster, nor has there ever been so much of it. Business culture need never sleep. Financial transactions and deals 24/7 are becoming the order of the day (and night). What is true of legal commerce is also true of international crime and terrorism. It is the quantum leap in our communicative resources, I believe, in addition to its consequences for almost every other dimension of culture, that convinces us that a qualitatively different level of globalization is upon us. The idea of "one world" just feels right.

As in every other arena of culture, the arts and entertainments are the beneficiaries of the communications-media explosion. American movies make a large percentage of their profits overseas. Often, a film, or even a TV series,

that fails stateside is able to recoup its losses internationally. At a visit in the fall of 2005 to a cinéplex in Porto, all the films save one were American. Moreover, the dissemination of film is not only by way of traditional movie screens. Cassettes and DVDs have extended the lives of movies behind their first run, and the devices that play these media are everywhere globally. Boot-legged video cassettes of *Jurassic Park* (Steven Spielberg, 1993) were available in subway stations in Moscow the day before the film was released in the United States.

However, the flow of mass art is not just one way. Many Americans, as well as audiences in other nations, have developed a taste for Japanese *animé* and martial arts films from Hong Kong. Hong Kong cinema has influenced the style of Hollywood movies, ranging from the works of Quentin Tarantino to the Wachowski brothers. If certain elements of American crime films have been appropriated by Hong Kong directors, ninja choreography is at home in Los Angeles, not only in movies but also in the dance moves on MTV. Increasingly, we are seeing the emergence of hybrid, mass-motion-picture art forms.

The Western taste for different national cinemas is also illustrated by the existence of the film festival in the Italian city of Udine, which advertises itself as "the world's largest showcase of popular East Asian cinema."[4] Reciprocating attention, Japan made the film *The Last Samurai* (Edward Zwick, 2003), a Tom Cruise vehicle of limited success in America, the blockbuster it was intended to be.

Indian films are screened in Africa, England, and even the United States, often catering to diaspora audiences, while also attracting a substantial non-Indian clientele as well; outside Philadelphia, in the suburb of Cherry Hill as well as in the Regal Barn Plaza in Doylestown, there are theaters that specialize in Bollywood cinema.[5] Indian film is becoming an industrial force to reckon with worldwide. And perhaps this cinema, too, is starting to have an impact on Western film producers; think of the musical numbers in Tim Burton's 2005 *Charlie and the Chocolate Factory*. Would they have even been there except for the example of Bollywood? And a Bollywood sensibility is also manifest in the British film *Elizabeth* (1998), directed as it was by the Bombay director Shekhar Kapur.

So far I have been alluding to *mass* movie culture. But the more artistically ambitious, putatively alternative, so-called independent film movement is also acquiring a global reach. One important factor in this process is the proliferation of film festivals. At present, according to Kenneth Turan, "there is barely a day where some film festival is not being celebrated in some exotic city somewhere in the world."[6] Though some of these festivals are devoted to popular cinema, more frequently they provide venues where foreign-language and independent filmmakers can present work that challenges the routine product of the mass media that holds most of the movie screens in the world captive.[7] At their best, they offer a "cosmopolitan," in Kwame Anthony Appiah's sense, countercinema.[8] That is, they bring sophisticated work from everywhere to serious audiences in search of something different.

Moreover, these film festivals are connected to tourism, another salient aspect of our global moment. Especially due to the vast expansion of the possibilities of air transportation, not only can art and artists travel almost anywhere in the urban world with ease; so can audiences. And one thing that attracts them to a locale is a film festival.

Undoubtedly, these festivals have contributed to a shift in sophisticated film taste. Whereas the cinéphile of the 1960s and early 1970s was preoccupied with American film and what came to be called the Art Cinema (which was mostly European), since the 1980s, connoisseurs, such as the late Serge Daney and Jonathan Rosenbaum, have been on the lookout for new developments in emerging national cinemas such as Iran, Taiwan, and, presently, South Korea.[9] In short, taste in film, both high and low, has never been so cosmopolitan.

What is true of film, also appears to have at least some relevance to TV. In Memphis, they watch *American Idol*; in Mumbai, they watch *Indian Idol*. Mexican telenovelas are popular in Ghana, while students from KwaZulu-Natal watch the American soap opera *Days of Our Lives* (Allan Chase, Ted Corday, and Irna Phillips, 1965–).[10] *Dallas* (David Jacobs, 1978–2001), as of this writing, is still running in Capetown.

Often, national television industries use American product to start up their operation, filling out their programming schedule with Hollywood until there is enough indigenous product to do the job. When the national industry develops, however, it still often uses American formats—such as the dramatic series—which results in the flow-

ering of a range of hybrid forms. Furthermore, American television has been hospitable to Japanese shows, like *Pokemon* (Masamitsu Hidaka and Kunihiko Yuyama, 1997–2002), *Yu-Gi-Oh* (Kazuki Takahashi, 1998–), and the *Hi-Hi-Puffy Ami Yumi Show* (Sam Register, 2004), and the influence of Japanese animation can be seen on the cartoon channels stateside.[11] The Japanese product is so familiar to Americans that a Pokemon figure can be satirized in the toon *Drawn Together* (Dave Jeser and Matthew Silverstein, 2004–) on the cable channel Comedy Central. And an American production company has recently launched an indigenous anime program.

It seems very appropriate that the impression of a global art market should be encouraged by film and TV, since these technologies belong to the category of communicative media that are making the world "a smaller place." Due to their mechanical and electronic reproducibility, they are by their very nature able to defy distance. In that sense, they are, at least potentially, global media. Moreover, the fact that the basic symbols in these media are pictures—the sort of symbols that require no special, prior training in order to be recognized—means that they have a level of accessibility unmatched by competing print media. Thus, it should come as no surprise that these media span the world and are readily able to penetrate cultural boundaries.

Of course, other media that have this capacity for electronic border crossing are aural recording and broadcast radio. By means of transistor radios, cassette players, Walkmans, CDs, iPods, and the Internet, music from everywhere can be heard anywhere. Indeed, there are more different audio technologies today that facilitate encounters with more world music than ever before, and this market is catered to by transnational music industries.[12] Rap music has been embraced and produced by Muslim youths in Paris and, in fact, this *banlieue* rap was said to have stoked the Arab insurgency throughout France in 2005.[13] Popular Indian music is garnering a following across the globe because of its connection to Bollywood cinema. The South Korean singer Rain (Ji-Hong Jung), who specializes in K-pop music, is about to attempt to crack the American market with a tour; he is described as a combination of Usher, Justin Timberlake, and Michael Jackson, but his performance integrates dancing inflected by martial-arts movements from his own culture, yielding yet another example of the sort transnational hybridization that at times seems omnipresent.[14]

Because the mass communications media are so integral to the experience of the transnational urban world—because they appear to be everywhere—the impression that the arts have gone utterly global is hard to resist. Some discern a tendency toward homogenization that they lament, while others find it liberating or, at least, promising. However, there are reasons to be cautious here. Motion pictures, for example, from diverse lands, including the United States, do manage to make their way around the world. However, they do not do so with equal saturation. The traffic in movies and TV tends to be regional rather than truly global. That is, one does not find movies from everywhere on the same marquee.

The reason for this is obvious, since movies and TV are not only moving pictures, but (since the third decade of the twentieth century) they are also talking pictures. Thus, their distribution tends to be partitioned into geolinguistic regions, dominated by players suited to the pertinent cultures. Mexico and Brazil, for example, are the centers of audiovisual mass culture for Latin America; Hong Kong and Taiwan for much of Chinese-speaking Asia, though mainland China is also attempting to play in that market; Egypt is the center for the Arab world; India for the subcontinent and for its far flung diasporas from Africa to America.[15] In sub-Saharan Africa, Nigeria is emerging as an important regional producer for audiovisual media targeted to equatorial interests. Suitably enough, it is being called Nollywood.[16]

Admittedly, to some it has seemed that American productions have dominated the airways of the emerging television industries of what was once called the third world. However, this typically only occurs in the earlier stages of the evolution of these industries. Once indigenous product becomes available, the ratio changes. It is true that there are a number of transnational media giants that bestride the world like colossi, but they favor reliance on local production. The American model of television as an entertainment predicated on attracting potential consumers to a relentless barrage of advertisements may be pervasive throughout the world of television; but Hollywood does not dominate the moving picture world.[17] In India, for example, the local motion picture industry still holds sway.

So, on the one hand, art—even mass art—is not a single, unified global phenomenon. It is transnational, but regional rather than global, if by 'global' we mean to refer to something homogenous in every corner of the world. Furthermore, on the other hand, though we may think of ourselves as immersed in a new era of artistic hybridization, a moment's thought reveals that the arts—including those labeled "high" arts—have perennially been susceptible to cross-cultural fertilization. Consider, briefly, the case of theatrical dance, for example.[18]

Starting on the Western side of the ledger, much early modern dance looked to the choreography of other cultures as a way to liberate and to distinguish itself from the dominant tradition of ballet. The dances of other cultures, in short, were appropriated as a marker of opposition to what was perceived to be the ruling form of Western dance. Loïe Fuller, Isadora Duncan, and Ruth St. Denis all attended the Paris Exhibition of 1900 and saw, particularly in the colonial pavilions, a wide range of dances from African, Near Eastern, and Asian cultures. This influenced all three artists, though the evidence is perhaps most striking in the work of St. Denis, who staged her own "orientalized" versions of Asia myths in pieces like *Radha*. Denis' orientalism was then further inspired by the performances of Sada Yacco's Japanese dances, which she saw in Coney Island in New York.[19]

Fuller's art nouveau style also owed much to the passion for Japonisme that was sweeping Europe at the time, while Mary Wigman's *Witch Dance* uses music reminiscent of the *Noh* ensemble and exploits the frozen, stylized (*mie*) pose of Kabuki.[20] In *Night Journey*, Martha Graham helped herself to what she called "Bali turns" and "Javanese foot movements." Not only is Merce Cunningham's choreography based on ideas from Zen—which Cunningham learned from John Cage—but his *Sixteen Dances for Soloist and Company of Three* derives from theories about the nine permanent emotions found in classical Indian aesthetics. In the 1970s, Deborah Hay employed Tai Chi Chuan in the construction of her circle dances and Steve Paxton was inspired by Aikido when he invented Contact Improvisation.

Perhaps what is most ironic about the avant-garde's reliance on choreographic hybridization as a means to separate itself from the ballet is that the ballet also has a long history of turning to other cultures for ideas. This is true not only of avant-garde ballets, including the orientalism of Diaghilev's productions of *Scheherazade* and *Le Dieu Bleu*, as well as the Africanisms of the

Ballet Suedoi's *La Creation du Monde*; it is also evident throughout the history of ballet. Russian classical ballet frequently incorporated the dances of the Other, often before royalty, as if to celebrate the vast dominion of the czarist empire. Recall the character dances by Coffee (putatively Arabian dancing) and Tea (Chinese dancing) in *The Nutcracker*, which, among other things, it is reasonable to speculate, expressed Russia's desire to dominate central Asia and the Far East.

Petipa's 1877 ballet *La Bayadere*, of course, is ostensibly based on an Indian temple dancer, while in the eighteenth century, *Les indes Galantes* has sections set in Turkey, Peru, Persia, and North America; it is what Lincoln Kirstein calls a *ballet geographique*, indulging, as it does, in orientalism, the sauvagerie of the New World, and Chinoiserie. Indeed, Noverre's ballet *Fetes Chinosises* is an entire spectacle comprised of non-European dance theater and ceremonial forms.[21] As early as 1605, there are reports of African imagery—specifically Ethiopian nymphs—in the ballet *The Masque of Blackness*.

My point in citing all these examples is not to suggest that these Western appropriations of non-Western dance have been done with genuine intercultural understanding. My point is simply that hybridity is not something new. The Western dance tradition has, to a certain extent, been hybrid almost from the get-go.

This is not only the case with the Western tradition. In the first two decades of the twentieth century, Western ballet and modern dance both made significant inroads into East Asia. White Russians, such as the Bolshoi dancer George Gontcharov, fled Russia after the revolution and founded dance schools in China and Japan. Similarly, Isadora Duncan and Denishawn toured the Far East and enlisted followers to the modern dance movement. In the 1920s and 1930s, Japanese dancers went to Germany to study expressionist dance, a heritage that helped shape the Japanese modern dance movement of Butoh.

Maoist China took on the tradition of the Russian ballet wholesale from its Soviet patrons and, by means of it, produced their own version of socialist realism. At present, a Chinese version of *Swan Lake* is on tour. Though the basic idea derives from the Western balletic tradition, by way of the choreographer Zhao Ming, the production is noteworthy for its unabashed incorporation of the acrobatics of the tradition of Chinese opera. In one

breathtaking moment, in a gesture of exquisite hybridization, for example, the dancer Wu Zhengdan essays an arabesque on pointe on the head of her husband Wei Baohua.[22]

In brief, interestingly enough, ballet and modern dance were becoming entrenched in Asia at exactly the same time as they were establishing themselves in North America, with both continents adapting these traditions in their own hybridizing ways.

Thus, as this very hurried review of dance history should indicate, the thought that there is something special about the art of our own times in terms of hybridization is hardly credible. Throughout the history of art we find that where there is cultural contact between different traditions, poaching and outright assimilation has been as likely as not.

III.   TRANSNATIONAL INSTITUTIONS

We seem between a rock and a hard place. On the one hand, we want to say that it is undeniable that we have entered a new era of globalization both in general and with respect to art. But, on the other hand, with just a little pressure, the notion of globalization in both respects appears to come apart. For, not every nation in the world is an equal partner in this global dance and even those parts that are involved in transnational enterprises are often more regionally engaged than globally. The world is not as pervasively connected as is often imagined. Moreover, the tendency toward cultural and artistic exchange, influence, and even borrowings that result in hybridization is not something recently arrived with the Internet. It has been happening at varying speeds whenever civilizations meet. So, must we give up the idea that something has changed?

I do not think so. Something has changed, but the concept of globalization, construed as a Hegelian *zeitgeist*, is not a fruitful way to articulate the change. Rather than thinking of the present in terms of a totality, governed by an animating essence that is refracted in its every dimension, we are better advised to think on a smaller gauge. First, let us think in terms of transnational relations, rather than global relations, where it is understood that there are many different, often very unlike, kinds of transnational relations, and that these do not add up to a cohesive global network playing the same tune in different registers. Un-doubtedly, one reason we speak of globalization has to do with the vast multiplication of actors and sites of exchange than heretofore.[23] And there are certainly more transnational activities going on than ever before, if only because there are more nations, more people, and more ways to connect them. But there is no reason to suppose that these fit into a neat package that can be labeled infor-matively with a summary adage like the Hegelian catchphrase, "In the ancient world, one is free." We cannot say, for example, that "today, all are connected in some ineluctably global way." Things are more fragmentary than that.

Nevertheless, there may be something unprece-dented about some of the fragments—some of the parts—that coexist in the present transnational moment. So rather than attempt to say something about the global condition as a whole, we may try to say something about some of the *forms* taken by the transnational relations that are starting to evolve in new directions.[24] That is, what is called globalization may begin to be parsed in terms of the increase of the available modes of organization for the transnational construction of new versions of the kinds of cultural structures that previously discharged their social functions more locally. Or, in other words, the question is better posed as: Are any novel transnational institutions or prac-tices coming into being? My own sense is that the answer to this question is *yes*. Specifically, I think that an integrated, transnational institution of art is assembling itself before our very eyes.[25]

IV.   A TRANSNATIONAL ARTWORLD?

Who could possibly be in a position to pronounce authoritatively upon the direction of art world-wide today? Although it is undoubtedly absurdly overreaching, given the sheer amount of work at issue, to pretend to be able to say anything in-formative about the present course of art inter-nationally, perhaps I can state my claims some-what less ridiculously by framing them as tentative hypotheses—provisional and certainly fallible hy-potheses. I do not believe that I am on top of nearly enough data to be certain of my conjectures; I am not sure who is. But insofar as we need conjectures to orient future research, if only critically, let me, in the hope of advancing the discussion, speculate on my suspicion that there is currently evolving

an integrated transnational institution of art or, at least, an interlocking set of transnational institu-tions.

One objection to the existence of something we might call a global institution of art is that not ev-eryone we are inclined to call an artist belongs to it. In Bali, there are traditional artists engaged in reproducing the statues of gods and goddesses that populate the many Hindu temples on the island. Because the native clay from the local riverbed is soft, these statues need to be replaced every thirty or forty years; they deteriorate so quickly. There is a whole cottage industry devoted to this project. But no one supposes that these artists belong to the same artworld as does Jeff Koons, even though they, too, are sculptors.

They are artists, but they are not part of the in-ternational artworld that stages biennales relent-lessly and that stocks those burgeoning museums of contemporary art that are sprouting up with abandon everywhere in the urbanized world. Nor are the Balinese artists who continue to make tra-ditional folk art for sale to tourists participants in the Artworld International.

Nevertheless, this objection to the notion of global art does not really touch my hypothesis that there is aborning an international institution of art. For, I wish to maintain no more than that this in-stitution is transnational and not that it is global, where that is assumed to entail that every artist be-longs to it. Not everyone we are disposed to label an artist belongs to this transnational institution. Indeed, not everyone who is an artist, properly so-called, is probably even admissible in principle to this transnational institution.

So the notion of a transnational institution of art dodges the first objection that is generally lev-eled at global hypotheses. How does it fare against the second type of objection—namely, that the type of transnational interaction we see nowa-days has been around for at least centuries, if not longer. My response is that what we are witness-ing now differs from the past insofar as what we see emerging is something like a single, integrated, cosmopolitan institution of art, organized transna-tionally in such a way that the participants, from wherever they hail, share converging or overlap-ping traditions and practices at the same time that they exhibit and distribute their art in interna-tionally coordinated venues. And this, I submit, is something worth considering as substantially unprecedented.

To appreciate what is new about the emerging international institution of art, we need to contrast briefly the modalities of transnational art exchanges in the past and those of the present—that is, we need to think about art on the international stage then and now.

Artworks have perennially crossed cultural and ethnic boundaries, if not as barter, then as plunder. In the 1460s and 1470s—that is to say, in the earliest stages of capitalism—cultural exchange between the East and the West abounded.[26] Artists such as Gentile Bellini and Costanzo da Ferrara were loaned by Venice and Naples, respectively, to Mehmet II after his conquest of Constantinople. Both subsequently returned to the West, bringing with them imagery and iconography that they encountered in the Near East.[27] The motifs imported by artists like these appeared frequently in European artworks. For instance, the carpet pictured in Hans Holbein's *The Ambassadors* of 1533 is of Ottoman provenance.[28] However, the specific artists who influenced Bellini and Costanzo did not thereby become part of the Western lineage; they were not, for example, cited by the likes of Vasari.

China was involved in a lively trade in porcelain long before Europe became interested in these artworks. Between 800 and 1450, Chinese porcelain was a valuable export item in markets as far flung as Japan, Southeast Asia, the Middle East, and Egypt. Indeed, Chinese porcelain is first thought to have arrived in Europe via North Africa. By the seventeenth century, these artifacts were highly prized in Europe as well, where the demand eventually resulted in the incorporation of Western themes.[29]

The trade in Asian luxury items, encompassing metalwork, furniture, and textiles, including textiles from India—useful art, but *art* nonetheless—became increasingly heavy from the seventeenth century onward. With the rise of the bourgeoisie and the coincident refinement of European taste, Asian wares were often the objects of their aesthetic gratification. Likewise, paintings and sculptures traveled Westward. What is noteworthy about this exchange from our contemporary perspective is that while Europeans appreciated these artifacts and collected them, neither the works nor the masters who produced them were incorporated into European art narratives or artistic canons. The narratives and canons remained stubbornly parochial.

A European might collect Chinese porcelain or drawings, or, for that matter, later, pre-Colombian art, but these collectibles and the artists who created them did not enter the "big story" of art as it was told in the West. That narrative and that canon remained resolutely local, as did the narratives and canons of the various lineages of non-Western art. Non-Western art could enter the story of art as an outside or external influence, but no non-Western artist was treated as a full-fledged citizen of the Western artworld and, to a large extent, vice versa. A parallel phenomenon is also observable in music, where composers such as Mozart adapted Turkish themes without any Turkish composers thereby figuring internally in the Western lineage. The various traditions, though open to outside influence, were each essentially local or regional. There were multiple artistic histories that, though sometimes tangent, were nevertheless discrete.

As is well known, the Japanese colored woodcuts of the Ukiyo-e School of the seventeenth through nineteenth centuries had a visible influence on Seurat, Manet, Van Gogh, Lautrec, and Whistler, but even though that influence is acknowledged in Western art histories, the masters of the Ukiyo-e School are not included in the same genealogy as Western artists. Though having a causal impact on that tradition, they were conceived to be as external to it.

Likewise, the influence of African tribal art on Picasso's invention of Cubism is widely acknowledged. But it is an outside influence on developments internal to the Western artworld; no African traditions were thereby regarded as part and parcel of the story of art, or modernism, as told from the perspective of the West or the Western insider. African art is not portrayed as one of the art-historical tributaries flowing into modern art. No African artist has a place in the story equivalent to that of Manet.

That is, the historians of the Western tradition do not, for example, track modernism as following from African art in the way in which we trace Cubism as evolving from Cézanne. Though Picasso was influenced by African art, there is no African artist or even African art formation in his lineage in the way that Cézanne is. Rather, we presume that we are dealing with at least two distinct artworlds here.

Similarly, Asian aesthetics figures in the narratives that we tell of Ezra Pound and poetic modernism and in our accounts of Bertolt Brecht and the evolution of theatrical alienation effects. But we think of these Asian influences as opportunities certain Western artists exploited in order to make certain moves within the Western art world. The relevant aesthetic strategies were appropriated in order to short-circuit various traditional Western approaches. They could function as counterstrategies. However, as counterstrategies, they do not have standing in their own right, on the basis of their own artistic identity, in the Western art narratives in which they appear.

Thus, this sort of artistic exchange, though transnational, is not part and parcel of a *unified* artworld, but occurs across different artworld institutions, such as *Japanese* theater and *European* theater. Alien aesthetic discourses, as dragooned by Westerners, were used to mark opposition to prevailing norms in the indigenous northern Atlantic practice. Alternative aesthetics were, in such cases, manipulated rather than integrated; they are deployed for tactical advantages rather than being contributions to a mutually reciprocal conversation.

However, it does now seem to be the case that the various national and regional centers of serious or ambitious fine art are beginning to be fashioned into a single world—a unified, transnational institution of art. Some evidence for this is the proliferation of biennales, of which, on a conservative estimate, there are more than fifty; it is said that there is now a biennale somewhere on the average of every two weeks.[30] Like film festivals, these high-art extravaganzas are partly predicated on attracting international tourism, but they also function to assemble a large number of artists from different geographical regions and cultural backgrounds and thus to showcase, especially for curators, a wide range of work that can, in turn, feed into the ever-expanding museum and gallery systems worldwide. Artists such as Shirin Neshat and William Kentridge, for example, came to prominence through this network.

Moreover, this institutional network has also constituted a readjustment in the balance of power in the artworld. As James Meyer notes:

Within the new dispensation, it's the curators who travel the most, who see the greatest range of work, who have the broadest sense of practice; the curators whose activity (exhibition) is closest to the practice and has the greatest impact on it. Many critics today wonder why criticism is so enervated ... [T]he vitality of critical debate appears to have shifted, at least for now, from discourse to curation. [I]t's the curator who is most informed, who is most able to articulate what's interesting and important in art practice.[31]

Given the enhanced possibilities of communication and transportation, these curators provide a constant channel of information that flows from large-scale exhibitions, to museums and galleries, and then back again. The faxes, e-mails, and telephone lines are always vibrating with art news and art deals. Video cassettes and DVDs of work are constantly orbiting the planet. There is without a doubt at present an interconnected, international art circuitry regulated by curators bidding nomadic artists hither and yon in search of recognition and frequent-flyer miles.

Furthermore, this is not just a distribution network. It has developed something like its own preferred idioms. A common reaction that many have during a visit to quite a few biennales and other large-scale transnational exhibitions is: Where is the painting and the sculpture? These shows tend to be dominated by video, film, photography, installation pieces (often multimedia in nature), conceptual art, and performance art (often recorded by means of some moving picture medium).[32]

For example, at the Fifty-First Venice Biennale, not one of the Chinese artists represented exhibited a painting. Of the artists from the People's Republic of China, Jun Yang showed a video installation titled *Hero—This is We*, Chen Chieh-Jen offered a slow-motion film called *Factory*, Xu Zhen projected DVD segments on the oil tanks in the Arsenale, LiuWei had an installation piece comprised of a battery of flashing lights triggered by motion detectors, Wang Qiheng presented a DVD of himself discussing *fengshui*, Sun Yuan and Peng Yu offered a performance piece called *Farmer Du Wenda's Flying Saucer* that they attempted to launch unsuccessfully, and Yung-Ho Chang created a massive environment.

Likewise, the Taiwanese eschewed traditional painting and sculpture: Kuang-Yu Tsui and I-Chen Kuo served up videos, Chung-Li Kao presented a looped animation cum projector, and Hsin-I Eva Lin proffered an interactive Internet installation. Hong Kong's anothermountainman and Chan Yuk-keung both presented installation pieces, while Singapore's Lim Tzay Chuan unveiled a piece of conceptual art—a bathroom designed to show that art is useful.[33]

The South Korean artist Yeondoo Jung's piece was *Bewitched*, a slide projection named after the 1960s TV show in which he asked people to imagine their future, which he then staged and photographed.[34]

Marcia Vetrocq's overall impression of the recent Venice Biennale was that "[f]rom full-room installations to individual monitors, video emerges as a dominant medium in both sections of the international show."[35]

Similar observations may be made of other influential scopic exhibitions. Documenta 10 was dominated by photography and Documenta 11 by photo and video projections and large-scale installations. It is noteworthy that in a recent review of the Istanbul Biennial, only one drawing and one sculpture are mentioned; everything else discussed is an example of installation art, photography, video, and so forth.[36] Moreover, some of the artists who have been significant beneficiaries of the biennale network are moving image makers. William Kentridge is a draftsman, but he is most respected for what he calls his "Drawing for Projection," including *Johannesburg, 2nd Greatest City After Paris*, and *Sobriety, Obesity & Growing Old*. Shirin Neshat's reputation rests on films, such as *Rapture*, and video installations such as *Fervor*.

Perhaps backhanded confirmation of the tendency in the emerging artworld that painting is being ousted from its pride of place is a recent biennale in Prague. Prague is a city with not one but two biennales; in order to distinguish it from other biennales, both worldwide and in the neighborhood, the co-founder of the second biennale, Giancarlo Politi, declared that it would be devoted primarily to painting because, he argued, painting is a critically undervalued medium to whose powers of visual gratification attention must again be paid.[37]

Supposing that in the emerging transnational artworld painting and sculpture are losing ground—perhaps not absolutely but more probably proportionately—to video, film, photography, computer art, conceptual art, performance art, and installation art, it is hard to resist the observation that many of these art forms have been constructed on the basis of some of the very technologies that are transforming the wide world into a small world. Obviously, film, video, and photography are the sort of mechanically and electronically reproducible media that make it possible for the same artwork to be everywhere at once. Though an artist like Chung-Li Kao may choose to screen his film *Anti.mei.ology 002* in one place at a time, it could be shown at multiple sites simultaneously.

As already suggested, it is, to an important degree, this very possibility of "overcoming" space—by means of these very sorts of media—that instills in many the conviction that globalization is upon us. Thus, the popularity of photography, film, video, and, increasingly, computer, digital, and Internet art is itself *emblematic* of the emerging cosmopolitan artworld insofar as these media are themselves cosmopolitan.[38] As one passes through the aisles of many large-scale international exhibitions with the walls covered with digital photographs and with monitors flickering down the corridor, one has the feeling that one is standing right in the middle of the so-called wired world. Sometimes, the images, like the photographs of empty airport lounges by Martha Rosler and of tarmacs by Andreas Gursky, document the quotidian experience of the citizens of this new republic of art.[39] But, in addition, the preferred idiomatic media of this emerging institution also bear the expressive traces of its world-spanning ambitions.

Though in an admittedly different way, conceptual art, another favorite contemporary art form—like video and photography—also defies space, since it is frequently not tethered to a particular place inasmuch as a great deal of conceptual art is designed with the intention that seeing it *in situ* is not always necessary. Often, you can get the point of a conceptual artwork by simply reading a description or seeing a picture of it. Where such conceptual art is essentially a matter of an idea, it is lighter than air and, like a joke, can move anywhere faster than the speed of sound.

Performance artworks and installation artworks, of course, are rooted to specific locations; however, much of the performance art at large-scale international exhibitions is there by the grace of video, while, at the same time, a lot of installation art is multimedia, incorporating video, photography, audio recording, and even computer technology.[40] These devices are deployed to represent and to probe the modern world. But they also manage indirectly—*in virtue of what they are*—to express something of its phenomenological pulse: its informational density and seemingly omnipresent communicative connectedness.

Needless to say, I do not mean to suggest by any means that painting and sculpture have vanished from the scene. My point is only that they are not the privileged art forms of the moment in the emerging transnational institution. Moreover, several of the art forms that would appear to maintain that position—like video and photography—are media that, in addition to whatever else they symbolize, embody the message of globalization as, what Frederic Jameson calls, "the sense of an immense enlargement of communication."[41]

The base of the emerging transnational institution of art includes its network of coordinated venues, its "always-on-the-go" curatorial-mangerial class, and its preferred productive idioms. But it is also held together by means of a number of shared discourses, both artistic and critical. Artists, presenters, critics, and just plain art devotées share a number of conceptual frameworks and hermeneutical strategies that facilitate understanding transnationally.

That is, the artist can presume that with respect to certain types of work, featuring certain types of iconography, the audience will be prepared to explore the work in light of various recurring concerns, preoccupations, or ideas. Often, these hermeneutical posits are articles of progressive politics, such as postcolonialism, feminism, gay liberation, globalization and global inequality, the suppression of free expression and other human rights, identity politics, and the politics of representation, as well as a generic anti-establishmentarianism. A recent exhibition at the Museum of Modern Art's (MOMA) P.S. 1 Contemporary Art Center in New York City, for example, takes day labor around the world as its theme and interrogates it from a generally radical perspective.[42] The critic and the informed audience member entering the gallery space can try out these hermeneutical keys to attempt to unlock the often obscure secrets of a rebus-like installation piece until she or he finds one that works, one that, in other words, yields a satisfying interpretation.

Perhaps needless to say, the dissemination of these concerns did not appear magically. On the one hand, the recurring political concerns are related to the fact that in urban centers around the world artists find themselves in many of the same contexts with their attendant problematics—including capitalism in particular and modernization in general.[43] Moreover, on the other

hand, these themes have been circulated widely through critical discourse and they have even been showcased by means of international artworld events like the "platforms"—the interdisciplinary lectures and conferences—that comprised Okui Enwezor's Documenta 11.

Of course, this process also involves assumptions on the part of the audience about what the artist might be up to. Much new art is involved in what is called institutional critique—critiques of the institution of the museum, of the system of biennales, of the commodification of art, and of the artworld in general.[44] Apprized of such motifs, gallery-goers attempt to use the critique-of-the-institution framework in order to organize their thinking about the often mysterious avant-garde object before them. Because the audience and the artist share some mutual assumptions about each other's expectations regarding the available range of possible subject matter, they are able to have a conversation. Indeed, since these assumptions have been broadcast so widely internationally, it is readily possible—without much effort—to have transnational "conversations" between artistic senders and receivers who speak different native languages.

Moreover, the artists, presenters, and viewers are not only aware of a number of recurring themes or frameworks; they also share knowledge of a battery of formal devices for advancing those themes, including radical juxtaposition, de-familiarization, and the de-contextualization of objects and images from their customary milieus. Though not a syntax and much looser than a grammar, these formal ways of articulating content are, nevertheless, sense-making strategies. The artist knows them and knows that the audience knows them, and so the artist uses them in the anticipation that the audience will recognize them and apply them to his or her work on the basis of its understanding that sense-making strategies like these are quite frequently operating in contemporary art.

These sense-making strategies or associative pathways are shared around the world by the producers and informed consumers of ambitious fine art. They are in large measure what make the emerging transnational institution of art an internally coherent practice. For this institution is not just a mechanism for moving artworks around the world. Shipping companies can do that. The artworks that are delivered from afar must be sent and greeted with shared understandings. To achieve that, the emerging transnational art-world has evolved a reliable set of themes and sense-making strategies that can be mobilized in Shanghai, Sydney, Rio, or Capetown.

One such sense-making strategy is pastiche. This may involve the juxtaposition of high and low, but in terms of globalization, the terms of the juxtaposition might be the local and the traditional, on the one hand, versus something of modernizing import, on the other. For example, Mona Hatoun's *Keffea* presents an image of a traditional, male, Palestinian scarf festooned unexpectedly with the cuttings of women's hair, thereby subversively prompting—through the culturally anomalous opposition—thinking about the sexist repressiveness of Arab society.[45] Informed, cosmopolitan art viewers are on the lookout for tensions like this one in Hartoun's piece and know to take them as progressively inflected openings on a conversation about the dialectical significance of the clashing elements.[46]

Of course, I do not mean to claim that *all* the themes and sense-making strategies in play in the transnational artworld are utterly fixed. Many are. Indeed, enough are so that an intelligible transnational conversation is possible. Furthermore, I do not mean to insinuate that the existence of this transnational institution of art suppresses the expression of the situated interests of artists in their place of origin, since the frameworks I have been considering place a high value on difference, resistance, and critique. The emerging transnational institution of art strives, though perhaps not always successfully, to cultivate a cosmopolitan appreciation of the local within the context of a conversation that is intelligible, due to the preceding factors, to participants in far-flung regions around the world.

Though scarcely frictionless and by no means comprehensive with respect to every interest serious artists pursue currently, the transnational artworld has put in place a language game replete with conversational presuppositions, hermeneutical gambits, recurring themes, and sense-making strategies. This is a worldwide discursive framework—a serviceable, though far from comprehensive, tool-kit, if you will, for approaching and deciphering if not all then at least a very great deal of ambitious art from all over. Moreover, with these shared conversational presuppositions also comes a shared tradition and history.

In the 1980s, the complaint leveled at MOMA's primitivism and modern art show was that it was ethnocentricity at its most arrogant to hang tribal art next to modernist art simply on the basis of their superficial, surface similarities. These were discrete artworlds, even if tribal art sometimes served as an inspiration for modernist artists.

Today, however, when the artworks that derive from nominally different cultures stand side by side, they are not necessarily artworlds apart. The works at large-scale international exhibitions generally are playing the same or related language games and share, to a great extent, the same tradition. When in 1999 two Chinese artists, Yuan Cai and Jian Jun Xi, urinated into the Tate Modern's version of *Fountain*, they were obviously playing the same extended language game the French performance artist Pierre Pinoncelli was playing in 1993 when he urinated into another version of *Fountain* in Nimes.[47] Whether the Chinese were quoting the Frenchman is unknown, but both gestures were capable of making statements because they were tapping into a common tradition, a tradition whose Dada, of course, was Duchamp. Indeed, the shadow of Duchamp falls in every direction. At the recent Times of India Kala Ghoda Art Festival in Mumbai, there was a piece called *The Loovre* in the series *Urbanization II* by Apnavi Thacker, which is an installation that uses a row of four gold and sliver painted urinals to open a discussion on the lack of basic amenities in the city.[48]

In the past, the artworlds of different cultures were distinct, segregated by virtue of their diverse traditions of making and meaning, of articulation and interpretation. Even where these distinct traditions touched and cross-fertilized each other, their genealogies and canons stayed separate. What seems to be changing in the present historical moment is that a unified artworld with shared language games and traditions appears to be emerging across the globe. Connections between museums, galleries, and large-scale exhibitions are becoming more intensive due to the veritable explosion in the means of communication and transportation. But this is more than just a distribution system. It is underwritten by shared presuppositions, sense-making strategies, artistic heritages, as well as a proclivity for the use of certain media. It is, rather, a common art culture, one whose lineaments require far more study than this preliminary sketch offers.

Of course, not every art-making activity today belongs to this emerging transnational institution of art. There is still folk art, mass art, and various national traditions. But, at the same time, there is this transnational institution of art that connects the artistic practices of urban centers around the world both physically and intellectually. It is not an institution of art in the sense that the philosopher George Dickie had in mind when he coined the term. Its function is not to enfranchise art. Its function is to consolidate a transnational or global artworld—a culturescape with its own language games and networks of communication, distribution, and reception.[49]

NOËL CARROLL
Department of Philosophy
Temple University
Philadelphia, PA 19122, USA

INTERNET: carrolln@temple.edu

1. On the issue of whether and what globalization is, see Fredric Jameson, "Notes on Globalization as a Philosophical Problem," in *The Cultures of Globalization*, ed. Fredric Jameson and Masao Miyoshi (Duke University Press, 1998, 2003), pp. 54–77.

2. Bryant Simon, "Up-Close in the Flat World: A Case of Malay Teens in Starbucks in Singapore," a lecture at the Center for the Humanities at Temple University, Philadelphia, PA, February 2006.

3. Jan Nederveen Pieterse, "Globalization as Hybridization," in *Global Modernities*, ed. Mike Featherstone, Scott Lash, and Roland Robertson (London: Sage Publications, 1995, 1997), p. 53.

4. Kenneth Turan, *Sundance to Sarajevo: Film Festivals and the World They Made* (University of California Press, 2002), p. 1

5. This information was given to me by Priya Joshi of the English Department of Temple University.

6. Turan, *Sundance to Sarajevo*, p. 1.

7. Turan, *Sundance to Sarajevo*, p. 7.

8. For Appiah, a cosmopolitan is someone who, among other things, relishes exposure to cultural and artistic difference. See Kwame Anthony Appiah, *Cosmopolitanism: Ethics in a World of Strangers* (New York: W.W. Norton, 2006).

9. See Jonathan Rosenbaum, "The Missing Image: Review of *La masinon cinéma et La monde*, Volumes I and II, by Serge Daney," *New Left Review* 34 (2005): 145–151.

10. Appiah, *Cosmopolitanism*, pp. 109–111.

11. Just as the development of the Japanese graphic novel, a near relative to the cartoon by way of the comic, has spurred the evolution of the American genre.

12. Philip Bohlman, *World Music* (Oxford University Press, 2002), p. 133.

13. See "Letter from Europe," *International Herald Tribune*, November 24, 2005.

14. Deborah Sontag, "The Ambassador," *The New York Times*, January 29, 2006, §2.

15. John Sinclair, Elizabeth Jacka, and Stuart Cunningham, "Peripheral Vision," in *The Globalization Reader*, 2nd ed., ed. Frank J. Lechner and John Boli (Oxford: Blackwell, 2000, 2004), p. 298.

16. Kwame Anthony Appiah made this observation in an interview on National Public Radio on January 26, 2006. In a related vein, at present, with films like Timur Bekmambetov's *Night Watch* (2004) and *Day Watch* (2006), Moscow, with the help of 20th Century Fox International, is trying to capture the market of Russia and the Commonwealth of Independent States, which has a population of 280 million people and is said to be the fastest-growing film audience in the world. See "From Russia with Blood and Shape-Shifters," *The New York Times*, February 5, 2006, Arts and Leisure section.

17. Sinclair, Jacka, and Cunningham, "Peripheral Vision," p. 299.

18. This review of dance history relies very heavily on Sally Banes, "Our Hybrid Tradition," in *Before, After, and Between: Selected Dance Writings of Sally Banes*, ed. Andrea Harris (University of Wisconsin Press, forthcoming). See also Shelley C. Berg, "Sad Yacco in Lond and Paris 1900: Le Reve Réalisé," *Dance Chronicle* 18(3) (1995): 343–404; Shelley C. Berg, "Sada Yacco: The American Tour, 1899–1900," *Dance Chronicle* 16(2) (1993): 147–196.

19. See the articles by Shelley Berg referred to in note 18.

20. Gabriel P. Weisberg et al., *Japonisme: Japanese Influence on French Art, 1854–1910* (Cleveland, OH: Cleveland Museum of Art, 1975).

21. Lincoln Kirstein, *Dance: A Short History of Classic Theatrical Dancing* (New York: Dance Horizons, 1969), p. 205.

22. David Barboza, "China's Bold 'Swan,' Ready to Export," *The New York Times*, February 2, 2006, Arts section.

23. Ulrich Beck, *What is Globalization?* trans. by Patrick Camiller (Cambridge: Polity Press, 2000), p. 36.

24. This emphasis on the forms that current transnational relations are taking is a theme of Roland Robertson. See, for example, his "Mapping the Global Condition: Globalization as the Central Concept," in *Global Culture: Nationalism, Globalization and Modernity*, ed. Mike Featherstone (London: Sage Publications, 1990, 1992), pp. 15–30. See also Roland Robertson, *Globalization: Social Theory and Global Culture* (London: Sage Publications, 1992).

25. Freely adapting the vocabulary of Arjun Appadurai, we might also call this integrated transnational institution of art a *culturescape*. See A. Appadurai, "Disjuncture and Difference in the Global Cultural Economy," in *Global Culture*, pp. 296–300.

26. Lisa Jardine, *Worldly Goods: A New History of the Renaissance* (London, 1996), especially ch. 5.

27. Lisa Jardine and Jerry Brotton, *Global Interests: Renaissance Art Between East and West* (London: Reaktioin Books, 2000), p. 32.

28. Jardine and Brotton, *Global Interests*, p. 51.

29. Rose Kerr, "Chinese Porcelain in Early European Collections," in *Encounters: The Meeting of Asia and Europe 1500–1800*, ed. Anna Jackson and Amin Jaffers (London: Victoria and Albert Publications, 2004), pp. 44–51.

30. Richard Vine, "Report from Prague: Biennale Gamble Doubling Down," *Art in America* Sept. (2005): 47. Higher estimates are also available. In his talk "The Glocal and the Singuniversal: Reflections on Art and Culture in the Global World," Thierry De Duve cites a low of eighty biennales per year and a high of 140. His talk was given on February 14, 2006, at the conference *Multiple Cultures in a Globalizing World* at the Mohile Parikh Center for the Visual Arts, Mumbai, India.

31. James Meyer, moderator, "Global Tendencies: Globalism and the Large-Scale Exhibition," *Art Forum International* November (2003): 152–163.

32. It should be noted that the situation changes somewhat if one focuses on international art fairs rather than biennales. One sees far less video and installation art (though still a great deal of photography) at events like Art Basle. The reason for this is obvious. Art fairs are about selling artworks to private collectors and noninstitutional collectors prefer owning and displaying paintings and sculptures rather than things like videos and installation art. Nevertheless, I believe my emphasis on biennales here is justifiable, since biennales give us a sense of what it is that artists and presenters think is "the now thing."

33. For descriptions of this work, see Susan Kendzulak, "Chinese Artists at the 51st Venice Biennale," *Yishu: Journal of Contemporary Chinese Art* Septempber (2005): 6–10.

34. Andreas Schlaegel, "Yeondoo Jung," *Contemporary* Special Issue on the Venice Biennale (n.d.): 107.

35. Marcia E. Vetrocq, "Venice Biennale: Be Careful What You Wish For," *Art in America* September (2005): 114.

36. Eleanor Heartney, "Report from Istanbul: Artists in the City," *Art and America* December (2005): 55–57. Likewise, *The New York Times* review of the "Of Mice and Men" festival in Berlin only seems to have had eyes for the videos, photographs, and installation art.

37. Richard Vine, "Report from Prague," p. 49.

38. It should also be observed that there may be an economic element in the gravitation of biennales toward mechanically and electronically reproducible art, since it is very expensive to insure a painting or a sculpture for shipping, whereas a video cassette of a performance piece is readily replaceable for almost no money.

39. Pamela M. Lee, "Boundary Issues: The Artworld Under the Sign of Globalization," *Artforum* November (2003): 167.

40. Though I am emphasizing the role that these art forms play in large-scale international exhibitions, I would also like to add that these art forms are spreading across the world gallery by gallery and performance space by performance space as well. For example, in 1998, Geeta Kapur noted the upsurge of installation art in India. See Geeta Kapur, "Globalization and Culture: Navigating the Void," in *The Cultures of Globalization*, pp. 204–206.

41. This quotation is cited by Pamela M. Lee, "Boundary Issues," p. 166.

42. Roberta Smith, "Agitprop to Art: Turning a Kaleidoscope of Visions," *New York Times*, November 11, 2005, Arts section.

43. I owe this point to Prashant Parikh made to me in a private communication.

44. In private conversation, Dominic Willsdon, formerly of the Tate Modern and presently the director of educational programs at the Museum of Modern Art in San Francisco, has indicated to me that curators of international shows prefer work from other cultures that evinces commitment to critique, thus reinforcing the spread of a converging language game worldwide.

45. My interpretation of the Hartoun piece follows that of Homi Bhabha in his talk, "Living Together, Growing Apart," at the Multiple Cultures Conference in Mumbai on February 15, 2006.

46. Similar strategies of juxtaposition are in evidence among Chinese artists. Wang Guangyi uses the approach of the propaganda of the Cultural Revolution but inserts capitalist imagery like Marlboro and Coke logos, while Jian Jiwei sculpts stone reliefs in traditional Persian and Buddhist styles but populates them with contemporary characters. (I thank Ales Erjavec for calling these examples to my attention in a private communcation.)

47. Alan Riding, "Conceptual Artist as Vandal: Walk Tall and Carry a Little Hammer (or Ax)," *New York Times*, January 7, 2006, Arts section.

48. See "Return of R. Mutt," *The Times of India*, February 11, 2006.

49. I especially thank Susan Feagin, Ales Erjavec, Prashant Parikh, Dominic Willsdon, and Margaret Moore for their help in the preparation of this article, and wish to express my gratitude to the very responsive and informative audience who attended my lecture at the Mohile Parikh Center for the Visual Arts on February 15th, 2006 in Mumbai, India.

Contributors

PHILIP ALPERSON is Professor and Chair of the Department of Philosophy at Temple University, where he is also Director of the Center for Vietnamese Philosophy, Culture, and Society. He was the editor of *The Journal of Aesthetics and Art Criticism* from 1993–2003 and has edited several books on the aesthetics of music and the visual arts. His interests include aesthetic theory, the philosophy of music, creativity, performance, and art education. He is currently completing a book on the philosophy of music for Blackwell Publishing.

NOËL CARROLL is Andrew W. Mellon Professor of the Humanities at Temple University. His most recent book is *Comedy Incarnate: Buster Keaton, Physical Humor, and Bodily Coping* (Blackwell, 2006).

ARTHUR C. DANTO is Johnsonian Professor Emeritus of Philosophy at Columbia University and was Albertus Magnus Professor at the University of Cologne in 2005. He is president as well as an editor of *The Journal of Philosophy*, art critic at *The Nation*, and consulting editor at *Artforum*. He has served as president of the American Philosophical Association (1984) and of the American Society for Aesthetics (1989). He won the 1985 George S. Polk Prize for Criticism, and his book, *Encounters and Reflections* (Farrar, Straus & Giroux), was awarded the 1990 National Book Critics Circle Prize in Criticism. His philosophical writings include *The Transfiguration of the Commonplace* (Harvard University Press, 1980) and *Mysticism and Morality: Oriental Thought and Moral Philosophy* (Basic Books, 1973). He lives in New York City with his wife, the artist Barbara Westman.

STEPHEN DAVIES teaches philosophy at the University of Auckland. His most recent books are *The Philosophy of Art* (Blackwell, 2005), *Themes in the Philosophy of Music* (Oxford University Press, 2003), and *Musical Works and Performances* (Clarendon Press, 2001).

JALE NEJDET ERZEN teaches aesthetics and criticism, history of art, and photography at the Faculty of Architecture, Middle East Technical University in Ankara, Turkey. Besides having published and lectured on Ottoman architecture, Turkish art, and comparative aesthetics worldwide, she is also an exhibiting painter. She studied painting with Lorser Feitelson at the Art Center College of Design in Los Angeles. She is the organizer of the 2007 World Congress of Aesthetics in Ankara, Turkey.

SUSAN L. FEAGIN is Visiting Research Professor of Philosophy at Temple University and the editor of *The Journal of Aesthetics and Art Criticism*. She is the author of *Reading with Feeling: The Aesthetics of Appreciation* (Cornell, 1996) and co-editor, with Patrick Maynard, of *Aesthetics* (Oxford, 1997). She writes generally on philosophy of the visual arts, emotions and art, and philosophy of literature.

KATHLEEN MARIE HIGGINS is Professor of Philosophy at the University of Texas at Austin. She has also taught at the University of California, Riverside, and the University of Auckland. She is author of a number of books, including *The Music of Our Lives* (Temple, 1991) and the forthcoming *This Merry Company: Music and Human Nature*. She has edited or co-edited anthologies on such topics as aesthetics, ethics, German idealism, Nietzsche, erotic love, and world philosophy, including *Aesthetics in Perspective* (Wadsworth, 1996) and (with Robert C. Solomon) *From Africa to Zen: An Invitation to World Philosophy* (Rowman and Littlefield, 1993, 2003).

DOMINIC MCIVER LOPES teaches philosophy at the University of British Columbia and participated in a faculty exchange at Ritsumeikan University in 2006. He is the author of *Understanding Pictures* (Oxford University Press, 2004) and *Sight and Sensibility: Evaluating Pictures* (Oxford University Press, 2005). He is now working on the ontology, definition, and value of interactive computer art.

ERIC C. MULLIS is currently Assistant Professor of Philosophy at Queens University of Charlotte. He has recently been published in *Contemporary Aesthetics* and has forthcoming articles in *Journal of Aesthetic Education* and *The Journal of Speculative Philosophy*. His research centers on pragmatism, somaesthetics, and Chinese philosophy.

NGUYỄN CHÍ BẾN is Professor and Director of the Vietnam Institute of Culture and Information of the Vietnamese Ministry of Culture. His is the author of hundreds of papers on Vietnamese literature, folklore, and cultural management.

YURIKO SAITO is Professor of Philosophy at the Rhode Island School of Design, as well as associate editor of *Contemporary Aesthetics*. Her work in Japanese aesthetics, environmental aesthetics, and everyday aesthetics has appeared in a number of journals and anthologies. She is currently writing a book on everyday aesthetics.

RICHARD SHUSTERMAN is the Dorothy F. Schmidt Eminent Scholar Chair of Humanities and Professor of Philosophy at Florida Atlantic University, Boca Raton. The books he has written include *Practicing Philosophy* (Routledge, 1997), *Performing Live* (Cornell, 2000), *Surface and Depth* (Cornell, 2002), and *Pragmatist Aesthetics* (Blackwell, 1992; 2nd ed. Rowman & Littlefield, 2000, and translated into twelve languages).

TO NGO THANH is Professor and General Secretary of the Vietnam Association of Folklorists. He has served as the Head of the Division of the Institute of Culture of the Vietnamese Ministry of Culture and as the Director of the Vietnam Institute of Culture and Information. His main interests are in Vietnamese folklore and musical traditions.

SUSAN PRATT WALTON has a Ph.D. in musicology from the University of Michigan. She is the director of the Javanese gamelan at the University of Michigan, where she also teaches ethnomusicology and South and Southeast Asian studies. She has authored *Mode in Javanese Music* (Ohio University Press, 1987), articles on gender issues in music and experimental ethnography, and has translated two treatises on *gamelan* music from Javanese.

MARY BITTNER WISEMAN is Professor Emerita of Philosophy at Brooklyn College and the Graduate Center of the City University of New York. She is the author of *The Ecstases of Roland Barthes* (Routledge, 1989) and has just completed a book-length manuscript, *Looking at Women (in Paintings)*.